A DAMN BAD BUSINESS

A DAMN BAD BUSINESS

The NHS Deformed

Jeremy Lee-Potter

VICTOR GOLLANCZ

LONDON

First published in Great Britain 1997
by Victor Gollancz
An imprint of the Cassell Group
Wellington House, 125 Strand, London WC2R 0BB

A catalogue record for this book is
available from the British Library.

ISBN 0 575 06310 6

Typeset by Rowland Phototypesetting Ltd,
Bury St Edmunds, Suffolk
Printed and bound in Great Britain by
St Edmundsbury Press Ltd, Bury St Edmunds, Suffolk

97 98   5 4 3 2 1

For Lynda,
and for Emma, Charlie and Adam

'Medicine is a noble profession
but a damn bad business'

Sir Humphry Rolleston

Contents

Preface

When I was first asked to write this book I had serious doubts. I had just left the NHS, believing that the changes brought about by Margaret Thatcher and Kenneth Clarke had so damaged the service that I did not want to continue as a hospital consultant. Having so recently shaken myself free there was a risk that raking over the memories of the last few years would induce a painful abreaction.

However, I soon realized that not to attempt it would be to pass up a unique opportunity to record what happened, and to explain why so many who work in the NHS are angry and disillusioned with the so-called NHS reforms.

In this I was strongly encouraged and supported by my wife, Lynda, who thereby has had to suffer a husband whose thoughts and conversation over the past year have been about the health service to the exclusion of nearly all else. To her, my fondest thanks, and, to the rest of my family and friends, apologies.

Thanks are also due to many others, especially colleagues from the British Medical Association. Richard Smith, the editor of the *British Medical Journal*, has allowed me to quote numerous passages from the journal and I am indebted to him and many of his contributors. In particular I would like to thank John Warden, the *BMJ*'s political commentator, and Gordon MacPherson, its columnist Scrutator. Both are always shrewd and well-informed. Other regulars like Tony Smith, Tony Delamothe, John Appleby and Linda Beecham have provided valuable insights, reports, and overviews on events as they occurred.

During my time as BMA chairman the advice of Pamela Taylor, head of the public affairs division, was invariably wise, and I am also grateful to her staff, including Sue Marks of the parliamentary unit, and Nigel Duncan, who took over from Pamela when she was head-hunted by the BBC. The expertise of Jon Ford, from the economics research unit, was also most helpful, although I absolve him from any economic misapprehensions that I may display.

While writing this book I received unstinted help from the BMA Library, whose chief librarian, Tony McSeán, provides a service nonpareil for medical authors.

To Mark Jessop, the editor of *BMA News Review*, must go the credit for being indirectly responsible for this book, as it was he who persuaded me to write the article, on my resignation from the NHS, which first aroused the media interest which led to my publisher's approach when its contents were prematurely leaked in the *Independent* newspaper. The *News Review* has published many surveys and reports which have been useful then and now.

There are many medical staff and office-bearers within the BMA too numerous to mention with whom I have worked, and argued, over the years, but I have consulted none during the writing of this book. Thus the views expressed are mine alone and not those of the BMA.

The published works and their authors to which I have referred are all recorded in the Notes and Bibliography at the end of the book, and I acknowledge them here with thanks.

I am very grateful to Margaret Mossop for permission to quote from her letter to me about my late grandfather, Dr Samuel Lee Potter.

I owe a special debt to Valerie Rickett, who interpreted this doctor's handwriting with such skill that the returned text on computer disk was nearly flawless, whatever happened to it afterwards.

And finally enormous thanks go to Vicki Harris, who commissioned this book for Victor Gollancz, and then had the task of editing it with me at long distance over the telephone, rather than face-to-face, due to the birth of her son, Ben. With her skilled plastic surgery the health of the book may have improved to 'as well as can be expected', but whatever its prognosis any mistakes found will be mine not hers.

Jeremy Lee-Potter
September 1996

Introduction

To innovate is not to reform.
EDMUND BURKE, *A Letter to a Noble Lord*, 1796

On April Fools' Day 1991 the National Health Service underwent its most radical change since its foundation in 1948. Because of the extremely controversial nature of the change, the Department of Health for months had been anxious to achieve a low-key start. Instructions had gone out for a 'smooth take-off', a 'steady state', 'no surprises'. Perhaps the Conservative government hoped that, as the day happened to be Easter Monday, media attention would be diverted by the public holiday. The media noticed all right, but battle fatigue among the health-authority and hospital managers struggling to turn the flood of paper instructions into action produced the desired muted beginning.

The fact that it was April Fools' Day did not go unremarked by the health professions, whose members had almost unanimously resisted the changes since they had been first announced in January 1989. The announcement had taken the form of a White Paper, *Working for Patients*, in which Margaret Thatcher, in her prime ministerial foreword, wrote that 'the proposals represent the most far-reaching reform of the National Health Service in its forty year history'.[1] Her use of the word 'reform' caused enormous resentment amongst those who provided the service. The various images conjured up, of young offenders' institutions, the removal of rotten boroughs in 1832 and of curing malpractice, compounded the monumental slight delivered to NHS staff in failing to consult them. We had been through three major reorganizations, now we were to be reformed. The British Medical Association was furious when the review turned out to be a White rather than a Green Paper, which meant that the huge changes set out were to all intents and purposes a *fait accompli*. During the White Paper's year-long gestation Mrs Thatcher had not talked to the BMA at all but only to a few individual doctors who were 'one of us'. Kenneth Clarke, the Health Secretary, now told us the reforms were not negotiable although he would meet us.

Despite the spirited challenge to the White Paper after its publication, carried on throughout the next year and a half by the doctors, nurses and other clinical professions and by the Labour parliamentary opposition, the National Health Service and Community Care Act introducing the internal market to the NHS received royal assent on 17 June 1990, and thus passed into law.

When the changeover to the new system took place in 1991, Robin Cook, the Labour Shadow Health Secretary at the time, called it a set of buffers rather than a launchpad. In a continuing war of soundbites he said that the government's hoped-for steady state was in reality a standstill and that the changes would deform the NHS, not reform it. The BMA concurred at least with the latter part of this view.

What happened in April 1991 was that 57 self-governing trusts, mostly acute hospitals, came into being, and 1700 family doctors in 306 general practices were given their own budgets for some of their work. The remaining hospitals and general practices, the great majority, stayed under the management and administration respectively of their separate health authorities. There was one big difference: all providers of secondary healthcare, that is hospitals, and a few other parts of the health service like ambulances, were to have these services purchased by the district health authorities, and to a lesser extent by the new budgetholding practices. This was the purchaser–provider split which created the internal market in healthcare. There would be written contracts for everything within this market – operations, outpatient attendances, investigations, ambulance journeys, and all that a particular provider could provide that was wanted or could be afforded by the purchaser.

Anomalies and problems were immediate. A district health authority might have within its area a self-governing trust hospital outside its control and several other hospitals which it continued to manage itself. The authority's overall budget would have been reduced by the amount that had been given to any GP budgetholders in its locale. With its remaining funds the health authority had to buy care for all the district's non-budgetholding GPs' patients, and those services outside the budgetholders' allocation. It also had to make sure that any hospitals it still managed directly did not fail to compete with the trust hospitals that had escaped its clutches. A Chinese wall had to be set up within the authority to ensure its integrity in carrying out these conflicting tasks, and this extra administrative division produced a further drain on its reduced resources. It was not long either before many of the more able authority staff were queuing up to become managers in the freer, more independent trust hospitals. Rumours that salaries and perks were better in the trusts soon hastened the exodus.

Meanwhile the family doctors with budgets were renamed fundholders. Only those practices that had 11,000 or more patients were allowed at that time to have their own budgets. They also had to have approved computer systems and management arrangements, for which generous allowances were paid. The average fundholding practice received about £1 million annually to buy quite a limited range of services. These were confined to planned (as opposed to emergency) surgical operations and to outpatient consultations, treatments and procedures including X-rays, pathology and other investigations. Everything else, and any costs of more than £5000 for any one patient during a year, would remain the responsibility of the local health authority.

For general practitioners, fundholding held two main attractions. One was that for the first time since 1948 they would be valued customers rather than supplicants at the hospital when requesting operations and outpatient consultations for their patients. They now had the money to insist on early attention, or they could take their custom elsewhere. The other was that any savings they made from their budgets could be used to improve the fabric of their capital investment, their surgeries. They could also fund other desirable activities and developments such as attendance at postgraduate conferences and strengthening their staff. If savings could be made on drug budgets the money could now also be used elsewhere in the practice. The savings retained by fundholding practices have actually proved considerable. The overall average for 1994/95 was £83,000 per practice.[2]

To the 300 first-wave practices which embraced fundholding the disadvantages of the administrative and time-consuming hassle involved were outweighed by the doctors' greatly increased sense of being masters in their own houses. The ethical considerations of gaining an advantage for their patients at the expense of those of their non-fundholding colleagues were ignored in the first entrepreneurial flush of enthusiasm.

On the eve of the introduction of the reforms, William Waldegrave, who had been Secretary of State for Health since November the previous year, was less than complimentary about the health service. 'The NHS', he said, 'is an administrative slum designed in the 1940s, and it needs to be updated.' He defended the £300 million put in to kick-start the changes and claimed that it was worth spending money 'to provide the information technology and higher quality of management required'. There was no mention of the new logos, stationery, glossy brochures and hordes of management consultants advising on mission statements and the like, that ate large amounts of the start-up costs. Naïvely, Waldegrave hoped that the NHS would not acquire more administrators, to which, characteristically, the *Sun* responded, 'We'll be counting, Willie.'

As chairman of the British Medical Association's Council I commented that 'a new massive bureaucracy is being cranked into operation which will consume even more of the scarce resources doctors need to treat patients'. The *Sun*'s cynicism was justified and events have borne us both out in this regard. In the autumn of 1995, the next Health Secretary but one, Stephen Dorrell, announced that managerial and administrative costs, which had burgeoned in the intervening four and a half years, must be cut by 5 per cent.

Quite apart from the extra bureaucracy needed to administer the new market, the NHS was not ready for the changes. Many non-fundholding GPs did not know where they should be referring their patients for specialist care because they had not been informed by their health authority where its contracts for treatment had been placed. Another snag that soon appeared was that a patient could reach the top of a long hospital waiting list for an operation, only to find that his local health authority now did not have a contract with that hospital. This happened particularly where London teaching-hospitals were concerned, and Robin Cook on the Opposition front bench was assiduous in embarrassing the government with documented examples.

The dissatisfaction of patients and doctors, repeated all over the country, allowed damaging political capital to be made out of one of the original slogans of the reforms touted by Mrs Thatcher: 'Money will follow the patients.' It was too often the other way round. The actuality also ran counter to two of the claims contained in the leaflet about the new NHS pushed through every letterbox in the land: that the reforms would lead to more choice for patients and more freedom for their GPs.

As so often happens when politicians drag new policy rabbits out of hats, the reforms had not been properly thought through. Their aim was ostensibly laudable. No one could do other than support better value for money and more choice for patients, whether expressed through their general practitioners or more directly, but there was a huge question mark over whether these changes would bring this about.

The medical profession's view, and that of most health economists, was that there was simply too little money in the system to achieve the kind of patient choice that was available in other leading industrialized countries, which used various forms of insurance to pay for healthcare. The BMA had long contended that if Britain's spending on medical care per head of population was raised even to the current average for western Europe, our existing tax-based system would outperform our neighbours, in terms of both quality and public satisfaction. The reasons for this were twofold. First, our patients had to be registered with a family doctor, who acted as a gatekeeper and thus limited unnecessary access to the more expensive hospital-based services. Second, the transactional costs of insurance-based systems were wasteful because they contributed nothing to the medical care provided.

It was widely conceded that the NHS could be made more efficient, but this could best be brought about in a gradual way by continuing to improve the management of the service, particularly by involving the doctors, who inevitably used most of the resources.

By introducing an internal market, in which a multiplicity of buyers and sellers had to spend thousands of man-hours haggling over guesstimated prices, Mrs Thatcher plumped for the worst aspect of continental insurance-based systems – high transactional costs. At the same time, their most popular feature with patients seeking specialist attention – choice and no waiting list – could be achieved (indirectly) only by a minority whose GPs were fundholders. For the majority of patients, equitable access was damagingly compromised by the existence of the GP fundholders, and the development of a two-tier service soon appeared in some parts of the country.

The underlying Thatcherite belief that competition always brings cost-efficiency is at the root of the 'reforms'. The fundholding GPs would supposedly lead the way and force hospitals to respond, benefiting all. Mrs Thatcher hoped also that a health service broken up into small, quasi-private, competing units would somehow cost less per patient treated. She believed private concerns to be more efficient than public ones, without considering the nature of the business, or indeed whether health can or should *be* a business.

Economists believe that for a market to operate optimally there must be an excess of supply. Only then can it work efficiently, with the good driving out the bad, winners defeating losers in the marketplace. Our health service actually has a shortage of supply: demand cannot be met, nor even can need. There is now also an imbalance between the buyers and the sellers, as there is little market pressure on the buyers in the health authorities who are remote from local opprobium. If their local hospital loses custom and dwindles, patients are likely to be losers, if for no other reason than geography and the resultant transport difficulties. One of the crowning merits of the old NHS had been the success of the district general hospital concept and the resultant even spread of good-quality specialist care throughout the country.

About two-thirds of the expense of providing a health service is the cost of the staff. The NHS is quintessentially a people-oriented organization. The service cares for people and relies heavily on team-work. Those who work within it are not driven by commercial concerns; they do not seek or expect huge financial rewards for success. More than in most jobs an element of altruism is necessary at times, and this is admired within the culture. The values embedded in the reforms and, particularly at their launch and in their early days, even the language of commerce used so freely, grated with doctors and nurses.

Thus, upsetting the staff seemed a crass way of introducing such radical changes, and confirmed for many that, for all their talk of efficiency and being businesslike, the politicians who introduced the reforms were in reality very bad managers and had little understanding of business or the health service.

It is true that better ways of managing the health service must be found. Doctors should be more involved with management, and managers more involved with doctors. The management structure must be sufficiently robust that ministers are distanced from the day-to-day running of the service. Government must forswear the appointment of political placemen and -women on health authorities and hospital management boards. The *provision* of a health service is inevitably a political matter, but managing it is not.

The core of the health service, its clinical staff, remains dissident and the great majority continue to believe that the reforms have done great harm. Few however have the stomach for further major change in the immediate future. This means that some form of separation between the providers and the commissioners of healthcare will have to continue. Contracting must be abolished and more care taken with balancing the two sides, so that planning drives out fragmentation but some creative tension remains.

Most important of all is that our health service requires more money, and the way we pay for it is in need of urgent review. The present, seriously defective, allocation of funding to different parts of the country should also be corrected.

In the ensuing pages I will set out how the NHS has arrived at its present imperfect state and how I believe it must be protected in future from the swirling currents of political dogma and ephemeral ideology.

CHAPTER ONE

The National Health Service
Origins and Ideas

*It is not possible to understand politics . . . without knowing
something of history.*
DENIS HEALEY, *My Secret Planet*, 1992

A national health service has been a long time in coming. Some
provision was made in common law for the welfare of the poor as
far back as the time of Athelstan, the first King of the English, who
died in A D 940. But it was not until the beginning of the seventeenth
century, under an Elizabethan statute, that relief was extended
beyond 'setting the poor to work'. For the first time, parish officers
were also directed to use 'competent sums' from parochial taxation
'for and towards the necessary relief of the lame, impotent, old and
blind'.

Even then the main object was to restrain vagrancy and begging,
and to punish idleness, but by the early 19th century these more
punitive elements had been gradually separated from those concerned
with welfare. Increasing sums were spent so that in 1832, when a
new Poor Law was enacted, £7 million was spent on a population
of about 14 million – 9s. 9d. per head. This was a considerable
increase on 1750, when it had been only 2s. 2d.[1]

Nevertheless, the Provincial Medical and Surgical Association,
which had been founded in Worcester a few months before the new
Poor Law was passed, and which in 1855 became the British Medical
Association, was critical of the parsimony inherent in the Act. It was
amended two years later, in 1834, as it was agreed that it had been
'founded on vicious notions'. England and Wales were divided into

21 districts, not so many more than the 14 health regions (including Wales) of the early NHS in 1948. Each Poor Law district had an assistant commissioner in charge, responsible to the three central Poor Law commissioners. This improved administrative structure resulted in a reduction in expenditure by a quarter over the next 12 years when compared with the 12 before 1834. The commissioners stated that 'on the whole medical attendance seemed . . . to be adequately supplied and economically'. They were more concerned with cost than the amount of care provided – *plus ça change*. In another parallel with today, non-parishioners were a charge on their original residence, so-called 'settlement', and doctors were very much encouraged to certify non-residents fit to travel back to their own parishes as soon as possible for continuing relief.

The first secretary of the new Poor Law commissioners was Edwin Chadwick, not the last barrister to make an impact on medicine and healthcare in this country. Sir Edwin, as he later became, published a seminal report on the public health in 1842.[2] Like Sir Douglas Black 138 years later he reported that poverty, disease and ill-health were connected.[3] Chadwick believed, also rightly, that effective sanitary engineering had a major part to play in improving health. He had little time for doctors' efforts at cure, and the medical officers of health, whose appointment under the Public Health Act of 1848 he inspired, were concerned largely with sanitary reforms. This separation of public-health doctors from the rest of medicine persists to this day. These doctors form one arm of the tripartite structure of medicine in Britain (the other two being general practice and the hospital specialties), which has influenced all developments since.

The Poor Laws were repeatedly amended, there being no fewer than 130 amendments between 1834 and 1885. Welfare legislation seems always to have been subjected to frequent change. The comment of Dr Richard Burn in his *History of the Poor Laws* in 1764 is as topical today as it was then: 'When a flaw is observed a patch is provided for it, upon that another, and so on, till the original coat is lost amidst a variety of patchwork. And more labour and materials are expended (besides the clumsiness and motley figure) than would have made an entire suit.'

It was not until 1911 that a new suit was made. This was the National Insurance Act of the Chancellor of the Exchequer, David Lloyd George. This Act was the first to provide sickness benefit, and offered the services of a 'panel' doctor to working men earning less than £2 a week, but not to their families or to the unemployed. It was a contributory scheme, with payments from the worker, his employer and for the first time the state – the so-called 'ninepence for fourpence'. It was run much as existing friendly societies and 'sick clubs' had been. Only later were hospital services included.

The British Medical Association had been considering a comprehensive national health service since 1909, when a royal commission on the Poor Law had revealed how unsatisfactory were the provisions for those unable to pay for healthcare. Doctors knew this very well, as some of this financial burden fell on them, leading them to operate more or less as Robin Hoods, waiving their bills to those too poor to pay. They hoped to earn enough from richer patients and the sick clubs to pay their way, but in many industrial cities this could be difficult.

These doctors were often revered in their communities for their charity. I recently received a most touching letter from a 90-year-old lady who, as a child, had been a patient of my grandfather, Dr Samuel Lee Potter, in Batley, West Yorkshire, who died in a motor-cycle accident in 1912.

> I would like you to know all the children of Batley loved Dr Potter, and I mean loved. When he died the schools closed and a memorial service was held at the parish church. All the children took their spending money, ours was two pennies. A stonemason made a horse trough [as a memorial] and we used to go and put flowers on – mostly field flowers on Saturday mornings. He never sent bills to families who were poor but I am sure he was repaid in the love and affection everybody felt for him, especially the children of Batley, and he was never forgotten.

The BMA's report on the *Organisation of Medical Attendance on the Provident and Insurance Principle* was also published in 1911 and went further than Lloyd George's Act. It demanded 'that adequate medical attendance shall be placed within the reach of all members of the community'. It recognized that this was 'not only in the individual interest, but also in the general interest', a very important point indeed, which was to be made again in 1937 in the damning *Report on the British Health Services* by the independent think-tank Political and Economic Planning.[4]

As a solution to the problem, the National Insurance Act was not received with unalloyed pleasure by the doctors. It strengthened the position of the intermediaries between them and their patients. They had been tussling for years with the businessmen, as they saw them, in the friendly societies and the insurance companies, and now similar middlemen were incorporated in the Act. They were also angry that they had not been involved before the Bill's publication. Lloyd George agreed to receive a deputation from the BMA before actually introducing it, but protracted negotiations were necessary before a compromise was reached. There are striking parallels between what took place between Lloyd George and the BMA then and the hostilities with a later Welsh firebrand, Aneurin Bevan, in the lead-up to the formation of the NHS 35 years later. In both contests a silver Celtic tongue and sensible compromise were to win the doctors over in the end.

It was not until after the First World War that further advance towards a national health service was made. The first Ministry of Health was created in 1919, and a Consultative Council of Medical and Allied Services established under the chairmanship of one of the most eminent physicians of the day, Sir Bertrand Dawson. Lord Dawson of Penn (as he was to become in 1920 after the publication of his report, *The Future Provision of Medical and Allied Services*) had been King George V's doctor since 1914 and achieved the unique distinction for a doctor of a viscountcy in 1936. He considered it nothing less than the duty of the medical profession to promote national health, although his report did not deal with how the recommended co-ordinated preventive and curative service was to be funded. 'We do not mean the services to be free; we exclude for the moment the question how they are to be paid for,' he said. How often since have such otherwise laudable documents omitted this most crucial matter.

In 1929 the BMA made another attempt to improve on its 1911 ideas, and on the Dawson Report, when it published *A General Medical Service for the Nation*. This pamphlet was revised and reissued in 1933 and was widely discussed. Five years later, in November 1938, a definitive version was produced with the same title. It contained four main principles: that the achievement of 'positive health' should be the aim as well as disease prevention and the treatment of sickness; that everyone should have a general practitioner of his own choice; that specialist services should be available to all; and that the various parts of the complete medical service should be co-ordinated under a planned national health policy. It also wanted National Health Insurance extended to workers' families, but it did not consider that the wealthy should be covered – no doubt reflecting anxiety about the effect the proposals might have on doctors' private practice. This became an issue again in 1946 with Mr Bevan.

The report was far-seeing, better than Lord Dawson's, but like his it ducked the question of finance. Sadly its 'hope that practical measures will soon be taken to make a comprehensive service available for the people of this country' fell on deaf governmental ears; and in less than a year the country was at war.

Despite the war, the BMA was not going to give up easily, and in August 1940 it set up, with the medical Royal Colleges, a Medical Planning Commission which produced a draft interim report in May 1942, based on the 1938 document and critical of the disorganized and fragmented nature of existing medical services. It recommended an extension of the National Health Insurance scheme but was against a salaried governmental medical service. Nevertheless its general suggestions concerning a suitable structure, and ideas for the payment of general practitioners and senior hospital staff, were very much what was eventually put in place in the new NHS in 1948. Michael

Foot, in his biography of Aneurin Bevan, called it 'the boldest document ever issued by the British Medical Association'.[5]

It is often forgotten that Sir William Beveridge, who is usually regarded as the first architect of the National Health Service, as part of his comprehensive social security system, based it on the BMA's proposals.[6] In *Assumption B. Comprehensive Health and Rehabilitation Services*, he says: 'Restoration of a sick person to health is a duty of the State and the sick person, prior to any other consideration. The assumption made here is in accord with the definition of the objects of medical service as proposed in the Draft Interim Report of the British Medical Association.'[7] Where he did differ from the BMA was that he foresaw that the cost of the proposed health service might not be included in the social insurance contribution, about which he knew a great deal. The 'five giant evils' of 'Want, Disease, Ignorance, Squalor and Idleness' had to be tackled, although his original brief from the government had been confined to reviewing 'social insurance and allied services, and workmen's compensation'. He got round this by claiming that 'no satisfactory scheme for social security can be devised [without] a national health service', amongst other things.[8]

The coalition government of the time accepted Beveridge's thesis that a comprehensive health service was needed. Winston Churchill, as Prime Minister in February 1943, said: 'This approach to social security . . . constitutes an essential part of any post-war scheme of national betterment.'[9]

Discussions between the BMA and the Ministry of Health continued throughout 1943, and in February 1944 a White Paper was published by Henry Willink, the Minister of Health. The 'Radio Doctor', Charles Hill (later Lord Hill of Luton and chairman of the BBC), had just become secretary of the BMA and played an important role then and in subsequent events. Not only was he a wise and accomplished politician but he was also, rare for a doctor, an effective orator. The White Paper defined the new health service as free to everyone, the responsibility centrally of the Minister of Health assisted by a Central Medical Board, but run by local government advised by local health councils. Doctors were to be salaried and there was provision for compulsory service for the newly qualified. While approving wholeheartedly of the concept of the national health service to be introduced at last, the doctors were alarmed that the government intended to control the profession. They were totally opposed to a whole-time state-salaried service, and it was this that was to lead to the all-out war that developed between the BMA and the government right up until the introduction of the NHS in 1948. Initially there was also dissent about what became known as the '100 per cent issue'. Doctors were concerned that, if the whole population was covered, opportunities for private practice would vanish. Memories of dependence on such practice earlier in the century died hard, and these fears were justified. However eventually the '100 per cent issue' was settled, and negotiations were nearly at an end when events took an unexpected turn. The general election of June 1945 resulted in an overwhelming victory for the Labour Party, and Aneurin Bevan became Minister of Health.

Mr Bevan was a man with a mission – the National Health Service was to be his epitaph. Without further negotiation he introduced a National Health Service Bill in March 1946. Its accompanying White Paper set out the taking-over of existing hospitals and premises, described health centres, and proposed the payment of a basic allowance to GPs with the addition of a fixed amount for every patient registered – the capitation fee. Compensation, thought fair by doctors at the time, would be paid for the loss of the right to buy and sell practices. The new health service would be financed 'partly from the Exchequer, partly from local rates, partly from . . . National Insurance contributions' and there were to be some charges.

Doctors were still extremely unwilling to work under Civil Service direction and become employees of the state, nor did they want their places of work to be taken over. GPs were against being salaried and wished to keep their surgeries. Hospital doctors were opposed to the independent 'voluntary' hospitals being absorbed into the new service and controlled by local authorities.

Despite this opposition, the NHS Bill passed into law in November

1946 but the BMA voted by 55 per cent to 37 per cent (with 8 per cent not replying to the postal vote) against co-operation with Mr Bevan in negotiating the necessary regulations. The presidents of the three medical Royal Colleges in London (Physicians, Surgeons and Obstetricians & Gynaecologists) wrote to Bevan wishing 'to do what we can to prevent . . . an impasse'. They brought down widespread medical anger on their heads by so doing, as their successors were to do again in 1990 when the profession was at loggerheads with Mrs Thatcher over her reforms. The feeling then and later was that it was not the colleges' role to get involved in political matters for which they were not suited nor established. However Bevan listened to them and eventually negotiations with the BMA reopened in early 1947. They were still going on in April 1948 when he promised that a whole-time salaried service would not be brought in. This stimulated the BMA to canvas its members again, but 52 per cent were still against accepting service under the Act, and 64 per cent remained against the Act itself. Nevertheless the closeness of the result led the BMA Council to call another meeting of the Representative Body (the doctors' parliament) in May and put a recommendation to them to co-operate in the introduction of the new service. The motion included the statement 'while continuing to negotiate outstanding matters', a subtle rider, and it was carried, despite the strong opposition of many representatives.

Many have been puzzled since by the fight the BMA put up against the introduction of a health service which it had itself been advocating for nearly 40 years. There are penetrating echoes in the medical profession's opposition to the 1990 reforms. Although in the two years before 1948 medical objections could be attributed to concern over how doctors were to be paid, they were in fact much more fundamental. They reflected the absolute nature of a doctor's commitment to an individual patient, without the interposition of a third party, be it the state, an insurance company, a provident association or any other individual or agency. Medicine is a profession which, like the Church or the law, marches to a different drummer than most other occupations. Whenever doctors are face to face with sick patients, duty, ethics and honour demand that no constraint be placed on them by an employer, government or anyone else. They must do the best that can be done – even to the extent that it is to the doctor's own detriment. In this regard it is worth recalling the instructions which the General Medical Council, the statutory regulatory and registration body for doctors, gives in its ethical bible, *The Duties of a Doctor*. The doctor is enjoined not 'to refuse treatment . . . on the ground that the patient suffers, or may suffer, from a condition which could expose [the doctor] to personal risk'.[10]

Fear of direction by remote forces in government, management and the civil service was at the root of doctors' opposition in 1948 and again in 1990, although at the earlier date it was compounded by financial factors and at the later by the commercial thrust of the proposed changes. An attack on professional values was detected in both Acts.

The new National Health Service came into being on 5 July 1948 to provide, in Bevan's words, 'medical treatment and care . . . to rich and poor alike in accordance with medical needs and no other criteria'. The Minister of Health was instructed by the NHS Act 'to promote a comprehensive health service designed to secure and achieve improvements in the physical and mental health of the people . . . and the prevention, diagnosis and treatment of disease'.

The new service was immediately enormously popular, as for the first time the ever-present worries of the mass of the population over the consequences of serious illness were relieved. It was indisputably the greatest social advance that the country had ever seen, and patients flocked to take advantage of the free care, spectacles and dentistry that they could not afford before.

Many general practitioners however viewed it with a more jaundiced eye as their workload burgeoned, and they became disillusioned with the new demands made upon them. This medical discontent is well illustrated by a novel, *Honour a Physician*, written by a Sheffield GP, Dr Bobby Burns, under the pseudonym Philip

Auld. In it he bitterly indicts the new NHS 'as a corrupter, primarily of patients, secondarily of doctors, and a destroyer of family doctoring, good clinical medicine and continuing medical care'.[11]

The cost of the service soon shocked the government, and they were even more shocked when the general practitioners, now in serious revolt over their remuneration, were in 1952 awarded by Lord Justice Danckwerts a salary increase of five times what the government had been offering. Charges for spectacles, false teeth, dentistry and drugs had had to be introduced the year before, which caused Bevan and the young Harold Wilson to resign from the government in protest. A ceiling on health spending had been introduced then, but, as Guillebaud was to confirm in his 1956 report, extravagance was not the cause of the cash shortage, it was the unsuspected extent of the previously unmet need.[12] In fact, as a proportion of gross national product, the NHS only accounted for 3.25 per cent in 1953, a reduction of 0.5 per cent on 1949, and only about half what it does now in GNP terms.

The tripartite structure of medicine was maintained, with the general practitioners retaining their independence, under contract to the new executive councils to provide general medical services. Thirteen regional hospital boards in England were established (with Wales having a similar fourteenth body), and slightly different arrangements were made for Scotland and Northern Ireland. These boards employed the salaried hospital doctors. Local government employed the third group, the community and public-health doctors.

District hospitals were run by management committees drawn from their local communities, with professional representation, appointed by the Health Minister. Bevan had bowed to the Royal Colleges and allowed the metropolitan teaching-hospitals to remain outside this structure and to report directly to the Ministry of Health.

The original structure remained in place until the first major reorganization occurred in 1974, soon after the Labour Party won the general election. The new Secretary of State, Barbara Castle, introduced changes which had been designed by her Conservative predecessor, Keith Joseph. The regional boards became executive, rather than advisory as before, and were named 'regional health authorities'. 'Community health councils' were set up as watchdog bodies. The new Act also introduced consensus management, creating 206 'district management teams' to run local services, whose membership was based on a kind of Noah's Ark arrangement of one manager, one treasurer, one hospital doctor, one GP and one nurse. These teams, while democratic in intent, were to prove mostly ineffective because of the vacillation that trying to achieve consensus caused. The reorganization perfectly exemplified Dr Burn's patchwork of 1764, and ignored Kenneth Robinson's attempts to achieve a unified structure. Robinson, the Labour Health Minister from 1964 to 1968, was the son of a GP, and was probably the only occupant of that post to be regarded with genuine warmth by the medical profession. He was responsible for the 1965 GP Charter, which revitalized British general practice. To David Owen, the Minister of Health, it was a traumatic experience and made him 'deeply sceptical of a further wholesale administrative reform of the NHS'.[13]

Despite the 1974 reorganization, the NHS was soon seen to be in a mess again, and Prime Minister Harold Wilson decided, as he was inclined to do, to appoint a royal commission, to be chaired by Sir Alec Merrison, Vice-Chancellor of Bristol University. Merrison reported in July 1979 and, as so often seemed to happen with NHS reports, by the time the report was finished another government was in power. After the spate of strikes called the Winter of Discontent, in which hospital ancillary workers had been much involved, the Conservatives were elected back into office. Merrison's report proved to be something of a damp squib and he himself was aware that it had 'no blinding revelation which would transform the NHS'. Nevertheless the new government published *Patients First* in response.[14] The resultant legislation in 1982 strengthened local management, abolished the 'area' tier, created 'district health authorities' and simplified the planning and advisory systems. As usual, Scotland was reorganized slightly differently but was to be essentially the same.

This second reorganization was more of a pruning and simplification exercise and thus was more easily assimilated by the service than the first, but it was disruptive and failed to solve the root cause of the NHS's difficulties, finance.

While not strictly another reorganization, the next development was much more significant – the first Griffiths Report of October 1983.[15] Margaret Thatcher's Conservatives had won a landslide victory in the June general election and she was ripe for Sir Roy Griffiths' ideas. These included replacing consensus with general management, establishing a central Health Services Supervisory Board and an NHS Management Board (including an overall director of personnel) and introducing management budgeting. As deputy managing director of Sainsbury's, the supermarket chain, Sir Roy was appalled at what he had seen in the six months he had spent looking at the NHS's management arrangements. As far as he could see there was no one in charge and there was no pressure on doctors to manage the resources which they commanded in any organized or effective way. He wanted the NHS to be run like Sainsbury's, and although he recognized that doctors and nurses must be involved in its management he wanted much clearer lines of control.

The DHSS implemented Griffiths' ideas in a circular, bringing in general management throughout the health service. It was a curious paradox that a simple circular was all it took to bring about much more far-reaching change in the health service than all the legislation which had been needed to introduce the two previous reorganizations. Griffiths paved the way for the 1990 reforms by altering the balance of power between the professional staff and the managers. Managers (and not the clinical staff) were now clearly accountable for the resources used, and they were biddable by government in a way doctors were not.

Soon after Griffiths was brought in to look at the health service, the Nuffield Provincial Hospitals Trust invited another guru, Alain Enthoven, Professor of Health Management at Stanford University in the USA, to conduct a short review of the NHS in 1984. Although his work was not widely noticed in the health service at the time, he proved to be the most influential of them all. Enthoven had wide experience of government, having at one time been President

Johnson's Assistant Secretary of State for Defence. He published his thoughts in 1985 as *Reflections on the Management of the National Health Service*.[16]

This paper was enthusiastically received by the *Economist*,[17] and also by John Redwood and David Willetts, then members of Mrs Thatcher's Policy Unit at 10 Downing Street, who met with Enthoven. Willetts later became director of studies at the right-wing think-tank the Centre for Policy Studies, which in 1988 published a pamphlet by Redwood and Oliver Letwin calling for radical reform, but also an 'apolitical NHS' and what amounted to health vouchers (to which Mrs Thatcher reputedly had always been opposed).[18]

Enthoven produced a most perceptive analysis of the NHS and suggested that, if radical change to its structure was desired by policy makers, then the health-maintenance organization in the United States was the most promising model.

After deciding that the NHS was 'caught in a gridlock of forces that make changes exceedingly difficult to bring about', his overall message was that there were too many perverse incentives operating which failed to reward the best and cushioned the less efficient, and that market forces would release the talents and energies that were being stultified by the system.

In the face of an ageing population and advancing medical technology, the NHS would have to produce even more value for money, and a 'supportive environment and some institutional innovation [would] be needed'. The increased resources required for the twin challenges were put by the Health Department at 0.75 per cent and 0.5 per cent annually respectively: less than the 1 per cent each suggested by Health Minister Barney Hayhoe, but large none the less.

Enthoven attributed gridlock to a combination of circumstances. First was that a government of any political party would be unlikely to let spending grow faster than the national wealth. Within that constraint, the way consultants were employed in the hospitals, the fact that GPs were autonomous and that unionized nurses and other staff had nationally agreed terms of service, gave managers little scope to make 'efficiency-improving changes'. He quoted the American economist Charles Schultze, who had commented on the paradox that while the public tended to accept that a private concern could close down or translocate due to market forces, it found a state-owned one like a military base or a post office doing so hard to stomach. There were therefore hazards for politicians, as well as health staff, in bringing about radical change like closing a local hospital or moving a service to another district. One of the problems of the NHS was its rigidity.

He correctly identified the perverse way NHS finance was distributed. Whatever the benefits of the existing formula, it did not compensate a district which developed an excellent service in a specialty and attracted more patients from other districts thereby. Money did not follow patients. On waiting lists the same drag chain pulled. The size of a consultant's operating waiting list, apart from being an indication of his popularity and the demand on his particular expertise, could also boost the number of patients seeking to avoid the wait by consulting him privately. This was also perverse and he wanted to see a system whereby a surgeon could be given some form of incentive payment to reduce his waiting list in the NHS. He thought that the referring doctors could in some way control the well-known danger of a fee-for-item-of-service leading to unnecessary surgery.

In a health-maintenance organization – and Enthoven had experience of one of the largest as a consultant to the Kaiser-Permanente Medical Care Program in the United States – pressure can be brought to bear on healthcare providers through a fixed-payment-per-case system, preventing overcharging. His experience of the Kaiser-Permanente led him to believe that medical needs are not limitless but finite, and supports those of us within medicine who have been irritated beyond measure by the relentless political parrot-cry of 'bottomless pit'.

There is very little in Enthoven's analysis that doctors would disagree with, although we might offer different solutions. There are many flashes of insight that strike a universal chord: 'Politicians can use performance indicators for "number games" that destroy credibility'. That surely should have been burned in pokerwork over Virginia Bottomley's breakfast table. He believes that 'the role of management is to create a culture and reward system that guides thousands of decisions in the direction of better quality care and service at reduced costs'. The 1985 NHS relied on dedication and idealism, he said, 'but it offers few positive incentives to do a better job for the patients'.

The main thrust of the 1983 Griffiths Report gained his support. In particular he approved of Griffiths' apparent wish to take the Secretary of State out of day-to-day operational matters by having an NHS supervisory board (chaired by the Health Secretary) setting policy, but an NHS management board implementing it. He was also in favour of Griffiths' introduction of general managers, who should be allowed to get on and manage. However he was not optimistic that the politicians could be kept out of operational detail. He thought the best way to use general management would be to give some enthusiasts their head in a few pilot districts or a region for a couple of years and see what came up that was worth wider adoption. These thoughts were very much those of the BMA later, when Kenneth Clarke shocked just about everybody who knew anything about the health service by insisting that his reforms were to be applied across the whole health service without trials of any kind.

Enthoven's essay included a section on private-sector contracting and competitive tendering for support services like cleaning and catering, of which he was in favour, but he thought the government had gone about introducing them in a particularly ham-fisted way. Coercion would not get the best results, and he quoted a newspaper report saying that the government had threatened to take to court district health authorities who had refused to put services out to tender, as precisely how to give the idea a bad name.[19]

As far as contracting with private sources for medical care was concerned he thought that the NHS should first be able to cost its own services. Without that ability it would not know what to pay and whether it was cost-efficient. Using private hospitals could be an effective way to bring waiting lists down but, until good accounting systems were in place, managers would not be able to deflect the hostile criticism likely to result. He was aware of the popular view that the private health sector in Britain is a queue-jumping mechanism for the well-heeled but, as an American, he found this irrational. It may be that his relative inexperience of private healthcare in the UK led him to equate it with that in the USA, where it is not predominantly confined to planned, so-called cold, surgery as it is here. Mrs Thatcher made the same mistake when she wanted to know why, if private hospitals were run like a business, the NHS could not be. As must have been pointed out to her, the private sector simply charged what it needed to keep the bottom line in profit, as in most parts of the country at that time there was little competition. Knowing what to charge was not the same as knowing what everything cost. When my partners and I set the prices we would charge for the private pathology company we set up in 1978, we knew roughly what the initial demand was going to be, and what we needed to service the capital loan, pay the staff and overheads, and make a small profit. We therefore knew what to charge, without at the outset knowing precisely what each test cost. Contemporaneously my NHS laboratory received an overall fixed budget from which we had to provide all that was demanded of us – quite a different proposition, especially as in the NHS department we could not simply stop providing a particular test because it was not requested sufficiently often to be economic. The contrast between the two was great, as it was between private and NHS hospitals.

Nevertheless Enthoven had a point when he said that if services could be bought from a private supplier for a good price then the NHS ought to do so. Those in the NHS would add the caveat that sub-contracting some of the work of a large, all-embracing organization does not always save money. Cream-skimming by private competitors can cripple a public service and lead to its deterioration or even collapse.

In typically transatlantic fashion, Enthoven was keen on a spirit of experimentation, free from the restraining hand of the bureaucrat. He was surprised at the degree of risk aversion he found in the NHS. I venture to suggest that he did not meet enough clinicians, where most of the innovation resides by the very nature of medicine, but of course his brief was structural not clinical. He quoted several American studies including one which examined the long-cherished belief that a constraining GP gatekeeper screening out specialist referrals is cheaper than allowing patients to refer themselves directly. It was found in this study that the gatekeeper had no significant effect on the *per capita* costs, although the study must be interpreted with caution because the US's insurance-based healthcare is not comparable to our system.[20] It is received wisdom in Britain that one of the main reasons, if not the single most important reason, for the cheapness of the NHS compared with other systems of similar quality in industrialized countries is the requirement that patients have to be referred for specialist attention by their general practitioner. Some of the HMOs in the United States now allow patients to refer themselves directly.

There are several other examples of pilot projects examining shibboleths of various kinds in Enthoven's paper, of which only a few have been tried in Britain. He was rightly damning of 'clinical budgeting', which seemed a cosmetic exercise to him. This half-hearted system was introduced into the health service several years before Mrs Thatcher's review, and involved allocating budgets, very much in a nominal way, initially for services like pathology. As I protested at being given one for my laboratory in the early 1980s: 'Where is the chequebook that goes with my budget?' How could I genuinely run a department with a paper budget that was held somewhere in the accounts department, with a monthly statement nearly always containing errors, arriving at least a month in arrears, and with no real-time buying power? Enthoven calls it 'fiddling with supplies', and it was truly that. (Despite the arrival of the reforms, and squads of new accounting staff, clinical budgeting is not much different now. There has always been a lack of trust in

NHS hospitals that professional staff can manage the money needed to run their departments. The risk-aversive culture that Enthoven identified remains deep in the NHS managerial structure despite the NHS reforms.)

Enthoven struck a chord with clinicians on medical leadership, and his views were not very different from Roy Griffiths' on this. He was aware that to be a good manager you need to be a leader, and that leaders have to enjoy the respect of those led. Consequent to this, in a medical context the necessary prestige 'goes with possession of skills to apply advanced technology'. For this reason, in my view, public-health doctors are not ideally suited to manage and lead clinical consultants, and the same principle applies in many other occupations. He was in favour of training a small number of clinical specialists in management, as his own university does in the United States.

It would need a 'prestigious consultant with knowledge and instincts for management' to tackle waiting list problems for instance. He was conscious, however, that not many of the doctor-leaders he was after would take management posts if they had to suffer a large drop in income as a result. This was one of the points that the BMA made to government repeatedly, but it always fell on stony ground.

Chapters on resource allocation in the NHS and 'an internal market' completed the paper. The Resource Allocation Working Party in 1976 had produced a 'RAWP' formula for distributing the health service's money more fairly, but spending on Greater London remained much higher than it ought to have been and disparities between districts within a region were even wider. Enthoven proposed that all districts should be given funds according to their RAWP allocation and then be allowed to buy care for their populations wherever they liked, not necessarily from the hospitals within their district. Even more importantly they would not have to accept patients from other districts (except emergencies) without payment.

He developed this idea in his last chapter on 'An Internal Market Model for the NHS'. Each district would receive a RAWP-based *per capita* revenue and capital allowance to provide a comprehensive service for its population. Non-resident patients would be paid for at negotiated prices. In short, he saw districts – presumably district health authorities – as health-maintenance organizations.

Although he thought wages and working conditions should be negotiated locally, this would not be essential. Doctors would contract with the districts for their services, and he proposed that many kinds of contractual arrangement should be allowed, including short-term contracts and incentive payments. Where GPs were concerned, they would have to refer to agreed hospitals. Districts would be run on business lines, with a balance sheet and an income statement, and they would be able to borrow prudently at government long-term interest rates. They should also be able to sell off unused property and keep the proceeds.

Overall he thought of his scheme as a kind of 'market socialism', not privatization. It would give district health authorities much more freedom and would encourage innovation.

An important appendix on HMOs was included in which he expanded his ideas to apply them to districts. An HMO's responsiveness to its subscribers is very important, as dissatisfaction leads to enrolment with another HMO. At the same time HMOs can cut the cost of healthcare by good management, typically reducing total costs by 25 per cent and inpatient days by 40 per cent compared to traditional private medical insurance. The main lever in achieving this is by reducing hospital use, and not by paying the doctors less, but it has to be said that they do not take on the expensive burden of long-term care of the elderly which is proving such a contentious issue in Britain.

HMOs achieve the integration of general and specialist practice, in which patient records are shared, a divide which may have served the NHS well in the past, but is looking more of an obstacle than an advantage now that the body of general medical knowledge has become so great. Enthoven believes that multi-specialty group practice is the way ahead and many would agree with him, or at least that it should be tried. Unfortunately the nearest the new structure of the NHS can get to this is to allow certain hospital specialists to provide occasional consulting sessions in general practitioners' surgeries, which is hopelessly uneconomic in terms of the number of patients that can be seen in a session.

He was also convinced that an HMO must have a medical director leading it, 'a doctor whose leadership is accepted by other doctors, to organize and control the delivery of services'. He should be a bridge between medicine and management. While there are now medical directors in the NHS's hospitals, they do not have the role and status envisaged by Enthoven due to the way Kenneth Clarke set up the health authorities and trusts.

Enthoven's study formed the basis of Mrs Thatcher's 1991 NHS reforms, but its adaptation to the service has been clumsy and ill-thought-out. By cherry-picking what appealed to her market instincts and ignoring questions of coherence, scale and suitability to Britain's healthcare system, and by allowing Kenneth Clarke to dismiss Enthoven's strong recommendations for the limited trial of his ideas, she jeopardized much of the huge progress that the health service has made since 1948.

CHAPTER TWO

Lead-up to the NHS Reforms

July 1984–January 1988

Gold is the key, whatever else we try.
MOLIÈRE, *The School for Wives*, 1662

Throughout the 1980s a combination of circumstances gave rise to the impression that the NHS was failing the public. Although the money spent increased in real terms throughout the decade, the annual increase was small, and the rate of increase was falling off. Within the health service this felt like the tightening of belts in the face of inexorably increasing demand. To the public it looked like cuts, and regular stories of disaster in the media reinforced its unease.

The rapid advance in medical knowledge and technology, the rising public expectation brought about by the information explosion and the 'greying of Britain' all made managing the NHS, and paying for it, more and more difficult.

The switch to general management started in July 1984, with the appointment of the first regional general manager. By May 1987 there were 687 hospital and other unit general managers. About 60 per cent of them had been NHS administrators and were simply transmogrified; 10 per cent were recruited from outside the NHS; and doctors and nurses made up 11 per cent each.[1] Of the 14 regional managers only one was a doctor, the redoubtable Rosemary Rue, who had been Oxford's Regional Medical Officer for 15 years. Dame Rosemary, as she later became, was an invaluable adviser to me as president of the BMA in my first year as chairman of its Council in 1990.

The new managers often found themselves in an uncomfortable position between the central NHS management on the one hand and those who looked after the patients on the other. They were a convenient buffer for the government. Mrs Thatcher's manifesto for the 1987 election very much took the line that the new management arrangements would solve the NHS's problems. Good management was what the service had lacked, and now it had got it all would be well. If things did not go well it was the managers' fault and not the secretary of state's.

Health became an important battleground in the election. Hospital waiting lists were lengthening and Labour claimed there had been a 15 per cent increase under Mrs Thatcher. The Social Democrat–Liberal Alliance presented an enormous computer printout said to contain the names of over three-quarters of a million patients waiting for treatment. The Conservatives were rattled. Hospital doctors were becoming increasingly vociferous about trying to make bricks with insufficient straw, and they felt threatened by the new managers, some of whom were making macho noises along the lines of 'We are the masters now.'

On election day, 11 June 1987, I attended the BMA consultants' conference, where we passed a strongly worded resolution that consultants were not professionally accountable to managers. Paddy Ross, chairman of the BMA's consultants' committee, the Central Consultants and Specialists Committee, nevertheless spoke strongly for consultants to become involved in management to avoid being sidelined.

Paddy had been fighting his own battle within the BMA for some time on behalf of the government's Resource Management Initiative. This scheme aimed to show that hospital doctors and nurses could and should take part in the management of hospital specialty costs. To this end sums of £1 million or more each had been put into six pilot hospital sites to help develop computerized costing of all specialist work. Consultants countrywide had serious doubts about the cost-effectiveness of RMI, with its accompanying rather primitive and costly computerization, and its labour-intensiveness (much of it their own). Paddy was well aware that he could be seen as fraternizing with the enemy, and it was agreed that RMI would go no further than the six pilot sites until it had been properly reviewed and assessed.

To many members of the consultants' committee, resource management was a Trojan horse. They preferred at that time to remain outside management and sensed that by getting involved they would simply compromise their own clinical freedom and lay themselves open to criticism, along with the managers, if RMI in their hospitals forced economies that they were unhappy with for their patients. It was a hard time for Paddy Ross. He had become chairman of the CCSC ahead of the senior deputy chairman, Brian Lewis, who might have expected to succeed the outgoing chairman in October 1986. Lewis, a leading Kent anaesthetist and a powerful speaker, although a member of his local health authority and thus familiar with the need for better management, was an opponent of the RMI. He had a considerable following in the committee and could sway meetings with his wit and his often ribald speeches.

Paddy Ross is strong-willed, dogged and sincere. He achieved results by being totally in command of the facts and of himself. His determination could sometimes lapse into injured querulousness, but he had cause often enough to be disappointed at the cavalier approach he met from some of his departmental adversaries, especially later on from Kenneth Clarke.

After the 1987 election Norman Fowler, at that time the longest-serving health secretary since Bevan, was replaced by John Moore, a right-winger, who soon announced that he was going to reform the health service. Moore had spent some time as an investment banker in the United States, and was known to be an advocate of private health insurance. Mrs Thatcher was not keen on a review at that stage:[2] she told the Tory party conference on 9 October that she wanted at least another seven more years in office. John Moore made his NHS audience uneasy with his references to healthcare as an industry, and he did not seem to be doing much to stem the trouble in the NHS either. Since September there had been many reports of hospitals having to close beds to save money. Doncaster needed to save £700,000, Central Birmingham £750,000; Darlington was £900,000 overspent; North West Thames Region was £9 million short and South East Thames even more; and so it went on.[3] It was also well known that all kinds of financial dodges were being used by health authorities to conceal what amounted to technical bankruptcy in some cases. The National Association of Health Authorities surveyed about half the 192 district health authorities in the autumn and found that just over half of them were in severe financial difficulties, and this was before the normal winter squeeze on beds and resources.[4]

Doctors were becoming angrier and angrier. Family doctors had been waiting nearly three years for a new deal for general practice that had been promised by Norman Fowler and signalled in a Green Paper the year before.[5] Controversially this was to be paid for in part by the abolition of free eye tests and dental check-ups, announced in November. Hospital consultants were intensely frustrated by the closure of their beds and cancellation of their operating lists, and their junior colleagues had become seriously militant over long hours of work and too little training and supervision.

In mid-November, with the crisis mounting, Secretary of State Moore fell ill. Tony Newton, the Minister, stepped into the breach and was almost immediately faced with the plight of a hole-in-the-heart baby in the Birmingham Children's Hospital, David Barber. Seven-week-old David had had his life-saving operation cancelled five times for lack of intensive-care nurses, and his mother had gone to the High Court for an order compelling the hospital to carry out the operation, but had failed. David got his operation on 25 November, but sadly died 11 days later.

Soon after, the presidents of the three senior medical Royal Colleges, led by Sir Raymond Hoffenberg, the physicians' president, went on the record with a damning indictment of the government's handling of the health service. Mr Newton's £100 million emergency cash injection on 16 December vanished without trace in a grossly overstretched system, and 1988 opened to a chorus of gloom.

The *British Medical Journal* published a stinging new-year leader by its deputy editor, Tony Smith.[6] 'How do we convince the government that it is wrong, that the NHS is moving towards terminal decline, and that innovatory thinking is needed to solve the crisis?' he wrote. The editorial hammered home the facts: Britain trailed its continental neighbours in health spending in terms of proportion of gross national product (UK 6%, France 8.5%, Germany 9.5%, Holland 8.5% and Switzerland 7.4%), and we spent far less money per head every year (UK \$493, France \$853, Germany \$1000, Holland \$828, Switzerland \$1111). Even the *Financial Times* was unhappy, saying, 'This gap is too large to be explained easily away.'[7]

Smith took the government to task for not even maintaining expenditure commensurate with the targets agreed by its own health ministers, and quoted the famous 1986 House of Commons Social Services Committee to which Barney Hayhoe, then Minister but not for long afterwards, had given evidence.[8] Hayhoe agreed that services needed to rise by 2 per cent a year: 1 per cent because of the increase in old people, who made greater demands on the health service; half a per cent for medical advances; and half a per cent for improvements, such as better community care. The committee calculated that there was a cumulative shortfall of £1325 million between 1980 and 1986. The editorial further reminded government that it had agreed pay awards for health workers but had not fully funded them, thus causing guilt among the staff, who felt that their not particularly generous pay rises (two out of every five nurses were paid below the Low Pay Unit's threshold) were closing beds. In 1987 over 3000 beds were closed because of a lack of money, a shortage of nurses or other unplanned contingencies. And Edwina Currie, the Parliamentary Secretary for Health, had typically stirred the pot by opining that NHS expenditure would fall rather than rise as a proportion of gross national product.

Dr Smith's only note of optimism was that there was a 'growing consensus among doctors, administrators and politicians that the time has come for a commission of inquiry into the financing and organization of health care'. Little did he know how soon this would be announced.

January 1988 continued the period of woe for the health service. Despite the Baby Barber affair, children were still waiting for vital surgery in Birmingham, where also 100 consultants started a campaign to save the NHS.[9] Night nurses went on strike in Manchester about a cut in their extra pay for working at night, and a similar attack on blood-transfusion technicians' meals allowances in Yorkshire caused them to ban overtime. Meanwhile Neil Kinnock, the Leader of the Labour Party, obtained considerable publicity by being photographed at St Thomas's Hospital, across the river from the Houses of Parliament, in an empty ward which had been closed because of financial stringency. John Moore had just returned to work from the private hospital where he had been treated for pneumonia, but it was soon obvious that he was still unwell.

Meanwhile there was much to-ing and fro-ing with the Secretary of State. The Royal College presidents got to meet him on 13 January, and a joint statement was issued. The anodyne text agreed the need for more resources (presumably the presidents' contribution) and for more efficiency (no doubt Moore's), but to some the press photographs of Sir Raymond and his colleagues resembled nothing less than Chamberlain's return from Munich. My predecessor as BMA chairman, John Marks, also went to see Moore, and the much more hard-headed result could be interpreted as 'no more funds' (Moore), 'but when you are talking nuts and bolts with the profession, please talk to the BMA, not the College presidents' (Marks). John Major, then number two to Nigel Lawson in the Treasury, confirmed the BMA's cynicism the same day by announcing that no extra money was going to be put into the NHS.

The Commons debated the NHS on 19 January, and although a Conservative motion lauding the service and the amount of taxpayers' money that went into it was easily carried, John Moore, almost whispering at the dispatch box, was not impressive. The three college presidents next put in an appearance at the Social Services Select Committee, which was in the throes of taking evidence from the world and his wife about the health service. The presidents floundered when they were asked for solutions. They had the diagnosis – lack of money – but not the treatment: how much was needed or where to apply it. They were not the only doctors to believe that finding the tools for them to do *their* job was someone else's job. The select committee had been less than precise themselves a year or so before when they had produced their earlier report.

It seemed obvious to everyone that, whatever improvements were made to the structure, more money for the health service would have to be found, over and above the small year-by-year increase that was occuring. The Commons select committee had said so, the BMA had said so and the National Association of Health Authorities, whose members were on the whole sympathetic to government, it having appointed them, had said so. Julia Cumberlege, a health authority chairman and NAHA's chairman, later to become Health Minister in the Lords, led a delegation to the select committee at the end of January. She estimated that the government's projected NHS budget for 1988–89 under-funded the NHS by £400 million, assuming that pay awards ran at 5.9 per cent.

If everyone administering, managing and providing the health service was primarily concerned with financial inputs, the government had increasingly taken refuge in looking down the telescope from the other end, at output. Patients inevitably are also more concerned with outputs, because they represent their treatment and their access to it, but unlike politicians they seem to be able to see the evidence for a shortage of input, often just by looking at the scruffy surroundings in which all too often their health service is delivered. The ministerial outlook was given limited support by the evidence to the select committee of Ken Judge, director of the King's Fund Institute, a long-standing, respected and apolitical health think-tank, but few others. Judge thought that current funding was adequate, but he did agree that there was a historic cumulative shortfall of £1910 million. A later paper from the King's Fund corroborated Mrs Cumberlege's estimate of the extra finance needed immediately – its figure was within £10 million of hers.[10]

Soon afterwards, the political committee of the Carlton Club, which is London clubland's equivalent of Conservative Central

Office, produced a confidential paper in association with the Conservative Medical Society, *The NHS and the Private Sector*. This was
leaked, and must have chimed well with John Moore's beliefs, as it
advocated an insurance-based healthcare system, tax relief on private
health insurance, and NHS opt-out for individuals and for hospitals.
Then Leon Brittan, erstwhile Home Secretary and a former secretary
of state for trade and industry, published a pamphlet on rather the
same lines. He believed that more money for healthcare could be
garnered by an expansion of the private sector and closer links
between it and the public sector.[11]

A less successful Conservative politician also contributed to the
debate by writing a book. Ray Whitney, sacked as a junior health
minister by Mrs Thatcher in 1986, advocated US-style health-
maintenance organizations financed by private health insurance and
health vouchers. (He wrote as 'one of the assassinated pianists'. Mrs
Thatcher had found it easier to shoot the pianist than to compose
a new tune, he said.[12] Later she showed that she was able to do
both.) The BMA issued a statement calling on the government 'to
recognize its obligations to fund the NHS essentially from taxation
. . . in accordance with the clearly stated wishes of the people' and
for 'an immediate injection of additional funds of up to £1500
million'.

The Social Services Select Committee, having taken evidence for
several weeks, finally produced its report. It recommended that all
staff pay awards should be fully funded, and the shortfall of £95
million for the 1987–88 pay round made up. It also wanted an
additional sum of at least £1000 million to be put into the NHS
over two years to go some way towards making up the overall
cumulative deficit, which so many had given evidence about, and
which it put at £1896 million. Its report was almost immediately
rubbished by the Secretary of State. 'We do not think it is sensible
simply to write blank cheques,' he said.[13]

What the select committee had given him, that Moore for whatever reason failed to use, was a strong lever to prise some serious
money for the health service out of John Major at the Treasury. It

is not every day a select committee, with a majority of members of his own party on it, provides a spending minister with such a weapon. The medical profession were extremely upset at what was seen as a dropped dolly catch by 'their' minister, and what his civil servants thought can well be imagined.

When Mr Moore spoke at the BMA's triennial Council banquet soon afterwards he again adopted the 'outputter' stance, which, having looked such a gift horse in the mouth, is really all he could do. He was otherwise emollient, and said that he would welcome a submission to the government's review from the BMA. Consultation was not offered, but this went unnoticed at the time.

The consultants' committee survey of acute-sector resources, published in the same week, told a sorry tale. Of the 5300 beds closed that year, some 3100 had been removed for financial reasons. The service was short of 3100 nurses and 370 medical secretaries – vital to the smooth operation of consultants' work – and there had been widespread cancellation of clinical sessions of all kinds. Comments from consultants around the country made gloomy reading: 'The provision of medical care is essentially emergency only in most surgical specialties' (Oxford); 'We are an "efficient" hospital and we've recently been told we are "too efficient" and must cut our throughput' (Mersey). The report contained a graph showing that spending had paralleled activity until 1981, but from then on it had stopped rising while activity had continued to climb. In real terms, while the financial plateau remained at 113 per cent of 1974 spending, activity had reached 128 per cent by 1985 compared to the 1974 baseline. This graph and later ones like it were repeatedly brandished at ministers in the future when they played the output card. How much more juice could be squeezed from the NHS lemon?

CHAPTER THREE

The Year of the NHS Review
January 1988–January 1989

There is a certain relief in change, even though it be from bad to worse.
WASHINGTON IRVING, *Tales of a Traveller*, 1824

On Monday 25 January 1988, Mrs Thatcher went on the BBC's *Panorama* programme for a wide-ranging interview with David Dimbleby. She amazed viewers, the health service and, it is said, her Cabinet by announcing an internal review of the NHS. It would not be a royal commission – that would take too long – but 'our own' inquiry. It was assumed by the BMA that this would take the usual form, including consultations with them, the medical and nursing Royal Colleges, health authorities, managers, patient organizations and the rest. The overwhelming view on that Monday night was that, at last, something was going to happen that would pull the NHS out of the slough of despond into which it had fallen.

There were niggles of doubt, and worry that a Thatcherite solution might not be what the doctors ordered, especially in view of the prevailing right-wing think-tankery that was in the political ascendancy at the time. But almost anything might be better than the crisis state the NHS was in; and surely any thorough-going inquiry would reveal the truth about the NHS's desperate shortage of funds?

It was known that the review was likely to introduce some form of internal market. Political commentators like John Warden were already pencilling one in as a near certainty[1] and David Owen, a former Labour health minister, was a strong advocate.[2] But it was assumed by most that such a market would be limited to dealing with cross-boundary patient flows between health authorities: it was well recognized that when patients were referred to distant hospitals, the home authority saved money at the destination authority's expense. Some teaching-hospitals were already flirting with the idea of charging for some services like second opinions on pathology specimens.

The review team under Mrs Thatcher consisted of the Chancellor of the Exchequer, Nigel Lawson; the Chief Secretary to the Treasury, John Major; and the two ministers from Health, John Moore and Tony Newton. Sir Roy Griffiths and John O'Sullivan, a political journalist then a member of the Prime Minister's Policy Unit, also attended many of the meetings. The group met weekly and was remarkably secretive; even its membership was not known at the time. When John Moore met the Social Services committee in late March all he would say about the review was that its members were aware of the 'efficiency trap': the more patients a hospital treated the more likely it would be to run out of money. 'This is something – whether money should follow patients – we would like to look at carefully. It is a difficulty clearly associated with efficiency improvement,' he said. He pooh-poohed the £1896 million deficit the committee had identified and claimed that improvements in efficiency made up for the gap between spending and activity. It was difficult to prove either way, but those in the health service would not have had much trouble rejecting his claim.

Any deficit would always depend on when you started counting. The committee had used 1980. Was that a well funded or a badly funded year? The government was well aware that where you start from has a major effect on any finance argument. They use the same tactics when giving evidence to pay-review bodies, always choosing to start their calculations from a year which included the largest pay rise possible to show how generous the cumulated increases have been.

Even the low health spending per head in Britain could be used as evidence of how effective our health service was, and Moore felt reasonably comfortable with his select committee performance, as he knew that the only true measures of governmental success or failure were health outcomes, which were next to impossible to quantify. There had been failings, of course, but these were isolated incidents and could be dealt with by injections of cash here and there as needed by his honourable friend Mr Newton.

This insouciance was very much at variance with other perceptions as to the extent of the problem. The 100 Birmingham consultants wishing to 'rescue the NHS' had swollen to 200, and in a second report they demonstrated that the dire situation in their city went far beyond isolated anecdote. 'All posts falling vacant are now automatically frozen for a period of three months irrespective of the need for the post'; 'the average waiting time to see an orthopaedic surgeon in north Birmingham is now seventy-five weeks' were examples of what was reported. This was part of the pattern of shortage of finance seen by the public as 'cuts'.

Meanwhile the BMA submitted a lengthy memorandum of evidence to the NHS review.[3] It ran to some 5000 words, and opened with the four principles of the 1938 report, *A General Medical Service for the Nation*, which had been so influential at the inception of the health service. The memorandum was accompanied by two annexes, amplifying the evidence the BMA had given to the Social Services committee, which more than doubled its length. The whole was an impressive document: reasonable in tone, well thought out and comprehensive. It wanted the government to be very careful 'before it takes any decisions about introducing other and relatively untried systems of health care which have not stood the test of time to the extent that the NHS has done over the past forty years'. The first annexe drew attention to the 1987 British Social Attitudes survey which showed a marked decline in those expressing satisfaction with the NHS – only 40 per cent were very or quite satisfied in 1986 compared to 55 per cent three years before;[4] and the second covered alternative systems including internal markets, health-maintenance organizations and the private sector very thoroughly. It was thought that financing should remain tax-based, as did health service managers in their later submission,[5] although other means of funding were considered, including a special health tax, social insurance and even lottery finance. The memorandum concluded that 'from the outset the NHS has been underfunded' and that 'the very large majority of people in this country would now welcome immediate additional central funding for the NHS coupled with new initiatives to ensure that even greater value for money can be achieved in the future'.

John Marks, chairman of the BMA Council, led a small delegation to meet John Moore so that he could convey their evidence to the government's review – direct access to Mrs Thatcher was not offered. Moore said that there was no intention of undermining the service's basic principles. The BMA's public stance remained as before, that it was underfunding that was crippling the NHS. Our annual representative meeting in Norwich in early July was quiet but determined in its support of this contention. Despite the failure to meet Mrs Thatcher's review team the medical profession were relatively content at the time that their views would be taken into account.

Not only was the question of the total NHS budget under review, but also its distribution between the different parts of the country. In 1977 a Resource Allocation Working Party (RAWP) had devised a formula using standardized mortality ratios as an indicator of what proportion of the available healthcare money a region needed. The SMR is the ratio of actual deaths to those that would be expected based on the age and sex of the region's population. But basing funding on this was widely criticized as it failed to reflect socio-economic factors like deprivation. Loser regions claimed they had been 'rawped' when the formula did not work for them. The NHS Management Board now published a revised formula, using eight new measures which had been devised by Brian Jarman, Professor of General Practice at St Mary's Hospital, Paddington. He had chosen them for a different task – to assess family-doctor workload in underprivileged areas, so they were not entirely appropriate for the new purpose, but they were an improvement on the old method. The factors built into the formula were derived from the 1981 census, and included amongst other measures the number of young children and of old people living alone, who made greater demands on GPs.

The resulting redistribution of the money in England would throw up some difficult anomalies. A major loser would be the West Midlands, which included some of the highest-profile hospitals running out of money, leading to politically damaging headlines like those in Birmingham.

By now the vultures were gathering over John Moore's career. After a parliamentary débâcle over housing benefits, which cost another £100 million, there were whispers that running two ministries might be beyond him, and that he could not last. These omens proved right because he was to be left in charge only of Social Security when the Department of Health and Social Security was split in July, and Kenneth Clarke came in to run Health.

Kenneth Clarke's takeover from John Moore as Health Secretary had coincided with the parliamentary summer recess. David Mellor had replaced Tony Newton as Minister, and Edwina Currie stayed on as the Parliamentary Under-Secretary. The recess gave Clarke a chance to master his brief and think about the NHS review, without having to face the formidable Robin Cook across the floor of the House for a while. He disappeared to Spain on holiday, leaving the nurses fuming about their new regrading exercise and many other problems besides. Clarke also had other things to think about. There was the long-awaited report of the Social Services committee, under its new and effective Labour chairman, Frank Field, and the recent House of Lords defeat on the imposition of charges for eye tests and dental checks. The Department of Health had also just received writs for negligence from the first haemophiliacs who had been infected with the AIDS virus by contaminated blood products used in the NHS. The family doctors were in sullen revolt, and the DHSS's own inquiry into doctors and their careers had revealed that a great many young doctors, especially women, wished they had never taken up medicine, conditions were so bad.[6]

At the October Tory Party conference in Brighton, Kenneth Clarke made a much better showing than John Moore had the year before. He professed to being a supporter of the principles on which the NHS had been founded. He said it would not be privatized nor was it a commercial business, although it must be businesslike. His descent into the language of commerce was yet to come. He had winkled £140 million out of John Major at the Treasury in an attempt to salve the nurses' discontent over regrading and relieve the anxious health authorities, and he sounded altogether like a caring health secretary should. However it was obvious that he was already thinking about some form of budgetholding for family doctors, but how it could be achieved had not yet crystallized in his mind.

He had a problem on his hands with the GPs. Protracted negotiations had been going on with them over their new contract ever since the 1987 White Paper, *Promoting Better Health*, had been published. Could he bring negotiations to a close by tipping the balance of power within the health service towards the GPs by allowing them to join an internal market, thus giving them control over the hospital consultants?

If these were his thoughts at the time, he either played the hand badly or Tory ideas on markets were never going to be widely popular in a caring service anyway. Perhaps the notion of GP fundholding, which is said to have to come to him on a Spanish beach,[7] could have done with more considered thought in the cold light of an autumn morning in Whitehall on his return.

Mr Clarke followed up his party conference success by announcing a large increase for the health service following the annual public-spending review. He secured an extra £1300 million of new money from the Treasury. So perhaps, unlike his predecessor, he had listened to the Social Services committee, Mrs Cumberlege and the health authorities, and even the BMA and the medical and nursing Royal Colleges. Despite a large number of Conservative MPs voting against in the Commons, including two members of the Social Services committee (the mavericks Nicholas Winterton and Jerry Hayes), he had also managed to get Parliament to reverse the Lords' rejection of charges for eye tests and dental checks.

Clarke was on a roll. Unfortunately, when the economists had had time to look in detail at the Treasury's largesse it appeared that inflation would reduce the funding increase to about 1.6 per cent; and health-service inflation was greater than the general variety because staff pay formed a larger proportion of its costs compared to the rest of the economy. This was therefore the lowest increase since 1981–82, apart from 1985–86,[8] and below the awkward Hayhoe 2 per cent.

Clarke had met consultant leaders for the first time on 5 October. Sir Anthony Grabham, chairman of the Joint Consultants Committee, and its two deputy chairmen, Bill Ross, chairman of the conference of medical Royal Colleges, and Paddy Ross, BMA consultants' chairman, went down to the newly refurbished Department of Health in Whitehall. The JCC is a curious body which meets regularly with the government's Chief Medical Officer to discuss all hospital matters except what could be called broadly trade-union matters, which would be the province of the BMA. It is joint between the BMA consultants' committee and the medical Royal Colleges, and the BMA committee sends its top eight members and the colleges their presidents. There are also some other members, representing junior and geographical interests. It is thus a strange mixture of politicals and academics, giving the former some professional kudos and the latter an opportunity to be political, which their charitable status does not normally allow them. Sir Anthony is a veteran medico-politician whose encounters with government date back to the all-night vigils with Barbara Castle over private practice. He is a former chairman both of the BMA consultants' committee and of its Council, and one of the architects of *Achieving a Balance*, the joint agreement between the government, the colleges and the BMA on improving the career structure for NHS doctors.

At the BMA consultants' committee meeting the next day, Grabham and the two Rosses told us there was no news of the review, but Clarke had confirmed that, although the agreed 2 per cent annual increase in consultants that was part of the aforementioned balance had not occurred in 1986–87, the government remained committed to *Achieving a Balance*. Because of the financial difficulties that health authorities were in, only 1.5 per cent had been achieved.

At the meeting I took over from Brian Lewis as chairman of the negotiating subcommittee, and thus became one of Paddy Ross's two deputy chairmen. The other was John Chawner, a gynaecologist from North Wales, later to succeed Paddy as chairman in 1990, when Paddy himself succeeded Grabham at the JCC and I became BMA Council chairman.

It is the task of the negotiating subcommittee to meet regularly with the DoH and its ministers to discuss and agree the way in which consultants work in the NHS. Consultants then had national terms and conditions of service, so the range of matters to be discussed was large, and the detail often tedious. However in terms of the insights gained into the workings of civil servants and their ministers the experience gained was invaluable. There were major advantages to the health service too in carrying out these negotiations nationally and not, as now happens, with myriads of meetings taking up the time of hundreds of doctors, reinventing the wheel week by week with personnel directors in the hospitals where they work.

This is not to say that the national process was an acme of perfection. When I took over the subcommittee that October, I made a list of the many matters outstanding and the general state of play. There were no less than 10 areas requiring resolution, ranging from how consultants were to be employed as part-time general managers, to which the last response had been in September 1987, more than a year before, to the failure to implement agreements locally over the priority repair of on-call doctors' telephones, on which nothing had been heard from the DoH to a letter sent in March. The longest delay was over the correct way for consultants involved in clinical trials of new drugs to charge pharmaceutical firms for the work, and what proportion of the fees should go to their hospitals. This had been outstanding since a meeting in June 1987, and a reminder sent in September 1988 had been ignored.

Delays such as these served to colour the reactions of doctors to the bureaucracy we were faced with, and the common sceptical response to ministerial exhortations for the sharp end of the NHS to be more efficient and more responsive to our patients' needs. Not only charity should begin at home. At the same time we had sympathy for the civil servants with whom we struggled because they seemed often to be overburdened by the same ministers.

The BMA got its first taste of the new Health Minister, David Mellor, on 11 December. Mellor had been given the job of looking after the hospital side and came to the consultants' committee meeting, where he gave a relaxed performance. Speaking without notes, he showed a considerable grasp of the issues which concerned consultants and spoke well. He would not be drawn on the review, of which he was now a part, but said it would be based on 'the NHS as we know it' – a fairly meaningless statement, but members were charmed by his skilful rhetoric and wrongly took it to mean little change. He was reassuring on the Resource Management Initiative, confirming that it would not be extended until the system had been evaluated at the pilot sites. He covered most of the contemporary enthusiasms, like medical self-audit of their practice and medical management, and he fended off suggestions that linking NHS funding to the gross national product, or increasing it in some other way, was unrealistic. He had not made the government's standing with consultants any worse, and in fact rather impressed the majority with his obvious intellect and facility.

However, when the Social Services committee report appeared, it included many of the less contentious ideas that were to be incorporated in the NHS Reforms, but with some very important differences.[9] It had much to say about the need for doctors to use resources efficiently, about medical audit and the related need for 'systems [to be] devised to provide the government, management, doctors and the health professionals with proper costings of the treatments and procedures undertaken, and with a means of measuring the outcome of treatment'. It was however only in favour of a limited use of internal markets, and these should be between health authorities only; and it rejected the idea of American-style health-maintenance organizations or allowing people to opt out of the NHS via tax concessions for private health insurance. Central funding of the health service should remain, and any move from general taxation as a source should be studied very carefully and agreed on a cross-party basis. Regional health authorities could probably be abolished, and family practitioner committees should be combined with district health authorities – both these changes eventually occurred in 1996.

Overall the report was not going to set the Thames, nor the NHS, on fire – for which many were grateful. However, the doctors were anxious about the implications for their clinical freedom subsumed in all the talk about their accountability and 'potentially inefficient use of resources'. The onward march of lay management of doctors' clinical work was getting perilously close to the heart of the medical citadel.

The GPs were also increasingly concerned about the unsatisfactory progress being made on their contract. Their meetings with the DoH were frequent but confidential, and only the few members of the GPs' committee who were doing the negotiating knew what was going on. It seemed that the government's intention was to tighten management control of family doctors through the family practitioner committees, in a way which was a potential threat to the independent contractor status they had agreed with Aneurin Bevan all those years ago.

There were constant fears also that the general practice review would get swept up into Mrs Thatcher's separate NHS review, and the GP negotiators were continually frustrated by not knowing what this was likely to say. They were, like everyone else, being subjected to a deluge of leaks about the internal review, culminating in what was essentially a complete revelation of its contents by Robin Cook, which annoyed Kenneth Clarke greatly.

Finally a date was set for the review's release, Tuesday 31 January 1989. It was to be accompanied by £1 million worth of razzle-dazzle, which many felt was quite inappropriate in view of the NHS's straitened circumstances. Would the leaks prove accurate or would the NHS really remain much 'as we know it', as Mellor had said at the consultants' committee?

CHAPTER FOUR

Working for Patients
January–February 1989

*Change is novelty; and whether it is to operate any one of
the effects of reformation at all, or whether it may not contradict
the very principle upon which reformation is desired cannot be
certainly known beforehand.*
EDMUND BURKE, *A Letter to a Noble Lord*, 1796

On the day *Working for Patients* was published, the BMA received
advance copies a few hours before Kenneth Clarke's river trip from
Westminster to Limehouse Studios, where he would launch his big
idea to over 2000 NHS staff waiting for the teleconference in studios
around the country. The consultants' chairman, Paddy Ross, and his
two deputies, John Chawner and I, had agreed to meet with the
committee secretary, Sally Watson, to go through the government's
proposals in detail. We met at Paddy's club, the Army and Navy in
Pall Mall, in the late afternoon. Sally, a very bright Oxford history
graduate, had already carried out a preliminary trawl through the
document, and was able to confirm that Robin Cook's press conference leak a few days before was substantially accurate.

Paddy, John and I buried ourselves in the document's hundred
or so pages of cobalt-blue type interspersed with garish yellow block
headings.

The cover was ominous: the National Health Service had dropped
its 'National' to become The Health Service, with CARING FOR
THE 1990's in small capitals beneath. The price was £8.80, and
I wondered whether, in the brave new commercial world we were
about to enter, the BMA had had to pay for its 50 or so copies. I

expect it did. The typography of Margaret Thatcher's foreword was strange too. It looked like an old-fashioned press release, with a dozen sentences each separated from the next by wide white space. The text was the routine PR-speak that we were to become so familiar with when the Department spin doctors got into their stride later: 'The patient's needs will always be paramount' was the last sentence. Others included: 'a National Health Service [we were glad to see the 'National' back] that is run better will be a National Health Service that can care better'; 'the proposals ... offer new opportunities, and pose new challenges, for everyone concerned with running the service'; 'Time and again, the nation has seen just how much we owe to those who work in it.' There was no mention of what had precipitated the review in the first place: a service failing the public for lack of finance. A rapid skimming of the document confirmed that it had nothing to say about improved funding at all, although the service was to remain financed by general taxation. This was a surprise and a disappointment.

The paper was divided into six parts: the government's strategy; the hospital service; general practice; other issues; the health service in Scotland, Wales and Northern Ireland; and a conclusion, which set out a very tight timetable for introducing all the changes by 1991. On page six came the unexpected statement that eight more 'working papers' (ultimately there were ten) were to be published shortly 'as a basis for discussion with interested parties' and to explain how the new system would be implemented in detail.

This profound absence of detail was one of the reasons why the BMA did not respond immediately, thus as it turned out wrong-footing the impetuous Mr Clarke, who, before the BMA had uttered a word, lambasted us on television for being opposed to all change at any time. Another reason was that these were proposals affecting all branches of the profession and it would have been foolish for any chairman of the BMA Council to react before they could be consulted.

The main features of this blueprint for the new NHS were: opted-out hospitals, which would have management boards appointed to govern them; budgets for the larger general practices which wanted them; an internal market in which care would be bought for patients by proxies (health authorities and budgeted GPs) from providers (NHS hospitals and community services, and private hospitals); and the dismantling of national pay structures and much of the professional advisory machinery. The audit of medical practice was to become mandatory, as would a new scheme of drug-budget targets for all family doctors, and there would be some money for better information technology. The Audit Commission's remit would be extended from local government to the NHS, and the Resource Management Initiative would start to be introduced into major acute hospitals countrywide.

All the changes would 'improve patient choice' – it was not clear how – and there were strong hints of the Patient's Charter to come in terms of ridding the hospitals of long waiting times and providing better information. Running through the whole document was the move towards managerialism set in train by the 1983 Griffiths Report, and what doctors saw as the deprofessionalizing of clinical staff.

The intention was for management to be local, but accountable to Whitehall for delivering the government's objectives. To this end there would be a new NHS Policy Board, chaired and appointed by Clarke. The board would set objectives for an NHS Management Executive, chaired by the chief executive, Duncan Nichol, who was to replace Len Peach in this post next day. Nichol was an experienced NHS administrator, who had recently been the General Manager of the Mersey region. The Management Executive would also be responsible for family doctor services, in order to try to integrate primary care better with the hospital service – a goal to be welcomed if it could be achieved successfully by such means.

It was recognized that the Management Executive could not possibly control all 190 district health authorities directly, and in any case the DHAs were supposed to gain more local autonomy. The Executive could however achieve greater control over the regional health authorities, and it wanted them slimmed down. The RHAs had been the essential planning bodies of the old NHS. They held the ring between their districts, ensuring the even spread of specialist services, in which the fact that they also employed all the hospital doctors was crucial. RHAs also ran region-wide organizations such as blood transfusion and ambulance services, as well as providing advice on legal affairs, architecture, hospital design and a host of other technical matters. The seeds of the eventual destruction of the region's role were there at this early stage, and it seemed to us that, because RHA planning did not fit in with the new market dogma, one of the key successes of the NHS, its equitable spread, was at risk.

Despite all the assurances that had been given on the proper evaluation of the RMI, it was to be 'rolled out', aiming to have it working in 260 acute hospitals by the end of 1991–92. Paddy was incensed at this, knowing as he did what an expensive and difficult business it had been to introduce it into his own hospital. Even the White Paper recognized that such a general roll-out was ambitious. Paddy would have called it foolhardy.

An important part of the review concerned capital. The NHS has always been hamstrung by Treasury short-termism on capital. It was one of the reasons why most of our hospitals were so dilapidated and out-of-date. In a study in mid-1988, the National Audit Office reported that there was a £2000 million backlog in maintaining the NHS estate, with up to a quarter of it no longer usefully employed. (The Public Accounts Committee later endorsed this view.) The White Paper maintained that because capital was essentially a 'free good', under-utilization of capital assets led to inefficiency. For example, old buildings were left to rot, rather than being sold off and the money obtained reinvested. Of course if hospitals did sell off redundant plant they never saw the money again, as it went to the Treasury, so there was little incentive to do so. The wish to knock down and rebuild also led to bureaucratic entanglement as all such decisions had to be referred up the chain.

The review introduced a system of charging for capital. All buildings, plant and equipment had to be valued, a mammoth task as it turned out. Interest would be charged on that value, so that an under-used asset would become uneconomic and therefore sold. There was also a slight relaxation in the rules requiring capital plans to be approved by government: the value of capital schemes that previously had to be referred to the DoH for approval was increased from £5 to £10 million. Only those over £15 million would now have to be approved by the Treasury, instead of £10 million. Finally, there was a tentative paragraph about involving private capital. Exactly how all this was to be brought about had to await one of the later working papers. We were surprised at how vague the White Paper was about finance, and as we were later to find out, Mr Clarke was very sketchy on detail and how everything would fit together.

On balance, we thought including the health service in the Audit Commission's remit was a good move. While the government paid only very selective attention to parliamentary select committees, the reports of an independent body concerned with cost efficiency would be much harder to ignore. The Audit Commission, then led by Howard Davies, later appointed as deputy governor of the Bank of England, was a highly regarded organization, and if it could learn something of the health service and report objectively, doctors would support the idea.

Paddy, John and I were particularly interested in the chapter on self-governing hospitals. Candidates were expected to be the major acute hospitals, that is those with more than 250 beds. There were 320 of them, and the annual budgets of the larger ones exceeded £50 million. The government believed that self-government for these hospitals would 'encourage a stronger sense of local ownership and pride, building on the enormous fund of goodwill that exists in local communities'. In fact, in most districts it was already strongly felt that the local hospital belonged to the people, and the strength of its League of Friends testified to the regard in which it was held. To achieve an even stronger sense of local ownership by self-government would seem to require some involvement by local people in the selection of the governors, but this was not to be. Governance was to reside with a board of executive and non-executive directors, the chairman of which would be appointed by the Secretary of State.

The non-executive directors would also be appointed by the Health Secretary, after consulting the chairman (his own appointee), except for two drawn from the local community and approved by the RHA. The executives would include the hospital's general manager, finance director, medical director and a senior nurse manager. No board would have more than ten directors, excluding the chairman.

Having had trouble in the past with over-independent chairmen of its health authorities, the government was not going to risk letting locally elected directors with different political views to its own getting their hands on its new self-governing hospitals. Trust hospital chairmen were going to be very carefully vetted to make sure they were politically compatible with Mrs Thatcher's aims. This did not necessarily mean that they had to be members of the Conservative Party, but the overwhelming majority of those eventually appointed proved to have strong allegiances to the party or its political thinking. It was understandable that the government, because the reforms were to be based so firmly on the primacy of business and the market economy, thought they could only be carried through in the hospitals by believers. In government eyes, local Labour councillors and university academics were unlikely to be sympathetic. The idea of bringing in successful men and women from outside the health service, especially from business, was by no means anathema to doctors: the quality of management in the NHS was acknowledged to be less than uniformly high, and hospital consultants who thought their own managers were below par looked forward to some new and dynamic chairmen who would cut out the dead wood.

The new trusts would have to fund their activities by selling their services through contracts with purchasers of all kinds. They would have to earn enough not only to pay their staff and all other costs, but also the interest charges on the capital they employed. Competition with other hospitals was to be encouraged, but the Health Secretary would have reserve powers to stop any hospitals becoming too successful, due perhaps to their monopolistic position. Kenneth Clarke was clearly scared of the potential for damage in the new market he was unleashing.

As far as staff were concerned, the White Paper expressed the usual hope that jobs could be delegated to less-skilled, and thus cheaper, staff throughout the clinical field: from junior doctors to nurses; from physiotherapists, speech therapists and others to non-professional helpers. Under the heading of 'Pay Flexibility' it was proposed that the new opted-out hospital trusts should be free to settle the pay of their staff, including those, like nurses, whose pay was determined nationally by pay-review bodies.

Performance-related pay was now to penetrate further down the managerial ladder to 7000 middle managers, a move which those who remained unconvinced of its motivational powers saw as another example of the NHS being forced to follow in the footsteps of commerce: because 'business is better'. We knew that performance pay for doctors could not be far behind, and we anticipated the rows that we were to have in the mid-90s with the idealogues who advocated it.

How consultants and other hospital doctors were to be employed particularly concerned the three of us huddled amongst the militaria of the Army and Navy Club. Trusts were to be allowed to settle the pay and conditions of all their staff, including those, like doctors and nurses, covered by national pay-review bodies. They could abide by national pay agreements or invent their own.

To us this choice seemed mad. Of all the achievements of the NHS, the even spread of highly qualified hospital specialists through-out the country has been one of the greatest. This was brought about by having a national pay scale for all hospital doctors, wherever they worked and whatever specialty they practised. Since its formation, an NHS consultant neurosurgeon at a London teaching-hospital was taken on at the same salary as a consultant microbiologist in Preston.

It seemed perfectly obvious to us that, if trusts could set their own pay, eventually an expensive transfer market would develop as in the Football League. We would have premier-division hospitals and third-division hospitals, and woe betide the patient who lived in a place with a non-league hospital. As I write in 1996, this is exactly what is now happening. Stories abound of consultants in shortage specialties like anaesthetics being enticed to take up appointments at greatly enhanced starting salaries, with packages involving inducements such as cars and generous relocation expenses widely on offer. An American anaesthetist was recently recruited from Missouri to Hartlepool General Hospital with a deal that included bringing over his rottweiler dog, its quarantine charges, and his old pick-up truck.[1] The chairman of the hospital trust was delighted to fill a difficult vacancy in this way, as the consultant was not asking for double the normal salary, which other hospitals had had to pay. The doctor has since returned to the USA, with the comment 'You need to de-Stalinise your politics and your hospitals a little bit.'[2] As in pre-NHS days, we predicted that the distribution of hospital specialists would eventually come to be governed by money and not by need.

We knew that few consultants would think the new freedom offered to the management of trust hospitals to escape from the overpowering NHS bureaucracy would outweigh the disadvantages of breaking up the proven method of employing the professional staff, like doctors, that contributed so fundamentally to the equity of our health service. Clearly this was one area where we would have to try and persuade Clarke to change his views. Of 48,000 hospital doctors, 17,000 were consultants, and the paper recognized that the decisions made by them were critical as to how the NHS's money was used. To this end, carrying out medical audit was to become part of a consultant's contractual obligation. Medical audit was defined in the White Paper as 'a systematic, critical analysis of the quality of medical care, including the procedures used for diagnosis and treatment, the use of resources, and the resulting outcome for the patient'. It accepted that it was a professional matter and amounted to peer review of medical practice. Paddy, John and I and, we were sure, our colleagues, could support this wholeheartedly. Discussing the details would be necessary but we were relieved that there was at least something in Clarke's proposals that we could be enthusiastic about. In the event, medical audit proved to be not nearly so trouble-free as we had hoped.

We were less pleased about what the document had to say on

managing consultants' contracts. Government thought it unacceptable that local management had 'little authority or influence over
those who are in practice responsible for committing most of the
hospital services' resources'. On the face of it, this might seem reasonable, but no one was more conscious of the limited resources available
to them than the consultants, and they did not need accountants to
tell them that. While it was true that consultants in most departments
did not know the cost of their activities in pounds and pence, they
could not spend money that was not there, and as far as they were
concerned they treated patients and operated on them as soon and
as well as they could; priorities were governed by waiting lists. In
the view of doctors, such lists, while upsetting to them as well as to
their patients, were first and foremost a matter for politicians to
respond to – by providing the resources of staff and money to bring
them down.

Nevertheless Kenneth Clarke thought that consultants should be
more closely controlled by the managers and to this end he wanted
much more defined job descriptions and disciplinary procedures. He
annoyed our colleagues unnecessarily by insisting that district general
managers should take part directly in the appointment of consultants.
No one had ever suggested that consultant appointments, which
were governed by statute, had ever been other than scrupulously fair.
Appointment committees were independently chaired by a layman,
usually a health-authority chairman, and had members from the
relevant Royal College and from the local university medical school,
as well as representation from those with whom the successful candidate would work for the next 20 or 30 years.

Managers were also to be inserted into the distinction award
system, which was to be changed in other ways not envisaged by
Aneurin Bevan when he introduced it in 1948. I was later to spend
many a happy hour with Paddy and John as we struggled to make
the DoH's negotiators understand the benefits to the NHS of the
original system, and that, whatever its malfunctions, managers and
bureaucrats were unlikely to know as well as their peers who the
best specialists were.

As a minor sop to the glaringly obvious shortage of consultants and the failure to keep its word on the staffing agreement *Achieving a Balance*, 100 new consultant posts would be created over the next three years on the back of the review. We were pleased with this but as it meant only about half a consultant for every acute hospital we were less than overjoyed at the government's parsimony.

When it came to discussing funding the hospital service, the government did identify one cause of difficulty. Money was allocated to the 14 regions using the RAWP formula. Theoretically, this had improved the fairness of the allocations, although the RAWP targets had still not been reached in many regions. Three regions were still receiving more than 3 per cent less than their calculated allocation. Once they received their money, regions tended to distribute it to their districts on a historic basis. Those districts that had received proportionately more in the past went on getting more because they had traditionally employed more staff and had more expensive facilities. The result was that the money a district got was not related to the number of patients it treated; money did *not* follow patients. The new formula would be based on population, weighted to reflect health and age distribution, and the relative cost of providing services. The four London regions would however receive proportionately more, but 'cross-boundary flows' between regions would be paid for.

Some services to which patients needed guaranteed local access would be deemed 'core'. These included accident and emergency departments, emergency admissions to all specialties and their related outpatient and support services, and public-health and community services. District health authorities and GPs with budgets would be able to buy other services from wherever they could best obtain them, including from private hospitals.

The GPs had been told, while they struggled with their own 1987 White Paper, that the NHS review was to be largely about the hospital service. However it had occurred to Margaret Thatcher that, if self-governing hospitals were allowed to escape from the control of the district health authorities, these same DHAs, if they were to be the only buyers of hospital care, could discriminate against the hospitals which had opted to run themselves.[3] Her Policy Unit was pushing the idea of some GPs being buyers too, and Kenneth Clarke had been in favour.[4] In *Working for Patients* it was announced that the new scheme of budgetholding GPs would allow 'money to flow with the patient to hospitals from the GP practice'. Simplistically, it said that 'practices and hospitals which attract the most custom will receive the most money'. What it did not say was precisely how the regional health authorities would settle each practice's budget 'within national guide-lines designed to ensure fairness and consistency', without the detailed information on each practice's existing activity that it was widely acknowledged did not exist. Each GP practice budget was to be based on its projected use of drugs and its expected hospital referrals, together with an allowance for staff and premises improvements.

Practices with at least 11,000 patients, twice the national average, would be eligible for budgets. It was estimated that there were more than 1000 of these, making up about 9 per cent of all practices, and covering a quarter of the population. Government anticipated that budgets would be in the region of £600,000–£700,000. An extra fee to cover management and other costs, including start–up costs, was part of the inducement. The money for a district's budgeted GPs would be deducted from the DHA's budget, and this meant that if the budgets allocated proved too high the resulting district shortfall could prove disastrous. An additional risk for a district's hospitals was that if the GPs did not spend their budgets locally there would be insufficient finance for them to maintain their core services and fund their overheads like rates, power and water charges, as well as staff costs and the new capital charges, leading to redundancies and ultimately insolvency.

The White Paper followed *Promoting Better Health* by announcing the government's intention to increase the proportion of a family doctor's remuneration that was based on the number and age of the patients on his list – the capitation-fee element – from 46 per cent to at least 60 per cent. Reductions in the basic practice allowance were therefore inevitable.

Also from *Promoting Better Health* came the targeted health-promotion incentives which were to prove so contentious; and moves to enable patients to change their doctor more easily; and for practice leaflets to give much more useful information, including the advertising of the special clinics and other services they offered. Medical audit was to be encouraged in general practice but, unlike in hospital practice, would not be part of a GP's contract until details had been discussed and agreed.

A major part of the costs of general practice is the prescription of medicines. The drugs bill is the largest single element and makes up over a third of total expenditure on primary care, amounting to £1900 million in the financial year preceding the review, 1987–88. Drug expenditure was rising steadily year by year, and had grown by an average of 4 per cent more than inflation over the previous five years. There was also great variation from one locality to another, and between practices. It was not clear whether patients in the low-cost areas and of low-cost practices were being under-treated, or those in the high cost areas were being extravagantly treated. However, family practitioner committees were to be given the task of setting indicative drug budgets for each practice and for their medical advisers to then monitor the results. A new prescribing information system, the Prescribing Analysis and Cost scheme (PACT), would be used to identify variations from the norm, and these would be investigated. The new scheme would not start until April 1991, but further details would be given in one of the projected working papers, including decisions on possible sanctions against GPs who persistently exceeded their indicative drug budget without good reason; and a carrot, to go with this stick, for those spending less.

Given the emphasis on stronger management of the NHS it would have been surprising if the White Paper had had nothing to say about managing general practice, despite the sensitivity of family doctors about their independent-contractor status. GPs were nevertheless incensed by the removal of their previously strong representation on family practitioner committees. The new FPCs were to be severely slimmed down from their existing 30 members, half of whom were from the health professions, the majority doctors, and half lay, with a professional or lay chairman. The new committees would have ten members, with a chairman appointed by the Secretary of State. Of the four professional members of the new committees only one would be a GP. He or she would be appointed like the others by the quango RHA and would not be, as in the past, chosen by local GPs to represent them.

As with the other authorities, and the self-governing hospitals' boards, the lay members would also be appointed by the RHA and would serve in a personal capacity without any local representative mandate; and there would be a chief executive in whose appointment the professional members would play no part. The inevitable antagonism which this structure created made the new FPCs' task in getting off on the right foot extremely difficult, and soured the continuing negotiations over *Promoting Better Health*.

Ironically in view of the unpopular new GP contract to come, and the continuing fall in morale in general practice and consequent fall-off in trainee GPs, *Working for Patients* announced the government's intention to 'seek reserve powers to control, if necessary, the number of GPs entering into a contract with the NHS' and 'to reduce from 70 to 65 the retirement age for GPs'. Did they expect a rush of new applicants, especially into the big cities where a high proportion of the over-65-year-old, often single-handed, family doctors were?

Finally, the family practitioner committees were to be made accountable to the RHAs, as the DHAs already were, instead of directly to the Department of Health. This proved to be a first step towards control of GPs at district level, as the FPCs were later merged with the DHAs when the RHAs were abolished in 1996.

The composition of health authorities, too, was covered, being the only issue under 'Other Issues'. It is worth quoting its second paragraph in full:

Chairmen and members of health authorities will continue to have a vital role in the management of the service and will need to spearhead the changes that the Government is proposing in their White Paper. Because so much management responsibility is now to be delegated to local level, the Government have decided that the membership of authorities should reflect this new role.

This was code for: 'The workers who deliver the service are likely to cut up rough about the new commercial management culture we are introducing, so we will need strong placemen in positions of power in the new system. We will also have to get rid of local-authority representatives on DHAs because in much of the country they will be politically opposed to what we are doing.'

RHAs and DHAs which had between 15 and 20 members were reduced to a maximum of 11 members: five non-executive and from two to five executives, with a non-executive chairman. All chairmen, and the RHA non-executives, would be appointed by the Health Secretary; and the DHA non-executives would be appointed by the RHAs. The non-executive members would be appointed solely on the basis of the skills and experience they could bring to the authority, that is to say it was preferable if they were businessmen and -women who might have Conservative sympathies, and the skills and experience they brought should be related to their business activities rather than the health service.

The executive members had to include the general manager, soon to materialize as the chief executive, who was appointed by the non-executives, and he, along with the non-executives, had to appoint a finance director and up to three other executive members. Teaching districts continued to have someone from the medical school on the DHA, and RHAs had to include an FPC chairman. Local community interests were now to be left to the watchdog community health councils.

Mrs Thatcher, having secured an administrative structure as sympathetic as possible to her beliefs, now turned her attention to ways of achieving a larger private health sector. She was initially impressed by John Moore's idea that NHS hospitals might opt out completely through charities, privatization or management buy-outs, or perhaps by being leased to operating companies set up by the staff. She was also interested in tax incentives to use private care, but this was strongly resisted by the Chancellor, Nigel Lawson.[5] She managed to persuade Lawson to agree to giving tax relief on private health insurance premiums to those aged 60 or over from April 1990. This was as far as Lawson would budge, but he regretted not putting up a stronger fight in resisting any tax relief for private health insurance; but he agreed it before Clarke, who would have supported him, was made Health Secretary.[6]

The tax concession to the over-60s was included in the section of the White Paper on the independent health sector, whose contribution to healthcare in the UK was called 'very substantial'. At the time less than 10 per cent of the UK population was covered by private health insurance (it is now just over 19 per cent), but 17 per cent of all non-emergency surgery, including nearly a third of all artificial hip replacements and a fifth of coronary artery bypass grafts, was carried out in private hospitals. To many this might seem to indicate that there was a shortage of provision in the NHS, but to a government desperately anxious not to put a higher proportion of the national wealth into healthcare it increased 'the range of options available to patients and their GPs'.

To support the private sector the White Paper gave a fair wind to NHS purchasers to buy from private hospitals and other providers, and to make much wider use of competitive tendering beyond non-clinical support services like laundry and catering. Along with joint ventures in leasing land to the private sector and sharing facilities, trading was to be encouraged, including selling clinical diagnostic services like pathology and radiology to private hospitals. There was a clear threat to the new chief executives and their performance-related pay that the government 'expects all health authorities to consider the opportunities for co-operative ventures as part of their regular reviews of performance'. In the new NHS, private was good, a sea change from the previous view that private was parasitic and thus bad.

The Scottish, Welsh and Northern Irish chapters mirrored the arrangements for England but were written in a less proselytising way. The responsible secretaries of state and their departments were protecting their turf and had got in the odd trumpet-blast for the excellence and far-sightedness of their respective health services.

The final chapter set out the 'formidable programme for reform which will require energy and commitment to carry it through'. The necessary introductory stages were planned to be carried out in three phases in 1989, 1990 and 1991. In the first year a fresh NHS Policy Board would be established and the old Management Board would become the NHS Management Executive (NHSME). The first self-governing hospitals would be identified; new job descriptions for consultants and the 100 new posts would be agreed; medical audit would start and the Resource Management Initiative be extended. In general practice, work would begin on practices wanting budgets and on indicative drug budgets, and regulations would be laid making it easier for patients to change their GPs. The Audit Commission would begin its work in the NHS. In the second year, changes begun in the first would 'gather momentum'. 'Shadow' boards for the so-called first wave of self-governing NHS hospital trusts would start developing plans, and the new RHAs, DHAs and FPCs would be set up. Regions would start billing each other for work done. In the third phase, 1991, the first trusts and budgetholding GPs would begin to operate with contracts, and DHAs would join RHAs in sending bills to and fro. Each general practice would be allocated a nominal budget for the drugs they used. The amount was calculated on the assumption that generic drugs, which were cheaper than their trade-named equivalents, would be prescribed as far as possible. The name 'indicative' was attached to these drug budgets so as to avoid the suggestion that GPs' prescribing was to be capped for the first time, which would have caused uproar. It was recognized that legislation would be needed for many of the changes and this would be set in train at the earliest opportunity.

When the consultants' committee met, two days after the White Paper was published, very few members had much good to say about it. Most believed that if all that was to be changed was the organization of the NHS and not its financing, then it would have been much better to have continued with evolution rather than have a revolution. Improvement to consultants' ways of working, including peer review in the form of medical audit and the fuller involvement of patients, did not need an internal market. Better information, especially about costs, greater investment in information technology, and consultants becoming more involved in hospital management could all have been achieved without cathartic change. Rolling out the RMI to 50 more hospitals in 1989, with 260 to be covered by 1991–92, would be extremely difficult and there was considerable scepticism about the government's commitment to putting up any extra money for it. Of the six pilot sites, at one, Arrowe Park Hospital in the Wirral, RMI had already failed and the DoH had withdrawn its support. If this ratio of one failure in six was to be reproduced nationally, over 40 hospitals would have trouble. There had been major and recurring problems with large computer projects in the NHS, and the omens were not propitious.

The only member of the committee who combined being a hospital manager with his clinical work, Russell Hopkins, who managed the Cardiff teaching-hospital, felt that much good could be identified in the paper, especially in giving more responsibility to local management. Hopkins, a medically and dentally qualified consultant oral surgeon, and one of the committee's most able and interesting members, was a management evangelist. He had practised what he preached by becoming one, but later struggled to maintain his influence and credibility within the BMA by becoming too closely identified with those seen as the forces of darkness – that is, Mrs Thatcher's marketeers. This was a great pity, because his views were always refreshing, if often unpopular. Mrs Thatcher soon rewarded him with an OBE, which was seen by his opponents as a typical if rather low-grade piece of Thatcherite patronage, and achieved the effect of reducing his influence further. He has now retired from clinical work and is the chairman of a hospital trust in Wales.

A leading psychiatrist member, Professor Robin Priest, was particularly vituperative about the review's anti-medical slant, and was deeply concerned about the absence of any mention of what was to happen to the community care of the disabled, and the mentally and chronically ill. It was true that *Working for Patients* seemed very much directed at the parts of the health service that generated the most news-worthy public concern, like excessive delays for acute surgery and long surgical waiting lists.

When the GPs' committee met, the prevailing mood was anger at the threats to their independent contractor status. They also viewed the move back to greater emphasis on patient list sizes in determining their pay as a seriously retrograde step. Members were not happy about their patients having to be referred to where the health authority had placed a contract (unless they were going to be budgetholders) rather than where the doctors wanted them to go, and their loss of representation on family practitioner committees was a direct attack on their advisory role.

I was at the meeting as one of the two liaison members from the consultants' committee, and its mood was black from the start, when members gave vent to their frustrations about the nine-month-long saga of the primary-care White Paper, *Promoting Better Health*. Their negotiators had decided that enough was enough, and relations with Mr Clarke were such that, despite the confidentiality of the meetings they had been having with him, they would have to tell the committee what was going on. Clarke had been informed of this and immediately sent his own letter to all the country's family doctors. With the further changes proposed in *Working for Patients* it was clear that trouble with Kenneth Clarke would not long be delayed.

Another brick in the wall of resentment that was being built within the medical profession was the government's treatment of the 19th report of the Doctors and Dentists Pay Review Body, which recommended an average increase of about 8 per cent in doctors' pay. The most senior consultants had been awarded an extra £1000, as the DDRB had 'no doubt that hospital [doctors] have contributed to the increased [hospital] activity'.

The government removed this recommended 'bonus', diverting

it to fund the 100 extra consultant posts promised in *Working for Patients*. The DDRB's improvement to consultants' distinction awards was also interfered with, the net result being that their recommended pay rises of between 10.8 per cent and 13.7 per cent were cut to 8 per cent.

The BMA consultants were understandably annoyed by this singling-out, which was believed to be the first time that a government had interfered with recommended relativities within the profession, the setting of which was very much a matter for expert decision by the review body. Yet another move had been made by government to damage the review-body system, and a stiff letter seeking a meeting with Kenneth Clarke was sent by the BMA secretary, John Havard.

When this meeting took place, Clarke was his usual ebullient self and, while he did not actually say so, it was evident that he was not much in favour of pay-review bodies anyway. Nor was he in favour of rewarding senior consultants more than other doctors, whatever the DDRB recommended. Yet another blow was dealt to any feelings of trust that the doctors might have had in what his government was likely to do to concepts of fairness elsewhere in the health service.

The first eight working papers arrived towards the end of February. They added another 160 pages to the mound of paper issuing from the Department of Health and were supposed to 'form [the] basis of detailed discussions'. They seemed to us to lack the sort of detail that could form such a basis. For instance, in the first of them, dealing with self-governing hospitals, on the vital matter of core services the reader was referred back to the White Paper itself which had placed them in five broad categories, of which examples had been given. The fifth category, for instance, was couched in the following convoluted and general terms: 'public health, community-based services and other hospital services which used to be provided on a local basis, either as a matter of policy, – for example, services for elderly or mentally ill people – or on grounds of practicability – for example, district nursing and health visiting'. As well as being vague, when reference needed to be made to the main document, no paragraph number or page was given to facilitate finding the text sought. The papers were not a triumph of administrative efficiency, and none was indexed.

Since core services were not given as a definitive list, very large question marks remained over whether certain major specialties were core or not, such as paediatric and maternity services. It seemed disingenuous to allow these decisions to be made locally without any national input. BMA Council was also concerned that competition to provide non-core services might well lead to important facilities becoming no longer available in some districts, and necessitate patients having to travel elsewhere at great inconvenience. Was this likely to cause the eventual demise of the linchpin of the hospital service, the district general hospital?

On the key matter of the contracts which were to be agreed between hospitals and the purchasing authorities and budgetholding GPs, 'three broad classes' were given. There was very little detail about these either. There were to be block contracts, cost-and-volume contracts, and cost-per-case contracts. Part of their definition was given in Working Paper 1 and part in Working Paper 2, and again only examples, not definitions, were given of the way contracts should 'reflect a variety of performance aims', like increasing the proportion of day cases, specifying waiting times and reducing length of stay and turnover intervals. (Because of the all-pervading vagueness, all sorts of disputes were to break out later about what could and what could not reasonably be demanded by purchasers when they negotiated contracts with hospitals. In Dorset, one of these disputes was about what sort of fuel the hospitals' vehicles would use: leaded, unleaded or diesel. The Dorset Health Authority wanted the hospitals' transport to be as green as possible, a reasonable aim, but not very much to do with buying services like hip-replacement operations for local patients.) In the first few years after the reforms came into effect, nearly all contracts were of the block type. With this the purchasers would pay a hospital an annual fee, in instalments, for a very broad category of work like outpatients. Whatever the service bought, other services like diagnostic investigations tended to be included, which proved very frustrating to departments like pathology which were quite capable of entering into a more detailed type of contract, like cost-and-volume. Cost-and-volume contracts generated a fixed sum for a baseline level of activity, defined in terms of a given number of treatments, investigations or cases. Once this baseline was reached, further cases would be paid for by cost-per-case. Very few cost-per-case contracts were entered into *ab initio*. They were regarded as risky by both sides, because imprecise costing would make a glaring hole in purchasers' budgets or hospital income respectively.

As for hospitals' own financial arrangements, some flesh was put on the bones of capital charging. Charges were to be made up of two parts: 'depreciation calculated on ordinary commercial accounting principles but based on the current value of the capital assets used by authorities', and 'interest calculated on the current value of capital assets used by authorities'. To accomplish this a considerable amount of work would have to be done if the tight timetable set by Sheila Masters (then the NHS director of financial management and recently made a dame to match the sundry knighthoods awarded to most of the reforms' other executors) was to be met. By the end of 1990 the technical details of asset valuation and capital charges had to have been discussed, and the asset values recorded provisionally. After that, between then and April 1991 the methods had to be refined and the valuations updated. Self-governing hospitals would be assigned an interest-bearing debt equal to the value of their initial assets, and those managed by district health authorities would have interest levied on them at a rate to be set by government.

Together with the introduction of the new contracting system throughout the health service, capital charging and the financial demands now placed on management led to an explosion in the number of accountancy staff employed. This is a major cause of the large increase in managerial staff now needed to run the NHS.

As chairman of the consultants' negotiating committee I was aware on reading Paper 7 (on consultants' appointments, contracts and distinction awards) that many difficult meetings with the Department of Health's negotiators would have to be held. The paper obfuscated the real reason for many of the proposed changes – the need for local managers to gain control of consultants' work and their contracts – by stating that existing management arrangements 'tended to cause confusion about the nature of a consultant's accountability to local management and the district health authority'. There was, in fact, no confusion. Consultants were appointed and employed at the regional level. This allowed the RHAs to maintain specialist services as fairly and evenly as possible across the part of the country for which they were responsible. The resulting arm's-length relationship had many benefits for all concerned, apart from equity for patients. The regional medical officer was accepted by consultants as their nominal head, and it was he or she who held disciplinary power over them, and not medical colleagues or managers in their hospitals. However, to carry through its controversial business-orientated plans, government realized that it would have to transfer control of consultants' contracts to its local centurions, the managers.

They therefore demanded much more detailed timetables from consultants and gave hospital managers the task of administering them. They made a 'commitment to management' a requirement for the lowest grade of distinction award to be bestowed, and awards would have to be supported by managers as well as a consultant's peers; to this end the regional committee which made recommendations would no longer be chaired by a consultant but by the RHA chairman, and senior managers would be members. The distinction award system had not altered in principle since the start of the health service. In 1948 it had been designed to bring the best specialists into the NHS. At the time of *Working for Patients*, the four grades, 'C', 'B', 'A' and 'A plus', increased a consultant's salary considerably, and they were especially valuable in that they were pensionable. At any one time about a third of consultants hold an award of some grade, and about two-thirds of individual consultants retire with one. It is thus a most significant part of consultants' remuneration and the proposed alterations to the system were highly resented.

At the time the lowest award, the 'C', added 20 per cent to the remuneration of a consultant at the top of the salary scale; the 'B' added 40 per cent; the 'A' 70 per cent; and the 'A plus' 95 per cent. Although when newspapers write about how highly hospital specialists are paid – 'top docs' in the tabloids – it is the 'A plus' holders whose salaries they usually quote, only a little over 200 consultants have them, about 1 per cent of the total. Just over one in five consultants has a 'C' award, so even the lowest award was not easy to come by, and few consultants under the age of 45 have one. The pay-review body recommends both the number of awards that can be made, and the amount each is worth.

To consultants, meddling with distinction awards was another instance of the government twisting their tails, *and* reminding them that they were to answer to the managers now. It certainly antagonized those on whom the hospital service most depended.

Hospitals would be the main site of medical audit, to which Working Paper 6 was devoted. The paltry sum of £250,000 would be set aside centrally to fund developments in the field. The paper recognized that professional leadership was essential but it was not clear on the practicalities. All districts were directed to set up medical-audit committees, chaired by a senior clinician, but how these would operate should there be self-governing hospitals competing with district-managed ones was not foreseen. The author did not seem to have anticipated that the new opted-out units would be extremely averse to allowing their audit studies to be shared with competing hospitals in the district. This cultural change to commercial ideas about competition was completely at variance with developments like medical audit that found ready acceptance by the medical profession. Another side effect of the proposed organizational and funding changes was the damage that the internal market was likely to do to medical research (which makes relatively poor commercial sense), but the working papers were silent on this.

Working Papers 3, 4 and 8 dealt with general practice. Not much was added to the information set out in *Working for Patients*. It was recognized that there would have to be discussion about precisely what treatments would be paid for out of GPs' budgets, for those that had them. Once a definitive list had been promulgated any disputes that arose would have to be settled by regional health authority adjudicators. The cost to the GP of a procedure would normally be fixed, so that, if unexpected complications arose associated with an individual patient's treatment, the hospital would have to bear the cost. This was clearly going to give hospitals difficulties: they would have to build into their prices some adjustment for the expensive treatment of the complications known to occur in a percentage of all procedures. This might not be too difficult with, say, the incidence of deep venous thrombosis or clots travelling to the lungs after various surgical operations that, although preventable to a large extent, could never be completely eradicated. However, calculating how much to add to the price of a hip-replacement operation for a rare complication was another matter. And as some complications were commoner where known risk factors like old age or obesity operated, should a loading factor be added? Car insurance is much more expensive for those under 25 because their claim record is greater; should poor-risk patients coming to surgery cost more to their general practitioner? Surely not.

Another area in which debate needed to take place was in the matter of health screening investigations. There is no unanimity of view on the value of most of these. The best substantiated is probably the cervical smear to detect pre-cancerous change, but even mammography for breast cancer, which is now widely available, is not universally acknowledged as a cost-effective use of scarce and prioritized NHS money. Disputes still rage as to the net benefit to those modifying their diet as a result of blood-cholesterol measurement to ward off coronary heart disease, and there is no incontrovertible evidence yet of the efficacy of measuring the prostate-specific antigen as an early sign of prostatic cancer, the second commonest cancer in men. When fundholding for general practitioners commenced, pathology laboratories found themselves in some ethical difficulty with fundholders who demanded to buy expensive biochemical screening procedures for their patients that were denied to non-fundholders' patients, whose district health authorities were unconvinced that such tests should be funded ahead of other better-proven interventions.

On the question of setting budgets for those practices which qualified on size and on the quality of their management and information-technology facilities, the working paper settled for the use of historic data. This meant that the previous year's figures for patient referral, the use of diagnostic services like pathology and radiology, staff and premises costs, and drug use were used. In a large number of practices some of this data had never been collected and hospitals began to receive anguished requests from potential fundholders wanting computer print-outs of all the biochemistry tests they had asked for over a given period, or how many of their patients had had which operations. As the exercise was on-going there was some potential over the next year or so, before budgets were finally set, to boost hospital use as much as possible to ensure the largest budget was allocated.

Such 'gaming' was also possible with the potential fundholder's drug budget. A recent example of this has led the Medical Practitioners Union, a small left-wing doctors' trade union affiliated to the TUC, to refer a Dundee doctor to the General Medical Council, alleging a misuse of public funds. Dr James Dunbar described how his practice maintained its high prescribing prior to becoming a third-wave fundholder, and then made savings of £137,000 in its drug budget in its first year of fundholding. It achieved these savings by increasing its previously low use of generic drugs, which are much cheaper than their branded equivalents. The MPU makes the point that he could have saved the health service money before he became a fundholder, and he should have done. Dr Dunbar is quoted as saying, 'Yes, we delayed making savings and yes, when we did make them we were able to reinvest them for the benefit of our patients.'[7] That the doctor felt this was a perfectly legitimate thing to do, in keeping with the spirit of the reforms, is evidenced by his publishing this method of boosting his budget.[8]

The episode aptly illustrates the effects the reforms are having on the NHS at large. If the service is fragmented into thousands of small units (the so-called primary-care-led NHS), all seeking to gain competitive advantage for their patients, the chances of securing a fair and equitable distribution of its resources will be much reduced. If Dr Dunbar could have reduced his prescribing by £137,000 in the year before he became a fundholder, this sum would have been available to treat patients elsewhere, and, because he would have received a smaller budget on becoming a fundholder, the benefits to other doctors' patients would have continued in future years.

Because the government wished to rein in as much as possible the rapidly growing expenditure on drugs, indicative prescribing budgets were to be assigned to non-budgetholding general practitioners. PACT was to be extended to six pilot FPCs to assist in the formulation of these indicative drug budgets. Individual family doctors' prescribing costs would be compared with the general level of prescribing, and FPC staff could then look in more detail at the reasons why some GPs were spending much more on drugs than others. If PACT was successful it should be possible for the FPCs' medical advisers to visit high-prescribing doctors, and help them bring costs down in a reasonable way, by using fewer higher-priced brand-name products and more generic unbranded ones. A tactful approach should not compromise the care of those patients who, for one reason or another, needed a branded medicine rather than a generic alternative, and indeed those who simply required very expensive medication. There were some incentives that FPCs could offer to non-budgetholding GPs if they managed to improve on their target, as half of any saving made could be spent on improvements in other areas of primary care.

Working Paper 8 announced the replacement of family practitioner committee administrators with chief executives, who would be appointed after open competition. Some of the long-serving administrators who could not, or would not, adapt to the new management culture would lose their jobs. The radical change to the committees themselves had already been described in *Working for*

Patients, and the new FPCs would be very different from the old ones. Not only would they have the *Working for Patients* changes to cope with, but also the primary-care White Paper to implement, when it was finally agreed.

Doctors could already see the manifest dangers to the health service threatened by the internal market. They could see the likelihood of a two-tier service developing due to the introduction of the contracting system, especially where the new budgetholding GPs were concerned. They were extremely worried that the government's true intention was to destabilize the NHS, fragment it and then privatize parts of it piecemeal. The eight working papers had added little detail to the original skeletal White Paper, and, if anything, less money would be available in future because of the increased proportion of the budget which would be swallowed up by the huge increase in administration needed.

Doctors had already been branded Luddite by the Secretary of State, in anticipation of their likely response to his unpopular proposals. Although John Marks had met him at the end of February and given him his personal reaction to the changes, the BMA had still not issued a formal response.

Meetings of BMA local divisions were being held all over the country, at which the turn-out had been massive. In calmer times, divisions would often only manage to attract a dozen or so doctors to their meetings. In February, 170 turned out in Barnet (John Marks' own division), 250 in Glasgow, 200 in Stirling, 80 in Sheffield and 100 in Lambeth. The Joint Consultants Committee held an all-day meeting on 28 February, at which some of the most distinguished doctors in the land expressed their serious alarm.

A two-day meeting of the BMA Council was arranged for the beginning of March to discuss what action the association should now take.

CHAPTER FIVE

Doctors Become Angry
March–July 1989

Anger may be foolish and absurd, and one may be irritated when in the wrong; but a man never feels outraged unless in some respect he is at bottom right.
VICTOR HUGO, *Les Misérables*, 1862

The Council of the British Medical Association is a large and unwieldy body. It has nearly 80 members, 52 of whom are elected members with voting rights, and up to 27 *ex officio* members of various kinds, who include its chief officers and the chairmen of the major semi-autonomous committees within the BMA. The voting members are chosen every two years, in elections run by the Electoral Reform Society, from constituencies organized geographically and by branch of the profession. The committee is exceedingly democratic and all-embracing; there is even a seat each for a medical student and a doctor who does not qualify for any of the thirteen existing constituencies.

Thus for Kenneth Clarke and David Mellor to dub the views of the BMA unrepresentative, which they repeatedly did, was mischievous. At the time, in 1989, more than three-quarters of all doctors belonged to the BMA – even more do so now – and although election returns of only about a third of those eligible to vote are usual in BMA Council elections, about the same as in most local-government elections, all members receive voting papers. Some doctors felt an almost irresistible urge to remind Mr Clarke that the government of which he was a part had only received about 40 per cent of the votes cast in the general election, so how representative was *he*? And the NHS reforms had not been in his party's election manifesto.

The Council debate that took place on 1 March was long and wide-ranging. A particularly important contribution was made by Sir Henry Yellowlees, who had been the Chief Medical Officer at the Department of Health for ten years, until he handed over to Donald Acheson in 1983. Sir Henry had had unrivalled experience in the medical administration of the NHS, including serving as deputy to the legendary chief medical officer Sir George Godber.

Sir Henry was a voting member of Council, and said, as one who might know, that he did not trust politicians. He was especially concerned about the projected increase in the direct power of the Secretary of State over the management of health authorities, and the imposition of cash limits on patients' treatment. Nevertheless he cautioned the BMA to be careful in its response, to concentrate on the government's stated intention of improving quality and hold them to this. Others were less circumspect. One veteran family doctor remembered the days before the 1966 GP Charter when GPs were forced to have more patients on their lists than they could cope with properly and were also tempted to add to them by poaching other doctors' patients to earn a satisfactory income. He thought the name of the White Paper should be extended to *Working for Patients to come out of the NHS*. The junior doctors were worried about their future, and thought that the proposals would damage the sort of NHS in which they wanted to work. Many consultants accurately forecast that the wishes of medical staff for their hospitals not to opt out would be over-ridden by managers and shadow management boards putting them forward for self-governing status.

There was much evidence that doctors were confused about what would actually happen, and that the public was much more so. There was a prevailing desire for the BMA to give a lead, particularly to the public, and several speakers advocated trying to influence back-bench Tory MPs, who might be anxious about their seats. The BMA had taken the precaution the previous autumn of approaching the well known advertising agency Abbott Mead Vickers, should a publicity campaign be necessary. At the meeting the mandate to mount such a campaign was contained in the Council's decision to 'take steps to inform the public, press, and Parliament of its serious concern at the consequences that many of the proposals will have for the health of the nation'. The results were to have an astonishing impact when the agency's ideas were put into effect.

In summing up, chairman John Marks expressed no illusions about the power of the government to force their changes through. It would be very difficult for doctors to resist, for example by striking, because of their unique responsibility to their patients. Although the BMA had been forced to become a trade union by virtue of government legislation,[1] to protect the responsibility it had to its members to negotiate for them, it was much more than a union, which was well recognized by the public. Patients knew that those who provided the medical care in the health service had their best interests at heart, and that the BMA was the true doctors' voice.

A Council statement was issued that 'many of the proposals . . . will cause serious damage to patient care within the NHS, will lead to a fragmented service and will destroy the comprehensive nature of the existing NHS, and ignore the critical issue of inadequate funding'. Far from increasing patient choice, Council was convinced the changes proposed would limit it, and the government's refusal to allow them to be evaluated by pilot schemes would lead to further problems and expense. The necessary information systems were as yet insufficiently developed, and they must receive separate funding. Governmental recognition of the importance of medical audit was welcomed and there was a somewhat platitudinous statement approving 'the government's objective to work with those providing the service to improve standards of patient care'. The battle was therefore joined, and John Marks went away to set up what was called in the BMA his 'war cabinet'.

Meanwhile Kenneth Clarke had published his response to the interminable negotiations over the new contract for family doctors, just a day after the eight working papers had come out.[2] A few days later he made his famous remark about wishing 'that the more suspicious of our GPs would stop feeling nervously for their wallets every time that I mention the word "reform"', during a speech at the annual dinner of the Royal College of General Practitioners. This could have been a deliberate attempt to stir up a matching insulting response from exasperated GPs, which he could then use to show how unreasonable they were. The remark was classic Clarke, and he made matters worse soon afterwards by saying how well-paid GPs were, illustrating this by including the sum they were reimbursed for their practice running costs with their personal remuneration. MPs are very sensitive about their own pay if their expenses are added in this way, because it gives them a potential income of £100,000 instead of £35,000 a year, so surely Mr Clarke knew what he was doing. There can be no doubting the sincerity of the doctors who believed that what Mr Clarke was about would severely damage the health service. Despite his slurs about wallets and self-interest, as John Marks said, 'our vested interest is in our patients'. The proposals in the White Paper would have a marginal effect, if any, on doctors' remuneration and would not reduce it. Some doctors would undoubtedly earn more as a result. What the great majority did not want was to practise in a system in which money again came between them and their patients in a two-tier system, as it had before 1948.

It is difficult to overestimate the dislike Clarke was beginning to attract in the health service. On his appointment he was seen as a strong and able minister, a supporter of the Welfare State who would fight the NHS's corner in Cabinet much more effectively than his predecessor, but his repeated gaffes were beginning to look more and more like purposeful acts stemming from a deeply aggressive and antagonistic approach to those who provided the service. His crude assaults on the GPs long predated the BMA's uniquely offensive billboard-poster campaign against him and his government launched in May, and at this stage only a leaflet about the reforms and the first surgery poster, SOS FOR THE NHS, were sent to all GPs to use in their practices.

The early BMA campaign in GP surgeries soon had an effect on Conservative MPs. Twenty-seven of them put down a Commons motion attacking the BMA for presenting a biased view of the White Paper. They questioned the morality and ethics of such an action, and there were not a few doctors who were uneasy about involving their own patients in the dispute. This moral bind in which the BMA found itself very much illustrates the difficulty ethical professions have in opposing governmental interdicts which clash with their professional values.

As was true right through the campaign by the BMA to counter Mr Clarke's glib assertions that he was bringing the NHS up to date, the better to care for patients, the public were sceptical. The BMA was to commission many polls of public opinion over the next two years, and early newspaper surveys showed that the government's £1.4 million launch was not paying dividends if it was intended to win hearts and minds. A week after the publication of *Working for Patients*, fewer than 30 per cent of the public believed that the changes would improve the NHS.[3] This figure had dropped to just over 10 per cent by late March.[4]

There were strong fears at the time that the opted-out hospitals, so dubbed by the BMA, would in effect become private companies, despite the government's denials. The credibility of Mrs Thatcher on this matter was not great. She seemed to think that private medicine was superior to public medicine, which showed that her view of the NHS was not based on in-depth knowledge. To her the BMA leaders were simply turbulent priests whom she would like to be rid of. Throughout her time as Prime Minister, she consistently refused to meet any of them.

Doctors of course were holding countless meetings themselves, at which the different branches of the profession expressed their serious forebodings about the principles of the changes the government intended to make, and about how they would affect all doctors in whatever field they practised. At a special meeting of the BMA in London attended by more than 300 representative doctors from all over Britain, the line that the Council was taking was approved, and it was agreed to hold another special representative meeting in July at the annual representative meeting in Swansea.

The profession's feelings at the time were beginning to consolidate towards the non-cooperation end of a spectrum of resistance. A motion put forward by a young surgeon that GPs should be asked not to volunteer for budgets and consultants asked not to take on management responsibilities was passed. But some, like the consultants' chairman Paddy Ross, were still calling for Kenneth Clarke 'to talk to us', as if the White Paper had been Green: 'We might well have come up with proposals that everyone would have found acceptable,' he said.

However, in May the BMA launched its new publicity offensive, which caused such a furore that the chances of negotiating with such a combative man as Clarke were much diminished. The campaign opened with newspaper advertisements, the first of which said, 'Mr Clarke wants to introduce a new spirit of competition within the NHS. The health of the patient versus the cost of the treatment.' It accused him of putting the principles on which the NHS was based at risk, and asked the public to tell their MPs what they thought about the White Paper: 'It's your Health Service, it's time you had your say.' Under a picture of Mr Clarke making a speech with his upright hand in an edge-on chopping gesture, the words 'The NHS – underfunded, undermined, under threat' were printed.

The cost of the campaign at that stage was estimated at about £600,000, which compared favourably with the government's launch publicity costs of over £1 million. (The eventual cost of the BMA's campaign was about £2.5 million, but it was a classic of its kind, and will go down in the annals of the advertising industry as a major success, even if it did not achieve its objective.) In early August the campaign was switched to billboard posters, which were to be pasted up all over the country for two months at a cost of £750,000. The bill had now reached nearly £2 million, but so far members had not complained about the cost.

The posters became increasingly abusive. An early one entitled 'Mrs Thatcher's plans for the NHS' and subheaded 'Don't let her steamroller the White Paper through. Write to your MP today' was relatively innocuous, if hard-hitting. It pictured, paradoxically, a modern road roller not driven by steam. The last in the series was the rudest and the most striking: 'What do you call a man who ignores medical advice?' The answer was 'Mr Clarke.' To some, such a personally directed attack, plastered up on hundreds of hoardings, was going too far. The Conservative press, and even the *Independent* newspaper, took the BMA to task for it. The *Sun*'s response was pithy – 'What a bunch of Hippocrates' was the headline above its editorial. However, many thought that the government had it coming to them. It lived by the media sword, so should it die by it. In John Marks, Clarke had found a worthy opponent from the same robust mould.

There were murmurings within the BMA too that this was a bridge too far. Marks was seen as a bit rough by some of the more sophisticated teaching-hospital consultants, and traditionalists among the general practitioners. Doctors did not behave in this unseemly way; we had always gone quietly about our business and patients respected us for it. What was not appreciated by those not meeting Clarke was his unique combination of affability and arrogance. It caused an overwhelming desire to put a bomb under him in those who had to deal with him, and bomb him they had.

On 26 May a deputation from the Joint Consultants Committee went to see him at Richmond House, the Department of Health's new headquarters in Whitehall. An extraordinary building almost opposite the Cenotaph, it resembles nothing so much as a pipe organ carried out in yellow stock brick. It is decoratively striped with horizontal stone courses, and its glassed lower frontage is protected, presumably for security purposes, by large black bollards. The temptation to ram-raid it must have occurred to many of the disgruntled NHS staff who have passed through its revolving doors.

We met Clarke in the long narrow room kept for these occasions. Beside him he had Health Minister David Mellor; Lord Hesketh, the minister in the Lords; and a handful of officials; and at his back a line of the obligatory but rather second-rate modern prints that decorate the more upmarket parts of the NHS. Opposite him on the window side, across an enormous length of light-oak table, sat a baker's dozen of the profession's finest. Sir Anthony Grabham sat directly opposite Clarke and opened proceedings with a short summary of the profession's position. He then asked him whether he would be prepared to listen to those he had brought along, to which Clarke agreed. It was quite difficult for later speakers to avoid repetition, but starting with an assortment of Royal College presidents, including Sir Ian Todd for the surgeons and Dame Margaret Turner-Warwick for the physicians, each gave three or four minutes of what the Health Secretary could not have wanted to hear. The message was: slow down, try a few of your ideas out in a small way, and listen to the medical profession. It was all very polite, and Clarke said very little, giving the appearance of listening although he was to take scant notice of what anyone said. I remember giving him the old saw, 'If it ain't broke, don't fix it,' but I said it *was* broke – not the structure, just its finances. I also said that it was generally recognized and accepted that the financial management of the health service did need improving and that doctors were keen to become more involved in hospital management, if a practical way could be found for them to do so. The modern hospital consultant was not a profligate waster of resources, careless of the cost of what he was engaged in.

Tony Grabham summed up after about an hour of this courtly harangue, and Clarke and his retinue trooped out. The meeting had been cordial, and Grabham had been particularly impressive, but it was to have no effect on Clarke whatsoever. It was a lesson I was to learn where talking to Mr Clarke was concerned.

On the hospital side opinion was hardening. We did not seem to be getting anywhere with the Department, so the consultants' committee decided to be as proactive as possible. In early 1989 it had written to all its regional committees setting out at length its objections to self-governing hospitals being able to employ consultants on contracts different from those that were nationally agreed. The committee foresaw that this would erode the even spread of consultants, for the time-honoured reasons first put forward by the Spens committee in 1948 that had been accepted by Aneurin Bevan. We now prepared and sent an information pack on self-governing hospitals to all the consultants in the health service.[5] In an introductory letter Paddy Ross wrote that the committee believed the proposal to enable hospitals to become self-governing was the 'most significant change in the running of the Health Service'. This was a slightly parochial view, as many thought that budgetholding GPs would prove to be more significant.

Paddy set out the main concerns as six. The first was that 'many of the apparent advantages [of SGHs] can be gained equally in a DHA-managed hospital'. Second, 'the composition of an NHS Trust is virtually identical to that of a DHA, with a chairman and non-executive members appointed directly by the Secretary of State, so there is no reason to expect less political interference'. Third, 'the financial risks of self-governing status are considerable within an untried internal market system. Capital charges in particular are likely to impose a heavy burden.' Fourth, 'the ability of self-governing hospitals to depart from national remuneration levels and terms and conditions of service threatens the professional independence of consultants and jeopardizes an even distribution of high quality staff throughout the country'. Fifth, 'self-governing status within a competitive market will reduce the priority given to medical education and postgraduate training, national agreements on medical manpower and other strategic matters'. And sixth, 'the provision of a comprehensive health service in relation to the needs of the local community will be adversely affected'. The introduction went on to announce a national conference on self-governing hospitals in September and hoped that consultants would make clear to hospital managers that they must be fully involved in all discussions about opting out. The working paper on SGHs had stated that applications for that status must 'demonstrate that senior professional staff, especially consultants, will be involved in the management of the hospital' and 'any successful proposal would need to carry the substantial commitment of those likely to be involved in the new management'.

Doubts about the merits of self-governing hospitals from bodies
such as the Social Services Select Committee, the Royal College of
Surgeons and the National Association of Health Authorities were
appended, and a particularly apposite quote from the Joint Consultants Committee was included:

These proposals inevitably change the prime aim of the
management of these hospitals, from the provision of adequate
care to the community as a whole to the financial success of the
hospital. The considerable experience of such hospitals in the USA
shows clearly that there will be pressure to encourage admission
of patients with conditions that can be treated with financial
benefit to the hospital rather than to admit those patients – often
the chronic sick – whose treatment is likely to lead to little or no
such benefit.

The information pack dealt in detail with the contents of Working
Paper 1 on self-governing hospitals and included preliminary details
of a survey the committee had conducted on the expressions of
interest which had been encouraged by Duncan Nichol, the new
NHS chief executive, and which had had to be lodged with Regional
Health Authorities by 8 May and forwarded to the Department of
Health by 31 May.

Nichol had caused controversy at the end of March by writing
an official letter to managers asking them to start looking for hospitals
that could meet the criteria for self-government. This was jumping
the gun because the legislation necessary to bring about self-
governing hospitals had not yet been presented to Parliament, let
alone passed into law. Nichol, a mild-mannered but tough manager,
had a difficult role. Although ranking as a permanent secretary, he
was not precisely a civil servant, but should surely be governed by
the same rules on political matters. The then Permanent Secretary
at the Department of Health, Sir Christopher France, could not
possibly have allowed such a letter to go out under his name. Nichol
was to have to run this particular gauntlet many times in the future,

and at one point just before a general election seemed to step fully into the political arena. The relationship between civil servants and their political masters has been called into question more and more in recent years, and the role of quasi-civil servants like the chief executives of government agencies has been much debated.[6]

Disquieting feedback was coming to the committee about the pressure by managers and health authorities to do Nichol's bidding. Kenneth Clarke had announced on 7 June that a large number of hospitals had expressed an interest in becoming self-governing. What pressures had been exerted? Examples were: hints that development monies would be withheld unless a hospital 'expressed interest'; that additional funding would be available if they did; and consultants had been told that a neighbouring hospital was applying, which would threaten the survival of their own unless they did too. In some cases managers had expressed interest either without the know-ledge of consultants, or in extreme cases specifically against their wishes.

The committee was well aware that these expressions of interest would be used politically to show how enthusiastic consultants around the country were for self-governing. This soon happened, as Question Time in the House of Commons on 18 May showed:

Mr Kinnock: Is the Prime Minister aware that according to 'the Daily Telegraph' this morning, support among doctors for her National Health Service proposals has risen to a new high of one per cent? What are her plans to double that support?
The Prime Minister: If the right hon. Gentleman had read other polls he would have noticed that at least twenty five per cent of doctors have shown interest – (interruption) – in taking their own practice budgets which is very different from the figure which he gave. We have indications that many hospitals are showing interest in becoming self-governing hospitals in the Health Service. Under the White Paper the purpose is better service for patients and an opportunity for doctors to choose whether they have their own practice budgets and for hospitals to choose

whether they will become self-governing. I am well aware that choice plays no part in Socialist policies.[7]

Clarke's list undoubtedly contained some optimistic bids from very small units, and some regions had submitted very few bids. Only one was allowed through by the Oxford Regional Manager as being realistic, and the common-sensical Brian Edwards in Trent had only accepted those from hospitals where the consultants had agreed.

In our survey, the first 182 replies from chairmen of hospital medical staff committees out of 370 polled showed that in almost a third of hospitals expressing interest the decision had not been approved by medical staff. In those where they did approve, half did so because they thought there would be a financial advantage to their hospital in going self-governing in the first wave; just over a third hoped to get more information by expressing interest; and about one in 10 did so as a result of management pressure. Only 5 per cent were in favour of self-governing in general. The balance of disadvantages outweighed the advantages. The most often cited disadvantage (from 74 hospitals) was the fear of fragmentation and loss of the comprehensive service they provided to the local community. Sixty-eight hospitals mentioned the adverse effect of local pay bargaining on an equal spread of specialists. Many also mentioned worries about medical education, financial risks and the additional administrative costs of an internal market. Of those who saw any advantages, most concentrated on the possibility of escaping from the constraints, especially on funding, of health-authority management. Some saw pay flexibility for staff who were hard to retain or recruit, like medical secretaries, as being of potential benefit. (NHS pay rates were uncompetitive in many fields where the skills required were not unique to the health service. Consultants particularly felt the impact of this where secretarial assistance was concerned, because a good medical secretary is vital to the running of a department where the doctor in charge spends most of his or her time with patients on the wards, in outpatient departments or the operating theatre. If telephoned messages from GPs and patients are not dealt with skil-fully, and correspondence not handled promptly, patients will be disadvantaged, however good the doctor.)

Permeating consultants' response to *Working for Patients* was the incompatibility between the devolution of power to the periphery and existing national agreements and legislation. An example was medical manpower. The self-governing-hospital working paper allowed such hospitals to employ what medical staff they wanted, with only a vague caveat about keeping an 'approximate balance' between training posts and substantive ones. This cut right across the agreement previously reached in *Achieving a Balance*, which was designed to ensure that the number of specialist training posts was matched by the appropriate number of trained specialists required (and there are over 60 hospital specialties practised by the 20,000 consultants in the NHS). Clarke was forced to publish a further paper on SGHs that required them to conform to *Achieving a Balance*.[8]

The original working paper had also absolved the SGHs from heeding DoH advice on a multiplicity of topics. There were strong suggestions that many hospital managers saw escape from the ticker-tape shower of paper from the Department as an irresistible reason for opting out. This freedom had to be curtailed as well because legislation such as the Data Protection Act, the Hospital Complaints Procedure Act and that governing the work of the Health Service Ombudsman could not be ignored. Nor could central guidance on some public-health and ethical issues be lightly cast aside.

Firming up what was and what might not be a 'core' service was also needed, so a clause was added to the later paper saying such services would be 'all those to which patients need guaranteed local access and where there may often be no real choice available on timing or location of delivery of that service'. More guidance on this was still needed and the DoH proposed to select some districts to work through a dry run to see what common core services might be.

Countless other lacunae in the structure were being discovered all the time, not least those to do with medical research, training and education, and capital charges and finance. In the case of the latter it was becoming clearer to government by the day that they could not allow market forces to run unchecked. Word began to issue from the DoH that it was a 'managed market' that they were seeking. To those of us familiar with the fudges we had so often seen from government there were mixed feelings. We were convinced that commercial-style markets had no place in medical care, but would it not have been better for the Health Secretary to have let the market rip, only for it to quickly fail, and then ditch the whole idea? However, the new capital charges paper set out many ways in which the Health Secretary could intervene if things got out of hand.[9] It looked as if the realists in the DoH, who were also centralists, were gaining the ascendancy.

By July, Kenneth Clarke was beginning to come to terms with the fact that he was not going to take the doctors and other clinical staff with him. General practitioners were now extremely disenchanted with the progress that their negotiators had made with their new contract. At a special conference of local medical committees – the bodies to which GP practices pay a levy quite separate from the subscription most individuals pay to the BMA – representatives turned down a motion by the BMA GP committee chairman, Michael Wilson, to get the compromise contract priced by the review body. Clarke had recently announced that the support of hospital staff was not going to be necessary for their hospitals to be allowed to become self-governing, and this marked a further deterioration in the relationship between not only health ministers and the medical profession, but also that between managers and doctors. The latter was the more significant, and the breach has not yet been healed in many of our hospitals. Most consultants felt that the hospitals to which they had dedicated their professional lives for up to 30 years were being taken away from them by an alien force in cahoots with an unpopular government.

CHAPTER SIX

The NHS Bill Reaches Parliament

July–November 1989

Those who are fond of setting things to rights, have no great objection to seeing them wrong.
WILLIAM HAZLITT, *Characteristics*, 1823

At the BMA's annual meeting in Swansea at the beginning of July a second special meeting about the reforms was held and supported the line being taken. John Marks urged that the BMA must not let up in its efforts to oppose Kenneth Clarke unless and until Parliament had actually made the changes law. There was still hope that by winning the battle for public opinion the BMA would force the government to draw back from the brink, and the BMA was winning this contest, he said, despite the Department of Health's greater resources.

The BMA held many roadshows around the country at which large numbers of the public supported its efforts, and a Gallup poll it commissioned showed overwhelming disapproval of the government's actions. Seventy-five per cent of the 900 people polled thought that the proposals would result in cuts in NHS services, and about the same proportion thought that they represented the first step in a process that would end in the privatization of the health service. Sixty-five per cent thought the NHS was not safe in Conservative hands, including about a third of the Conservative voters.

Clarke's response to the GP surgery leaflet for patients, *An SOS for the NHS*, had been to accuse the BMA of lying about his intentions. At the special representative meeting, John Marks' wife and practice partner, Dr Shirley Nathan, received considerable support when she refuted Kenneth Clarke's protest in detail. She said there was only one minor inaccuracy in the leaflet (about Scottish maternity services), and this had been corrected. There can be little doubt that the paper was alarmist, but in this it had taken a leaf out of the party political book of spin-doctoring. Russell Hopkins was attacked for taking John Marks to task over its question 'If your doctor runs out of money who will prescribe for you when you are ill?'. Hopkins' OBE had just been announced and he was seen to be in the enemy's camp. In the overheated atmosphere of the Brangwyn Hall in Swansea that day the point he was making was submerged in the great anger that Clarke had generated in the medical profession. A few cooler heads wondered whether the BMA was becoming too political for the profession's good. But in his opening address to the annual meeting, John Marks had shown that he was conscious of the BMA's need to maintain credibility. He was sure that the association was winning the propaganda war and had 'got it right politically'. The BMA's support from its members was strong. Their number had increased by 4000 in a year, and was now at its highest percentage of all doctors since the 1950s. The meeting should have been Marks' last as Council chairman, as he had been in office for five years, and he was intent on going out with a bang. He got a foot-stamping standing ovation for his speech, and it was genuine and not of the customary conference type intended for the media.

However there were complications should Marks stand down after his five years in the job. When the Council elects its chairman the initial term is for three years, with re-election necessary thereafter annually for a maximum of two more. Traditionally the chairmanship alternates between the two main divisions in medicine, the GPs and the hospital consultants. Marks' natural successor would have been the consultants' chairman, Paddy Ross, but he could not be persuaded to stand. His interests were largely confined to hospital practice, and in any case he hoped to succeed Sir Anthony Grabham as chairman of the prestigious Joint Consultants Committee in a year or so. If Ross had taken the BMA chair he would have given up his chance with the JCC and, probably, the knighthood that had gone to all previous incumbents that anyone could remember. The consultants' committee could not field a candidate apart from Ross who was sufficiently *papabile* at that stage, although there was much tea-room gossip about re-electing Marks' able predecessor, Tony Grabham. By a twist of fate, upon which so much political fortune turns, Grabham's father was very ill and Tony was unable to attend the meeting. Even supposing he would have accepted nomination at that time, Grabham would have to have been present for anything to have come of the idea. There was another consideration. Although his five-year term was up, for Marks to be replaced at that juncture might have sent the wrong message to the public, the media and not least to Clarke, who was distinctly on the back foot at the time. With the usual ingenuity that Byzantine constitutional rules allow, and the BMA's are nothing if not complicated, a way was found for Marks to stand again for a further final year, and he was re-elected unopposed.

Soon after the BMA's meeting in Swansea, on 10 July, Kenneth Clarke held a meeting in the large hall of the Institute of Mechanical Engineers in Birdcage Walk about how teaching and research would be affected by his reforms. Having failed totally with the 'trade union' part of the profession, the BMA, he probably thought a change of tack to try and sweep in the apolitical intelligentsia, the Royal Colleges' élite and the medical academics, might help his cause. He was emollient, and offered a little extra money so that the service costs of research and teaching students could be helped. He would not allow the teaching-hospitals to duck out of their educational responsibilities but he would prevent them from becoming uncompetitive in the new marketplace.

If he expected rapturous approval he was disappointed. There had hardly been a word about teaching and research in his White Paper and the academics had been simmering about their neglect for about six months. Geoffrey Chisholm, president of the Royal College of Surgeons of Edinburgh and Professor of Surgery in that city, excoriated him in the most civilized way. Why hadn't Clarke asked for their advice before, as they had been eager to talk to him? Others – including Keith Peters, now Sir Keith and holder of another ancient chair, Regius Professor of Physic at Cambridge – bowled him with questions about the practical application of some of the White Paper's opacities on how research could be carried on in a market situation. Even Clarke's customary chutzpah failed to stand up to a barrage of detailed questioning from some of the cream of the profession's intellects. He appeared seriously under-briefed, and if this was an attempt to win over an important section of the profession it was a failure.

The Birdcage Walk meeting had not reassured the medical academics, and when a tenth working paper on education and training was published in October there was considerable chagrin when it was found not to include doctors and dentists. The initial guide to self-governing hospitals had, it is true, declared the Secretary of State's intention to take such powers as were necessary to make sure that trust hospitals did not evade the expensive business of paying for professional staff training in some part, but exactly what pressures could be brought to bear remained unclear. Direct funding had been proposed in Working Paper 2 to take training and research costs out of the market.

The problems of paying for education and training in a market system had also been briefly acknowledged in Enthoven's paper. When he wrote his paper, a special addition for medical teaching responsibilities known as the Service Increment for Teaching (SIFT) was in place. Later an R for 'research' was added, converting it to SIFTR. Would SIFTR remain the mechanism, and would it be enough to protect some of the leading hospitals in the country from pricing themselves out of the market?

The next day, the government's intentions on Sir Roy Griffiths' report on community care were published.[1] In his pithy report, Griffiths drew on the facts about community care elicited by the Audit Commission in 1986. 'At the centre', he said, 'community care has been talked of for thirty years and in few areas can the gap between political rhetoric and policy on the one hand, or between policy and reality in the field on the other hand have been so great.' There was 'a feeling that community care is a poor relation; everybody's distant relative but nobody's baby'. 'In short,' he said, 'we have to be satisfied that it is not the roadblocks to achievement which are the major problems, but the vehicles themselves.' In a reference to the large mental hospitals, which inexorably were being closed down, he stressed that 'no person should be discharged [into the community] without a clear package of care devised and without being the responsibility of a named care worker'. He recommended that there should be a single minister responsible for all aspects of community care, but unfortunately this advice was not followed. He wanted social services authorities funded by a specific grant, and he thought that it was the role of the public sector to ensure that care was provided, but that how it was provided was a secondary consideration. He himself was certain that local authorities should do it and be held to account for it. He was nevertheless realistic about the difficulties. There is 'no neat perfect solution waiting to be discovered – no Rubik Cube which will be perfectly solved if one can get the various components appropriately related. It cannot be managed in detail from Whitehall, but it has to be managed. The move to specific grant is important, [it is] an instrument of central control, but not an instrument of constraint'.

Clarke persuaded Margaret Thatcher to bite the bullet and delegate the social care of the elderly, handicapped and mentally ill to local authorities very much as Griffiths had suggested. The report had been with government for well over a year and there had been much talk that Mrs Thatcher did not want to allow local authorities to control the large funds that were involved. The annual bill for residential care alone had already reached £1000 million. Those involved with care were worried that the central direction of standards that Griffiths had wanted might be sacrificed to the government's evident aim in other fields to escape responsibility for what actually happened on the ground. Subsidiarity was a convenient fire escape, but the debate on what are operational matters and what are policy matters when public services are hived off to agencies and the like had not yet taken off. The government decided they could not take the financial risk of letting the local authorities run community care as proposed, and this part of the new NHS Act was excluded from its April 1991 start. It eventually arrived in April 1993.

Matters were also coming to a head over the GPs' new contract. The ballot of all GPs decided on by the GPs' committee delivered a resounding raspberry to the Secretary of State. In a high 82 per cent turnout, three-quarters of the GPs responding rejected the contract on offer. The main features were remuneration based more on patient numbers registered than previously, for prescribed immunization and cervical smear targets to be reached, and an alteration in how night visits were to be paid for. To Michael Wilson, the GPs' chairman, the poll result was a blow because he believed that it was the best package that could be negotiated, and that Clarke would simply impose it if it was not agreed. He was right, but that did not make him popular with his committee.

Clarke had said in response to a question on another occasion that he was not going to act like the Grand Old Duke of York and march his men back down the hill over the reforms. Nor did Wilson want to retreat, but to carry on up the hill into battle would have meant collecting GPs' signatures for mass resignation from the health service, as had been done when James Cameron was negotiating with Kenneth Robinson in the early 1960s. Wilson did not believe GPs would go that far on this occasion, and he was proved right on this too, eventually. Clarke's advantage over Wilson was that he did not have to take 29,000 general practitioners with him. His troops in the Department of Health and in NHS management had no choice but to follow.

After a difficult time in the committee, Michael Wilson was re-elected as chairman and instructed to reopen negotiations. However a few days later Clarke's response was to refuse to talk any further. Soon after that he imposed his new contract.

The consultants were also discouraged. They had had a great number of meetings at the Department of Health, mostly with civil servants, but many questions remained unanswered or unsatisfactorily resolved. We had talked endlessly about self-governing hospitals, consultant contracts, job descriptions, management, appointments, distinction awards and how the regions would be funded. On the latter the new simpler RAWP formula seemed not to measure social deprivation effectively as a factor requiring extra funding, a fact known ever since the Black Report of 1980.[2] We were also unconvinced that the existing medical manpower controls could survive the new staffing freedoms to be offered to self-governing hospitals, and, like the medical academics at the Birdcage Walk meeting, we had not been sufficiently reassured about education and research. A very important imponderable was how quality, as opposed to quantity, of healthcare could be safeguarded in the new contracting system. How could quality be measured, and supposing it could, how would the managers largely responsible for contracting be able to specify it when they had no medical training? What plans did the Department of Health have for advising those involved in the new contracting process on setting up the necessary measurements of clinical outcome? Were any pilot studies for monitoring agreed outcome-measures planned?

The department could not answer these questions and it became increasingly clear that knotty problems like these would be left to the overstretched managers on the ground to sort out. There was also no answer to the obvious corollary: where would the extra money come from to pay for the quantum leap in management time that was going to be needed by the new system?

The civil servants seemed to have very little freedom to negotiate anything: they were continually looking over their shoulders and having to refer back. Negotiating in the real world requires principals more than it requires principles. The DoH's principals were the health ministers back in Richmond House, but we often wondered what principles were motivating them. Nevertheless we stumbled on with John Shaw and David Walden, the department's civil servants who dealt with hospital matters. They were an interesting pair, both very able but presenting a complete contrast in styles. Shaw, the senior of them and an under-secretary, later became director of corporate affairs on the NHS Management Board for three years before retiring with a CB in 1996. He was an Oxford graduate and had an acerbic, schoolmasterly manner, but his subdued dress was always set off by a flash of bright red socks. (The significance of this was intriguing. Was it a symbol of occult left-wing rebellion in an apparently staid civil servant serving a government of whom he did not approve? His wife was a Liberal Democrat councillor, but plenty of husbands and wives had very different political views. In negotiations one tries to know as much about the opposing side as possible but we never resolved the question of John Shaw's red socks.) David Walden was altogether a less confrontational character, prepared to explore the territory that lay behind his own negotiating ramparts. He had acted as personal assistant to Sir Roy Griffiths and had a very quick mind. We made better progress with him. I already knew him as he had at one time been involved with the pathology specialty when I was chairman of the BMA's pathology subcommittee.

It seemed to the leaders of the consultants' committee that our colleagues in the regions still needed to be warned about the choppy waters they were headed for should their hospitals opt to become self-governing. We decided that we should visit hospitals around the country, both to ensure that consultants were as well briefed on the situation as possible, and to advise them as strongly as we could not to let their managers take them down the self-governing road while so many questions remained unanswered. For the next year, Paddy Ross, John Chawner and I, and many other members of the consultants' committee, traipsed round the country talking to hospital medical staff committees.

Sometimes, as at Milton Keynes and Ipswich, both of which I visited in June, the meetings were simply with consultants, and those present were nearly all for keeping the status quo. Occasionally one or two were strongly in favour of going self-governing, nearly always on the basis that early 'first-wavers' would obtain strong financial support from a government desperate for the success of its new idea. Most of these enthusiasts had lost patience with the bureaucracy of the old system and saw the coming shake-up as a way of injecting new capital into their worn-out hospitals and inadequate equipment budgets. The majority, who were against, did not want to take on the rest of the baggage that came with self-governing, and could see that a new bureaucracy would simply be substituted for the old.

At Brighton, where I spoke the following May, the hospital manager was at the meeting and, although more consultants were against opting out than in favour, a sizeable minority wanted to chance their arm and become self-governing. By that time managers were actively working towards self-government, and were looking for those consultants who would be allies when the new Jerusalem arrived. Debates were beginning to be less free than they had been, and whether your hospital opted out of the district health authority's control had become more a matter of 'when' than 'if'. Ironically the manager at Brighton left to join a healthcare consultancy outside the NHS some time after the hospital became a trust.

Doctors are by the nature of their clinical experience independent and pragmatic, and if there were to be self-governing hospitals and budgetholding GPs, however much they believed that damage to the NHS would follow, individuals had to look to the particular circumstances of their hospitals and practices and decide for themselves.

Many politicians are also independent pragmatists, especially those not picked for office (there may be a connection), and select committees are fissile because of it. The Social Services committee had first reported on *Working for Patients* in May.[3] Its report urged the government to cool things down, but it was not unanimous. Frank Field, the Labour MP in the chair, had not been able to keep two of his Conservative members on board. Marion Roe, later to become chairman herself in 1992, and Ann Widdecombe, who in 1996 was to attract the soubriquet Doris Karloff for her stern mien as Prisons Minister within the Home Office, dissented from the report's criticism of Mr Clarke's haste. They, like him, rejected the idea of pilot studies, and were in favour of self-governing hospitals and budgetholding GPs. The other seven members of the committee, including three Conservatives, had taken more note of the enormous amount of evidence they had received from a wide range of authoritative sources, including the Joint Consultants Committee and the managers' professional body, the Institute of Health Service Management. The committee was most worried about the crammed timetable that Kenneth Clarke had set, but it was also unhappy about the climate of acrimony which was now poisoning constructive dialogue. They rightly drew attention to major flaws in the White Paper, especially that there was nothing about funding, and there was no analysis of future developments and demand. They believed that family practitioner committees and district health authorities should be merged, and that tax relief for the private health insurance of the over-60s should not have been included. Cabinet solidarity would not have allowed Clarke to have made his disagreement with the latter publicly known at the time. On this occasion the select committee put a figure of £1000 million on the extra funding the NHS should have. It was announced that they would report further in the summer, which in August they did.

The committee still thought the reforms would not work but this time another Conservative, the flamboyant iconoclast Jerry Hayes, joined Marion Roe and Ann Widdecombe in a minority report dissenting from some of the committee's conclusions. Two other Conservatives, the patrician elder statesman Sir David Price and the maverick Nicholas Winterton, remained with the majority. Interestingly the report thought that a two-tier service would result, but from unfair competition between health authority-managed hospitals and self-governing ones rather than, as did happen, because of fundholding in general practice. The committee was concerned by the possibility that fundholding GPs might beat the system by declaring their patients to be emergencies and thus outside their budgets, an area that the BMA consultants' committee was also worried about.

*

The operational principles relating to contracts for health services were published in September.[4] A letter had gone out in July from Sheila Masters, the NHS director of finance, acknowledging that sophisticated billing systems could not be in place by 1991, and the approach to contracting would have to be 'pragmatic'. This must have caused horse laughs among the desperately under-prepared managers in districts, hospitals and potential budgetholding general practices. The letter also mentioned 'diagnosis-related groups' or DRGs. This American concept had been part of the Resource Management Initiative. The idea was that a generalized costing system could be developed based not on individual medical interventions but on a package in which all the activities surrounding the treatment of a patient with a certain diagnosis could be amalgamated into one DRG. To achieve this, contractors were to be offered help with a computerized cost-allocation model and DRG 'grouper' (which would enable a hospital's work to be coded into DRGs), and a computer-based training package for staff. It was the practical difficulty of doing this that had made the RMI such an arduous task for the pilot hospitals that had tried it. It was crucial that the coding should be very accurate, and naturally it proved difficult to train clerical staff without medical knowledge to do it with sufficient precision to be used for financial contracts, on which the viability of hospital might depend.

The main paper gave a little more detail about the practical difficulties that would arise from contracting but was full of such phrases as: 'Guidance on a proposed system of shared funding [relating to specialists' services that were not provided in all districts, like cardiac surgery] will be issued in due course after consultation with interested parties.' The paper was full of 'mays' and 'mights' and inadvertently demonstrated on every page why piloting should have been tried. The Treasury probably thought so too when they weighed in with doubts about the existence of sufficient information technology to make the new system work properly.

The Joint Consultants Committee prepared a searching series of questions on contracting for Duncan Nichol to answer. This he did in a very general way, which made it clear that 'Suck it and see' prevailed in DoH thinking. He could not put even the vaguest figure on the additional cost of the new contracting system, the computers needed, nor on any aspects of the internal market. He *could* say that £82 million had already been spent on work for the reforms in the nine months since they had been announced, and that SIFT would be raised by £5.6 million from the £276 billion for 1989–90, a 2 per cent increase. Reading between the lines it seemed that he himself was doubtful about some of the underlying governmental assumptions of greater cost-efficiency. At these points he switched from a direct answer to 'The government is convinced . . .' and 'Government also expects . . .', which was not very reassuring.

Professor Enthoven himself had more explicit doubts when he paid another visit to the UK in September 1989. He said again that pilot studies should have been set up, and that a timescale of about 10 years would have been reasonable. Instead Kenneth Clarke's politically driven timetable allowed only two years.

Enthoven was also less than enthusiastic about the size of the proposed general practices that would be allowed budgets. He envisaged 100,000 patients as a suitable minimum, not 11,000, although a comprehensive HMO-type span of care was not involved. It may well be that some of the extremely large so-called multi-fund, total purchasing general practice groups that are now being tried equate better with his ideas. In total fundholding all care must be bought, including emergencies and other core services, and a multi-fund involves a group of practices pooling their budgets. Multi-funds may have 100,000 or more patients registered with them, about half the size of a typical health district. There are risks in total fundholding as, even with a much larger budget, unless practices join with others and become multi-funds, they can be swamped by a few very expensive events. For instance, in 1995 in Berkshire five out of six total fundholders spent an average of £25,000 a year on neonatal care, but the sixth had to pay £500,000 because intensive care was needed, which costs over £1000 a day.[5]

A very important point that Enthoven made on his visit was that, if doctors do not trust management, 'Then forget it.'[6] The proper relationship between doctors and managers remains the single most important unresolved factor in the NHS structure as we approach the millennium.

It was disastrous that Mrs Thatcher ran her review privately in the way that she did. It is universally acknowledged that politics cannot be taken out of healthcare, but the chance that five government ministers, most of whom had exceptionally heavy responsibilities elsewhere and little or no experience of the subject, could devise a new structure for the health service, even with help from Sir Roy Griffiths and a few advisers, was always going to be vanishingly small.

By taking the health professions into her confidence and asking if and how Enthoven's and others' work could best be adapted to the health service, years of conflict and anguish for patients and staff could have been avoided. Even if, at the end of the day, much of Enthoven had been found untransplantable, some improvements were bound to have followed. He repeatedly advocated small pilot studies, and there can be no question that he was right.

It was at about this time that Professor Harry Keen came on the scene by organizing a meeting of London consultants and academics that was highly critical of Kenneth Clarke's plans. Professor Keen, an internationally renowned diabetologist at Guy's Hospital, went on to found the NHS Support Federation, and was to be a thorn in the side of government for years over its plans for the NHS and for Guy's.

Events and personalities at Guy's could be regarded as paradigms for much connected with the NHS reforms. As one of the most famous teaching-hospitals, not only in Britain but in the world, Guy's had a very high profile from the beginning because it was regarded as the flagship for the changes. It had been a pioneer of the Resource Management Initiative and was seen as a model for the integration of doctors and nurses into hospital management: the various clinical specialty groups had been organized into clinical directorates, each having a consultant as clinical director, a nurse or paramedical as manager, and access to trained financial expertise. The directors formed a management board with an overall medical director. The first occupant of this post, Cyril Chantler, a paediatrician, was an apostle of medical management and was later appointed to the main NHS management board. He remained on the NHS board until 1996 when he left with a knighthood.

From Guy's also came two recently ennobled life peers, Tony Trafford and Ian McColl, both a year ahead of me there as students. Trafford had had an unusual career. He had left Guy's to go to Brighton as a consultant physician 20 years before, but soon after his appointment he had become Conservative MP for the Wrekin in Shropshire. How he managed to combine the two was a mystery to his friends but he only remained an MP between 1970 and 1974. He came to prominence after the Brighton IRA bombing of the Grand Hotel during the Tory party conference in 1984, when as a consultant at the local hospital he was involved in the care of many of the casualties, including Norman, now Lord, Tebbit. Trafford became a life peer in 1987, and had only just taken on the role of Health Minister in the Lords when he died very suddenly in September 1989. Not only was this a tragedy in itself, but in the two short months of his appointment there had been signs that he might have become a moderating influence between Clarke and the profession. His Lords health brief included the care of the elderly and therefore his input into community-care arrangements would have been valuable, and he was also responsible for medical manpower and junior doctors, both of which could have benefited from his cool head and personal experience.

Ian McColl's elevation to the Lords in July, without any intervening honours or official political experience, was if anything even more of a surprise than Tony Trafford's. He was a leading light in the Conservative Medical Society and had been recruited by David Willetts to give his views to Mrs Thatcher's Downing Street Policy Unit in 1988.[7] As Professor of Surgery at Guy's, McColl was a well-known academic, but rumour had it that he had advised Barbara Castle too when she was Health Secretary, so what exactly were his politics? He is undoubtedly an idealist, interested in new ideas. His integrity has never been doubted, but he was seen as a collaborator with the enemy by many doctors, and later he was to be heavily involved with Kenneth Clarke in working through ideas for self-governing hospitals.[8]

Nicholas Timmins, in his book, *The Five Giants*, suggests that McColl's nostalgia for the old days at Guy's, when the hospital was independent and run by a medical superintendent and a board of governors, can be detected in the concept of self-governing hospitals, and this is almost certainly correct. The Guy's medical superintendents were highly respected members of the hospital's senior consultant staff and were chosen by their colleagues. The superintendent lived in a rather grand part of the main building just inside the front gates, and had considerable power well into the 1960s. In a way, memories of the superintendent probably helped to gain acceptance also for the post of medical director which Sir Cyril Chantler later occupied.

David Willetts himself, who became heavily involved with the NHS reforms as director of the Centre for Policy Studies before becoming MP for Havant, has a Guy's connection too in that he is married to the daughter of Lord Butterfield, another physician from Guy's, who became Vice Chancellor of Oxford University.

Thus Guy's became not only a test bed for the reforms (especially when Peter Griffiths came from the NHS management board to become its chief executive), but also a hotbed of the resistance movement led by Harry Keen, who in the heady days of late 1989 carried the majority of the consultant staff with him. The days of *Schadenfreude* for Guy's Hospital's rivals, when the standard was torn from its flagship mast and many of its functions were transferred to its closest rival, St Thomas's Hospital, were some years off.

The great deal of money that Kenneth Clarke had allocated for work on the reforms was to be legally challenged by Harry Keen. To pay for judicial review of the legality of spending the money before the legislation introducing the reforms had been through Parliament, he wrote to all the consultants in the NHS asking for a minimum of £10, which about one in five paid, raising £40,000. Ultimately this endeavour failed, as will be related later.

*

At the Conservative Party conference in October, away from the main event – where Kenneth Clarke attracted the plaudits of the rank and file with his answer of 'Healthy' to the BMA poster question 'What do you call someone who ignores his doctor's advice?' – the BMA delegation was savaged at one of the fringe meetings. The BMA group had been introduced by the new BMA secretary, Ian Field, who had spoken for too long and should have left the floor earlier to the medico-politicals he had with him. Consequently the audience which Paddy Ross and the others addressed was already restive. Paddy was a natural Conservative himself and he found it difficult to cope with the verbal assault he suffered at the hands of the wildly partisan members of the party attending the meeting. The atmosphere was quite unlike that usually met in the fringe meetings at the main political party conferences that the BMA attended every year. Paddy publicly tore up his party membership card soon afterwards, in disgust. (The BMA tended to send those it hoped might be compatible with the particular party. Our more demotic leaders tended to be assigned to the Labour Party; I on the whole found myself with the Social and Liberal Democrats or later the Liberal Democrats, who were interesting but had some unorthodox outriders concerned with such less political matters as alternative medicine and diet. I always found it ironic later as Council chairman to be typecast as a right-winger, as, although not a member of any political party, unlike Paddy Ross and some other prominent consultant Conservatives, I felt more at home in that part of the political rainbow where orange changes to blue, always excepting the rather specific appeal of the Green Party which occupies that position prismatically.)

About this time the government were taking such a pasting in the public-relations battle that committed Conservatives in the constituencies and within medicine were starting to hit back. Shortly after the party conference, Conservative doctors formed a body in opposition to Harry Keen's NHS Support Federation, called the NHS Reform Group. Its chief architect was Dr Clive Froggatt, a family doctor from Cheltenham and leading light in the Conservative Medical Society. Clive already had the Prime Minister's ear, and regularly met with the Health Secretary, even deputizing for him at a press conference on one occasion. Along with Dr Michael Goldsmith, another even more entrepreneurial GP from the same political stable, Clive was one of the 'us' whom Mrs Thatcher consulted about the ideas that were coming out of her review group. He was heavily involved in Conservative affairs in the Cheltenham constituency, and very friendly with its MP, the late Sir Charles Irving. He had also worked with the Downing Street Policy Unit on the GP White Paper in 1987, and that following Roy Griffiths' report on community care.

Despite the activities of the pro-reform lobbies, hearts and minds were not being won, and at the end of October 1989 Mrs Thatcher took the opportunity provided by the resignation of her 'unassailable' Chancellor of the Exchequer, Nigel Lawson, to break up the bruising team of Clarke and Mellor and introduce someone who might be expected to look more like one of their own to the embattled health service staff. David Mellor's replacement as Health Minister, Virginia Bottomley, had been an MP for only five years, but had been a psychiatric social worker dealing with children in south London for eleven years before becoming an MP, so knew something about the health service. She had had a meteoric parliamentary career, having been a parliamentary private secretary to ministers in three departments of state, and a junior minister at the Department of the Environment.

Kenneth Clarke's own concession to the widespread opposition coming from the health service was to soften his language a little. On 22 November he introduced the NHS and Community Care Bill for its first reading in the House of Commons, and this Bill suggested that contracts were in fact simply service agreements. This may have been because of the flurry that there had been when the question of the legal enforcement of health service contracts had been raised. GPs with budgets would be called 'fundholders', as this sounded more encouraging than 'budgetholders'. There were no concessions to the BMA about clinical staff or the local community having a say in whether their hospital became self-governing – a 'trust' as it was now to be called – and no firming-up of Mr Clarke's assurances that medical training and research would be protected, beyond giving him powers to intervene if necessary. Legislation to introduce the changes set out in the recently published community care White Paper was included.

The Bill set out on its course through Parliament with a view to its inclusion in the Queen's Speech in November.

CHAPTER SEVEN

Opposition and Negotiation
January–June 1990

He that wrestles with us strengthens our nerves and sharpens our skill.
EDMUND BURKE, *Reflections on the Revolution in France*, 1790

The National Health Service and Community Care Bill reached the committee stage in Parliament in early January 1990. Opponents still hoped that important amendments could be made, since not all the Conservative members of the standing committee considering it were doctrinal purists. However, although some 900 amendments were tabled, no changes of any significance were made to the Bill, and Clarke was able to sound triumphant when its final clauses were approved at the end of February. Typically, he was unable to resist gilding the lily by claiming that the opposition parties and those in the health service were really in favour of what he was doing to improve the NHS. The public certainly were not in favour, as a third Gallup poll for the BMA showed. The percentage of people who approved what the government was doing to reform the NHS had dropped further to 11 per cent, down from 13 per cent two months before.

The lie to Kenneth Clarke's optimism was also given in March when the leaders of half a million NHS staff, including nurses and doctors, issued a document, *The Way Forward for the NHS*, which called for the reforms to be tried out in just two regions, and very carefully evaluated by an advisory body that would report to the soon-to-be-appointed NHS director of research and development. The signatories were 'ready to support proposals if properly costed and funded which can be shown to provide a better service, a service whose main defects are due to historic underfunding rather than defective organization'. This was followed by a statement expressing similar opposition to Kenneth Clarke's changes by the staff side of the General Whitley Council, which represented over a million more NHS employees.

Because the reforms were so far-reaching, and so potentially catastrophic, the BMA had always believed that, rather than bring them in all over the country at once, a smaller area might be chosen. Perhaps a small region like East Anglia, or two combined, could pilot the changes to start with? If things went badly wrong, money and management could have been pumped in and lessons learned. Clarke would have none of this. He probably saw such suggestions as a plot to cripple the reforms and cause confusion and delay. He believed that the health unions, including the BMA, would be able to muster all their fire on one small front rather than have to disperse it over the whole country. Politically he may have been right to have the NHS swallow its bitter medicine all in one go, but operationally he was wrong and the service has paid the price ever since.

The BMA's high-profile publicity campaign had ended in the summer with a bang, and it had switched its attention to mobilizing the opposition of its members locally and to lobbying members of both Houses of Parliament, where Kenneth Clarke was now embroiled in the national ambulance dispute over pay and conditions. Although much of the flak was being taken by Duncan Nichol, including regular television interviews, Clarke's attacks on ambulancemen as 'just professional drivers' had not gone down well. Those in medicine wondered whether he had sufficient grasp of all the pieces which made up the NHS jigsaw. He had accused the BMA of spending £3 million on its campaign against him, which was half a million pounds more than had actually been spent (and how would he know anyway?), and he seemed to be confusing Harry Keen and his fund-raising with the BMA, which had no need to seek funds to oppose him. It is true that some leading GPs in the BMA were setting up a NHS Supporters' Party to fight parliamentary elections, but this was not sponsored by the BMA in any way, nor was it connected with Professor Keen. A prominent GP, Christopher Tiarks, was to create a considerable diversion by standing in the Vale of Glamorgan by-election as an NHSSP candidate, and a leading member of the GPs' committee, Judy Gilley, had decided to oppose Mrs Thatcher in Finchley when the time came.

Harry Keen's writ for judicial review of the legality of what the Department of Health was doing to advance the reforms before the necessary legislation had been passed was heard in early February. The BMA had not felt able to support Keen because Anthony Scrivener QC, from whom it had sought advice, had believed there was not much chance of applying the brakes on Clarke in this way. Whatever the legal position, the fact that the case was brought at all must have been annoying to Clarke. The QC whom Harry Keen engaged, James Goudie, established that at least £40 million had been spent so far on setting up the reforms, with more than £250 million to come before the planned start date of April 1991. In fact the government were to publish figures considerably in excess of these a few weeks later. Since April 1989 they had spent £85 million to fund initial work on the White Paper, and planned to spend £300 million in 1990–91, excluding the enormous computer costs needed, which were estimated at an extra £165 million. Thus at that stage, about £550 million was the projected cost of introducing the changes, and this itself included nothing for the associated extra workload that had descended on everyone in the health service. The costs were therefore enormous and to date attempts by government to justify them have owed more to the *modus operandi* of the spin doctor and the snake-oil salesman than to that of the chartered accountant.

Goudie argued that Clarke did not have the power to spend all this money before the legislation introducing the changes had been passed. He said that the new NHS proposed was so different from the old, which was covered by the 1977 NHS Act, that Clarke could not proceed. Clarke's barrister thought he could, because he was simply acting with the powers his state office gave him to provide effective health services. Judges Woolf and Pill concurred with that view and £100,000 of Keen's fighting fund disappeared in costs.

The NHS Bill finally completed its committee and report stages in the House of Commons at the end of March with rowdy scenes and a midnight guillotine. There was a titanic row between Kenneth Clarke and his Labour opponent Robin Cook, in which the latter accused the former of a breach of faith.[1] Cook also, at a press conference later, warned hospital managers that they had better slow down in their attempts to take their hospitals down the self-governing road. If Labour won the next election, which would be within a year of the reforms' start date, they would reverse the changes. The internal market would be abolished, self-governing hospitals not voted for by local people would be returned to their district health authorities, and the businessmen appointed to authorities would be replaced by people truly representative of the community.

Cook's threats to managers were widely reported and drew much criticism from moderate opinion. They were nevertheless a sign that the gloves had come off in the political battle between Cook and Clarke, and any opposition to the NHS reforms was immediately pressed into the mould of party politics. In Clarkian terms the BMA were 'those lefties from Tavistock Square' and the Royal Colleges not much better. This traduced the BMA, and the stereotype Clarke created enabled him to rubbish informed criticism from any medical source. The course chosen by the BMA was to step up its lobbying in the House of Lords, where the Bill would go next, knowing that the main planks of the reforms could not now be altered. Damage limitation had to be the best option. Was there still a slight chance that the peers would pick up the piloting ideas from the Royal Colleges' *Way Forward for the NHS* and advance a thoughtful amendment that would succeed in slowing Clarke down? Those of us who had had any contact with him thought 'Not a chance,' but the Lords remained our only hope. On 24 April the Lords rejected building in such formal evaluation by 109 votes to 86, having previously rejected an all-party amendment that consultation must take place before a hospital could become self-governing. In May, at a meeting organized by Professor Keen's NHS Support Federation, I spoke on self-governing hospitals and the less than ethical reasons why some of our hospitals were, in the jargon, 'expressing an interest'. Interested hospitals wanted to be winners, and there was nothing wrong with that in the sense of being successful, but for there to be winners in a market there had to be losers too, and this was unacceptable in a health service one of whose founding principles was equity.

Conflicts among hospital staff over whether to become self-governing were dividing colleagues and damaging important relationships between those to whom friendly rivalry had been a useful spur to better performance. Rivalry was ceasing to be friendly in some places, and was downright destructive in others. Productive co-operation between doctors and managers had been dealt a serious blow by an insensitive, and in many ways sinister, document leaked from the Trent Regional Health Authority. In it managers in the new self-governing hospitals were invited to deal with those staff who opposed the reforms, and referred to them as 'renegades, subversives and opposers'. Another ringing sentence also sounded alarm bells: 'If a self-governing trust values teamwork – it needs to confront the obstructive and the prima donna when all else has failed to persuade individuals to sign up to a corporate philosophy.'

My response to this was: 'I think we have a corporate philosophy in medicine and that it has something to do with Hippocrates.' The meeting was not a rabble-rousing event. It was thoughtfully chaired by Sir Henry Yellowlees, and included a speaker from the Patients Association, not always unstinting in its praise for doctors but worried about the reforms, and a leading manager, Lorne Williamson, who strongly supported the proposed changes. Mr Williamson had a high profile at the time as he was District General Manager of the Tower Hamlets DHA that had the London Hospital (now The Royal London, which, with apologies to its alumni, I always think sounds more like a hotel than a hospital) within its territory. He was in charge of the London's bid to become self-governing and was expected to become its chief executive if the bid was successful. His personal career path was to be blighted later but the London's application succeeded and was indirectly responsible for the tragedy that was to overtake Bart's. Mr Williamson said that it was not his intention to take on the BMA as 'it would not be sensible to do so, initially'. Cautious words, but the terminal qualifier was noted by the doctors present.

At around this time Kenneth Clarke made what seemed to the Joint Consultants Committee an attempt to separate the Royal Colleges from the BMA. He proposed an advisory body that would monitor the new NHS and make sure that the reforms did not cause the damage to patient care that his opponents were widely predicting. The body, eventually to be called the Clinical Standards Advisory Group (CSAG), was set up with a lay chairman appointed by Clarke and appointed members, and in the event was to have a low profile. It was a purely political move, as I and others said in the JCC at the time, and the BMA, excluded from any involvement in its terms of reference and its membership, were cynical. But as long as Clarke did not expect agreeing to the setting-up of CSAG implied approval of his reforms, college presidents like Terence English thought they could not reject it and therefore should participate. Terence had already made a stand over Clarke's obvious intention to try and split off the BMA component of the JCC and deal just with the Royal Colleges. He had written several times to both the Health Secretary and the Chief Medical Officer about Clarke's failure to involve Sir Anthony Grabham, the chairman of the JCC (who came from the BMA side), in what he had in mind. Ultimately English wrote to Clarke refusing to attend a meeting with the college presidents that he had arranged for early April to discuss clinical standards and the NHS review. This firm stand by probably the most distinguished and publicly well-known president (he was one of the two leading heart transplant surgeons in Britain) had its effect, and the JCC chairman finally joined CSAG, but only as an observer.

The argument the medical profession was having with the government about the reforms was exacerbated when the doctors' pay-review body recommendations were again interfered with, for the eighth time in 10 years, and in the same way as the previous year.

This reinforced the doctors' view that they could not rely on their employer, the government's, integrity – a very serious charge. The review body for doctors' and dentists' pay was set up following the report of the Royal Commission in 1960 to Prime Minister Harold Macmillan. It was intended to resolve the unseemly and potentially dangerous clashes over their remuneration between doctors and government. The idea was welcomed by both sides and had worked reasonably well until the Thatcher governments from 1979 onwards. Mrs Thatcher was thought to be philosophically antipathetic to review bodies because of her belief in markets. Throughout the 1980s, tension developed because it became more and more clear that pay in the public sector was being used *pour encourager les autres*, despite the founding principle of review bodies that their recommendations must remain outside such considerations. There was a phrase of which we were regularly forced to remind health secretaries when we went to hear what the government's decisions were on receiving the DDRB's reports every year. This was, in the Royal Commission's words, that DDRB recommendations 'must only very rarely and for most obviously compelling reasons be rejected'. Eight times out of 10 did not seem to tally very well with 'rarely'; nor were we at all often persuaded that the reasons offered by government were compelling. The Royal Commission had anticipated bad faith by governments in using public-sector pay, including that of doctors and dentists, as an economic regulator, and specifically said that it should not be. It even amplified this by saying, 'Their earnings should not be prevented from rising because of fears that others may follow,' which is precisely what Clarke had in mind. A sour meeting was had with him, at which he was able to offer no meaningful response to our question about what Sir Graham Wilkins, the DDRB's chairman, had actually written in the body of his report: that he did 'not find the government's explanation convincing' for its removal of the additional £1000 recommended for senior consultants the year before. We found Clarke's explanation that it was to pay for extra consultants to be appointed even less convincing than Sir Graham. In short we did not believe one word of it, and another nail was knocked in the coffin of Clarke's credibility. As the BMA leaders left Richmond House many members of the delegation must have reflected on the falling standards in public life that allowed ministers to be so economical with the *actualité*, in Alan Clark's later famous words, whenever it suited them. This deterioration has continued unchecked, as the Scott report in 1996 so depressingly demonstrated.[2]

On 7 February some of us were at the Department of Health again, this time to see Virginia Bottomley on junior doctors' hours of work. Dr Graeme McDonald, the juniors' chairman, thought that the government might support an amendment to the NHS Bill, then in committee, preventing the exploitation of junior doctors, but it had to be left to the Labour Party to propose one (unsuccessfully) at the report stage. Mrs Bottomley professed sympathy for those juniors who were working excessive hours, but there were semantic difficulties over hours of *duty* and hours of *work*. The Department considered being available on call to be of such little consequence compared to treating patients on the wards that it was not prepared to intervene effectively with those hospitals which exploited their young doctors. The juniors were offered more discussions, but they had been having these for years and nothing concrete ever seemed to get done.

The trigger for this meeting had been the Dowie report, commissioned by the DoH.[3] Dr Dowie's report was a depressing document. She had interviewed 522 junior doctors in 1987 and 1988 about their work and found that more than 40 of them were on duty on average for 90 hours a week, with the most junior of them averaging 97 hours. A large proportion regretted ever having taken up medicine and, whilst this feeling was more common amongst the most junior who were going through a baptism of fire and fatigue, many doctors quite far advanced on a specialist career felt the same. Mrs Bottomley pleaded that time was needed to set things to rights, but the cynicism expressed by Graeme McDonald and his three junior-doctor colleagues was overwhelming, and he had no difficulty in getting his case across to the journalists who attended the press conference he gave immediately after the meeting.

In fact, junior doctors' hours of work were eventually reduced somewhat, but what many of them have found is that the same, or usually more, work has to be squeezed into a shorter period of time and thus their levels of fatigue have not lessened much.

Working conditions for consultants were on the agenda in May, when I and my colleagues concluded the negotiations with the Department of Health on Working Paper 7, *NHS Consultants: Appointments, Contracts and Distinction Awards*. We had succeeded to a large extent, against the odds in the view of some commentators, in defending the professional nature of consultant work. Our negotiating position had been much strengthened by the publication, with the 1990 pay-review body report, of a survey of consultants' workload by the Office of Manpower Economics. The OME provides the working secretariat of the review body and is therefore independent of the profession and of government. What the survey showed was that consultants worked on average about 10 hours more per week than their contracts required them to, without counting their on-call commitment for emergencies. A sample of one in 16 of all consultants had been taken in order to avoid bias towards any particular specialty. Sixty per cent of those sampled had provided useable data. Weekly hours worked ranged from 40 by ophthalmologists to 52 by accident and emergency consultants, and while emergency recalls added only 12 minutes for pathologists, five hours were carried out by paediatricians. What the survey was saying to those in the Department who had ears to hear was that the NHS was getting a great deal more work out of the consultants than it was paying for. This was only to be expected from senior members of a profession with whom bucks stopped, but enforcing a rigid, industrial type of contract on such people would risk losing far more than any apparent managerial advantage gained.

A most important feature of a consultant's work is that it can never be governed by a time clock or a factory hooter. Nor would patients expect it to be. Another aspect is that in the hospital situation a consultant is really his own manager. He or she will normally have to work as part of a team, often including his peers, and will need to co-operate with others of all disciplines. But it is to misunderstand the nature of medicine to imagine, for instance, that a surgeon's contract could be sensibly written specifying that every Tuesday, between nine a.m. and one p.m., he will perform one colectomy, one appendicectomy, one mastectomy and two inguinal herniorrhaphies. Once we had agreed how 'job plans' were to be applied, we were able to concede a greater role for local managers in monitoring them. In practice what was to happen in most hospitals was that this task was given to the medical director, and the system has worked perfectly well since.

We were not able to agree so easily on appointment procedures or on distinction awards. We were concerned at what we saw as the unnecessary insertion of managers into what were largely or entirely professional matters. On the question of consultant appointments, the Department had one major change in mind. This was that the district general manager should join the appointment panel as a full voting member. There were two reasons for this proposal as we saw it: first, to raise the status of the DGM *vis-à-vis* consultants, a largely cosmetic change; and, second, to enable a manager to ascertain how amenable a potential appointee might be to managerial priorities if they differed from medical ones. This second reason was significant and, in our view, potentially unacceptable. It was the duty of the specialist medical members of the appointing panels to ensure that the chosen candidate was the best qualified for the job, and of the lay chairman to act on behalf of the employing authority, of which he was usually the chairman or at least a member, to prevent bias or special pleading amongst the medical members leading to the wrong appointment. Nevertheless we eventually gave way on this point, hoping that managerial common sense would prevail.

On distinction awards, admittedly an arcane system even among doctors (not excluding recipients), we thought many of the Department's ideas unfair and uninformed. The main proposals were that awards would be regularly reviewed and could be withdrawn if performance was shown to have fallen; that an award must be held for three years before it became pensionable; that the lowest, 'C', award should only be given to those who had a commitment to management and the 'development of the service'; that no one should be allowed to obtain a higher award without joining the ladder at the 'C' award level; and that managerial input should be increased on the regional 'C' award committees which recommended who should receive one. In addition, the regional health authority chairman would now chair these regional committees instead of a senior consultant, and he would be joined by five senior managers.

As chairman of the consultants' negotiators I had had lunch in November the previous year with Sir Gordon Robson, the anaesthetist chairman of the National Central Awards Committee, which oversaw the whole system, to find out what he thought about the government's White Paper proposals on distinction awards. Many of them did not worry him overmuch, but like us he thought the idea that an award would have to be held for three years before being pensionable seemed unfair, especially if a consultant died (as his widow would be penalized) or had to retire because of ill-health before the three years were completed.

The idea behind the proposal was that the Department believed that awards were given as 'retirement presents' to boost pensions. We believed that the gap between us was largely due to a different perception of the nature of a distinction award. Consultants saw them as an increase in salary given for outstanding work over a long career. The DoH seemed to regard them as performance pay, to be assessed regularly, and raised and lowered like managerial bonuses.

Sir Gordon believed that the civil servants within the DoH were actually quite sympathetic to the consultants over the matter of distinction awards. Although he did not say so, it seemed to me that civil servants, who retired on full pension at 60, and whose most senior and outstanding members commonly received (admittedly non-monetary) awards in the shape of knighthoods, CBs and CBEs, might very well see the matter with eyes not much different from ours. It seemed the intransigence was coming from the Secretary of State.

As far as the necessary transition from 'C' upwards was concerned, it was exceptionally rare to start higher, although there was once a brilliant researcher who had gone unnoticed by the system for 17 years before going straight on to an 'A plus'. We negotiated a get-out clause for researchers and academics who could not claim the now necessary commitment to management and development, so that they could still get a 'C', and we persuaded the DoH to withdraw the necessity for all consultants to start with a 'C'.

We eventually agreed also to the RHA chairman taking over the chair of the regional 'C' committees, with the previous medical chairman acting, as in the past, as the committee's eyes and ears in the new role of vice-chairman; and ensured that the five senior managers who would join him did not become fixtures, but rotated off the committee after a few years like the medical members.

We came away from the final negotiation on awards feeling we had done the best we could, but that most of the evident criticism of the system was due to its built-in lack of openness. We hoped that the DoH had learned enough about the system during the negotiations to leave it alone for a long time. They did not, of course, and a major renegotiation on 'C' awards took place in 1995 as a *quid pro quo* to ward off the introduction of performance pay, to which the BMA remains vehemently opposed.

The distinction awards system's compatibility with self-governing hospitals, local pay and managerial input is questionable for a number of reasons, but if it founders, finding a more equitable way to identify and reward the best and provide a worthwhile carrot to the aspiring will not be easy.

Meanwhile, managers around the country were beginning to worry that they had only a year in which to work out what to do if the internal market did not work. It was all very well for the airily confident Clarke to ring full steam ahead and leave the jeremiahs in his wake, but it was the managers who would have to sort out the organizational mess if the theoretical did not translate into the practical. Thus the Rubber Windmill was born.[4]

The Rubber Windmill was a workshop set up by the East Anglian RHA with the Office for Public Management to work through events brought about by the White Paper.[5] A computer simulation took all the participants through the three years 1990 to 1993 at break-neck speed – a month took only 15 minutes. The title was inspired and the study valuable, even if the trappings of role-playing games were not to everyone's taste. The 40 individuals taking part were all issued with coloured T-shirts emblazoned with the Rubber Windmill logo, the colours depending on the role group they were in. The players adopted roles close to their duties in real life: managers and civil servants from the DoH and health authorities; doctors from public health, general practice and hospitals; and staff from local authorities and social services. There were moderators, rapporteurs, and the BBC journalist Niall Dickson provided news reports of what was taking place to mimic the real-life impact of the media on the proceedings. Some of the most influential operatives from the managerial side of the NHS took part, including Peter Griffiths, Duncan Nichols' deputy on the NHS Management Executive, Dr Graham Winyard, then the Wessex Region's Director of Public Health, but later to become a deputy chief medical officer and medical director on the NHSME; and two regional general managers, Alasdair Liddell from East Anglia and Christopher Spry from South West Thames. The moderators included the American Jo Ivey Boufford, who became director of the King's Fund College, and Professor Anthony Culyer, one of the country's leading health economists from the University of York.

The role players were required to set their objectives and try and achieve them. This involved negotiating contracts between purchasers and providers and arguing over everything laid down by the White Paper, including whether to be self-governing or to be a fundholder, and maintaining financial control. Real data from two health authorities had been provided. After the first year, which took an afternoon, it was apparent that everyone was so taken up with getting the mechanics of the reforms in place that there was little time to devote to what was actually happening to patients. After the second, 1991–92, alliances had been formed and the system was beginning to function. However, after the third year the market collapsed. Hospitals had their beds completely blocked by the many treated patients who could not be discharged into the community because the local authorities had run out of money and could not accept them. The health authorities had been neutered by the GP fundholders, whose funds had been subtracted from the authorities as laid down by the system, with the result that only the fundholders had enough money left to buy elective admissions. Only emergency admissions were being taken by the local hospitals, and the region was threatening to resile on the budgets it had previously agreed with the GP fundholders. The net effect of all this was that purchasers were having to ask providers to cut corners on quality to meet contracts and stay in the black.

This disastrous market crash stunned all the participants, none more so than those from the DoH. It is true that the third year had been tuned by the moderators to produce a worst-case scenario. They had boosted the GP fundholders and put financial pressure on the local authorities, and it was this that was largely responsible for the spectacular failure. But the results must have given serious pause for thought in the DoH at the very least as to whether the community-care section of the NHS Bill could be allowed to proceed along with the rest of the Bill.

What was particularly significant was that for all the expressed intentions of the reforms to increase the *quality* of care available in the health service it looked as if this might be one of the first casualties. To the government's critics it reinforced the view that the cogs and shafts of Clarke's reforms were truly made of rubber and that they just would not mesh.

Most of those taking part returned a year later to mull over the lessons they had learned. The resulting report is a masterpiece of NHS jargon, full of 'establishing agendas' – usually for 'change' – and 'developing new strategies'. The lessons were contained in 'key objectives': 'Creating a new role for purchasers; Involving service consumers and the public; Managing the process of change; Achieving health gain; and Creating effective provider units'.[6]

There is hardly a mention of patients in the whole document. Instead of dealing with the treatment of cancer or heart disease, the talk is of 'providing "health assurance" for local populations' and that 'the elements of "excellent" purchasing would include assessment of health needs'. Hospitals become 'provider units' which 'have gained a far stronger focus as a result of the purchaser–provider split'.

The paper's final conclusion is that 'the problems associated with the dislocation of long standing institutional traditions could outpace the real opportunities presented by a new focus on achieving health gain'. If that means that the reforms were likely to be disruptive the authors were absolutely correct. Another disruptive influence was actually the widespread use by management pundits like this of an abstract language quite foreign to the clinical staff in the health service, who strongly suspected that it concealed ignorance of the real world of patients, doctors and nurses.

The Rubber Windmill exercises provided a salutary lesson to all concerned, and the fact that the findings were very largely ignored has always interested me, given the prominence of many of those involved and the conclusions reached. The reason must be that political deaf ears were turned to anything which might have cast doubts on the wisdom of driving on with Kenneth Clarke's all-embracing plans.

June is the conference season for the BMA. In the earlier part of the month the conferences of its main constituent groupings are held: the GPs, the consultants, the juniors, the academics and the public-health doctors. At all of them the NHS reforms headed the agenda, although naturally the new contract imposed on them took up much of the GPs' time, and the lack of progress on their hours of work occupied the junior hospital doctors. At the end of June comes the main meeting of the BMA's year, the annual representative meeting. In 1990 about 450 doctors converged on my own divisional town, Bournemouth.

The annual representative meeting is opened, after a courtesy visit from the mayor of that year's conference borough, by the chairman of Council's speech. It was John Marks' real swansong as chairman this time, and he made it count. He strongly defended the BMA's campaign, attacked Clarke for his bully-boy tactics and reminded him of the facts concerning the BMA's attitude to the foundation of the NHS. Clarke had recently repeated the politically convenient but historically inaccurate accusation that the BMA had opposed the introduction of a national health service. Marks took the opportunity to remind Clarke what the *Daily Telegraph* had reported in March 1946, before the NHS Bill had been passed, when the Conservatives were in opposition: 'The Conservative Party . . . will attack the Bill on the grounds that there has been no adequate effort to secure agreement with the medical profession and that it will break the traditions of the profession.' John was not a medical historian for nothing, and on ceremonial occasions proudly wore the scarlet gown of a doctor of medicine of Edinburgh University, which he had earned for his thesis on the history of GPs' local medical committees. How curious it was that the Conservatives, now that they were in office, were doing exactly what they had accused their opponents of doing when they themselves were in opposition long ago. He ended his speech with a characteristic soundbite: 'NHS will stand not for National Health Service but for No Hope Service, and ultimately for No Health Service.'

It was an effective performance, and although strong on anti-reform polemics made quite clear that the root cause of the health service's problems was its insufficient funding. But he did make plain that, once the reforms were passed into law in a few days' time, doctors would work within the law however much they disliked the changes. At the debate on the reforms two days later a defiant motion calling for non-cooperation was avoided procedurally and ones on under-funding, regretting the internal market and its cost, and calling for the BMA to continue its opposition to the reforms, among others, were passed.

Throughout the meeting corridor negotiations were going on as to who should succeed John Marks. It seemed to me that I stood as good a chance as any. According to precedent, the next chairman should be a consultant as John was a GP. Our chairman, Paddy Ross, still wanted to chance his arm for the JCC chair later, and as one of his two deputy chairmen I would be qualified to stand. The other deputy chairman, John Chawner, had always wanted to succeed Paddy as the consultants' chairman, and like him was very much hospital-orientated and not much of a Council man. He decided not to stand.

The Scottish Council chairman, paediatrician Angus Ford, had been considered as a candidate briefly, but, although skilled in the smoke-filled-room aspects of medical politics (and he was a smoker, which did not fit the BMA image at all), he might be less effective on the more public stage that the BMA's chairman was increasingly having to occupy. It was my good fortune that the meeting was being held on my home territory and I was able to invite the 20 or 30 members of the consultants' committee who were attending the ARM to my house for a drinks party on the conference eve. If any had it in mind to support my candidacy they at least would have a chance to assess my suitability in a different setting to the usual narrow confines of meetings and political debates. The only other possible contender remained Tony Grabham, but it seemed to the great majority of my colleagues that recycling him for another term as BMA chairman, six years after he had completed five years in the office, would make the consultants' committee appear bankrupt of talent, and would have been unprecedented.

Eventually the consultants held a private meeting to which Grabham and I were not invited, and I was informed that I had gained their support decisively. Once this had been established the consultants went to the GPs' leaders and the other committees for acceptance of their candidate. Having passed this test I was elected chairman unopposed at the Council meeting which is always held immediately the conference has finished its business on the last day.

I became chairman of the BMA Council on 28 June 1990, the day before the NHS and Community Care Bill received royal assent.

CHAPTER EIGHT

Into the Council Hot Seat
July–November 1990

You cannot step twice into the same river, for other waters are
continually flowing in.
HERACLITUS, *Fragments, c.* 500 BC

Coming into office as I did, just as the NHS Act became law, presented an interesting challenge but also many difficulties. John Marks had personified the BMA's objections to what the government was planning for the health service. He had traded blow for blow with Kenneth Clarke, but although he had won the argument he had lost the battle, because the only remaining weapon the doctors had was the nuclear one of resignation from the NHS, and they were not going to use that.

I could see that the only gains that could be made in this situation, and they would be limited, lay in trying to re-establish some sort of negotiating platform with Clarke and his department. The main structure of the new NHS was now enshrined in legislation. There would be some self-governing hospitals and some fundholding GPs, and the internal market would operate, no doubt in a considerably fudged manner, in nine months' time. Clarke had already signed regulations bringing in the new membership arrangements for health authorities, including the family health service authorities which replaced the old family practitioner committees.

The BMA's policies are made at the annual representative meetings, and its Council, although elected by a national vote of all its members, is only their guardian through the year, responding to events in a way that is in line with them. The Council chairman is expected to represent the Council's views, and thus the association's policies, at all times. To assist him he has an executive committee and a finance and general purposes committee made up of the leaders of the constituent, so-called craft, committees: the GPs, consultants, juniors, academics and public-health doctors. The chief officers of the BMA – the president, the chairman of the representative body and the treasurer, along with the head of the BMA's civil service, its secretary – and the editor of the *British Medical Journal* also meet with the Council chairman at least monthly to ensure that a comprehensive overview on all the association's activities is maintained.

While having the great merit of democracy there are serious defects in this type of constitution, as the Labour Party has found with its own conference in the past. The Conservative Party, for instance, does not allow its party conference to make policy, and thus tie the hands of its leaders so tightly that they cannot be flexible and respond to events appropriately. Continuing the political analogy, BMA Council is not a cabinet and nor is its executive committee. Trade-union legislation demands that BMA Council is elected directly by all the association's 100,000 members, organized into craft-based and geographical constituencies, and the fact that it has to carry out policy made by the (arguably less democratically based) Representative Body remains a historical anomaly, predating the legislation. This is because the representatives are not always entirely typical of those they represent, as they are mostly activists and political and ethical enthusiasts. As in most trade unions it is not difficult to become a representative of your colleagues if you always turn up and are prepared to shoulder the unpopular load of organizing the meetings, running them and attending to all the administrative nuts and bolts that need maintenance. BMA divisions often find it quite difficult to persuade someone to give up a week in the summer to sit in a stuffy auditorium somewhere in Britain and make and listen to speeches about everything under the medical sun.

It is the view of many in the BMA that it is the craft committees that most nearly reflect the views of the profession at large, and it is from the leaders of these bodies that the bulk of the Council comes. Nevertheless inter-craft tensions always remain beneath the surface. The junior hospital doctors may wish to put one over the consultants and seek the support of the GPs, who may themselves have a particular matter to settle with the consultants. The hospital doctors, junior and senior, may on other occasions form an alliance to defend their territory against the GPs. The Council chairman has to be aware of these threats to unity and try and help resolve them before too much blood is spilled. As he himself will inevitably be identified with the craft from which he comes, it is vital that he does not allow himself to be typecast as pursuing craft interests or always viewing things through craft-tinted spectacles. As things turned out, I often found myself more in tune with what the GP leadership was saying than with some of my ex-colleagues from the consultants' committee. I often had much sympathy for the junior doctors' position too, especially when they were led by one of the ablest young medical politicians in the BMA, Stephen Hunter, a psychiatrist who is now a consultant in Wales.

My purpose in giving this thumbnail sketch of the BMA is to explain the situation I was in when I became Council chairman immediately after an emotional annual representative meeting, fired up by its dislike of the government's reforms. The momentum of the meeting and the policy it had made laid down that strong resistance to the government's plans should continue. I, along with some of the more experienced committee chairmen, thought that any chestnuts that could be retrieved from the fire were more likely to come from personal dialogue with Clarke and his ministers than by continuing a noisy public campaign. At the same time I realized that if, like the representatives and in reality most of the Council, you have no personal voice in the corridors of power, the only thing that makes you feel better is if your proxies, the BMA leaders in this case, say in public what you want to say, and damn the diplomacy and the consequences.

Nevertheless, I had just spent a year chairing negotiations with the Health Department over the working arrangements for consultants in the new NHS, and I had learned that those with whom agreement is sought must be allowed to claim some success for their side. Those who wish to advance on a battlefield without losing too many men must leave a route open for their adversaries to retreat. To drive your enemy to the sea, with no boats available to him, will only result in a bloody conflict in which you too will lose troops, and if your own force is not overwhelmingly strong you may well be defeated to boot, as many armies have found when they have trapped an apparently weaker opponent. Despite the huffings and puffings at the ARM and Marks' announcement of a 'summer offensive', we were going to have to sit down with Clarke and try and get him off the hook on which he and we were both impaled.

I gave a large number of interviews in which I tried to reach Clarke, and see if some fences could be mended. There was a terrible risk to my own position if I was seen to be softening the BMA's opposition to the reforms themselves, for which I had no remit. Both I, and the BMA's public affairs division, PADIV, tried to encourage the line that there was a change of *style* at the BMA, rather than that opposition to the reforms had departed with John Marks. (PADIV was led by Pamela Taylor, who was so good at her job that she was head-hunted by the BBC a couple of years later.) We were partially successful in this but some journalists, like David Brindle from the *Guardian*, were tapped in to some of the hard-line activists who thought that I would be too placatory and I never shook off this description. More successful was an interview with Anthony Clare, who was then writing a weekly piece for the short-lived *Sunday Correspondent* and came down to see me at my hospital. After we had finished the interview he discovered his tape recorder had not been working, which probably explains why a strange anec-dote about the Prince of Wales being refused admittance to an American casualty department before his credit rating had been checked was attributed to me. The story sounded unlikely and I had certainly not heard it before nor told it to him. Despite the faulty tape recorder, Clare faithfully recorded my passionate belief in the NHS and my hopes that reasoned dialogue could ameliorate the helter-skelter rush to chaos that I believed was going on. When I later met Alan Pike of the *Financial Times*, he told me he had heard that Kenneth Clarke hoped it would be possible to 'turn over a new page'. I hoped to meet the Health Secretary soon but I was not encouraged by the cavalier way he was dealing with the opposition in the House of Commons, nor by his offhand appearance before its Social Services committee. When pressed by Frank Field to give a little more detail on how the success or otherwise of the new self-governing trust hospitals would be measured, he claimed quite ludicrously that there would be no central machine and that it would be entirely up to local judgements.[1]

Meanwhile the BMA's summer offensive was largely taking the form of trying to dissuade hospitals from becoming trusts. PADIV had produced assorted leaflets, keyrings and badges picturing a despondent gingerbread man in striped pyjamas sitting in a hospital bed captioned 'People lose out if our hospital opts out.' Again, this effectively encapsulated medical and public opinion on the reforms and infuriated Mrs Thatcher and her Health Secretary.

Final firm applications for self-government from hospitals, community and ambulance services now numbered 65, and included a combined one from Guy's and its satellite hospital Lewisham. At Guy's 64 per cent of the consultants voted for self-government and the remainder were against (in a 90 per cent turnout). Interestingly, two-thirds of them voted also that the proposed NHS changes were not in the best long-term interests of national healthcare, with only 15 per cent approving them. The medical and dental senior staff committee, which was very large, had appointed its own select committee to examine the question of applying for trust status. The select committee met 34 times and was subjected to a welter of documents, including some from the DoH, which was taking a keen interest in its flagship, much of it extolling the supposed advantages of opting out. In the end the select committee voted to recommend trust application to the main committee as offering the least damaging local option, with only one of its members voting against. Steuart Cameron, the one who had held out, was Professor of Renal Medicine and one of Britain's leading nephrologists. He was also the most brilliant student of my year, and a friend who had devoted his life to Guy's since we had started there straight from school in 1952. Cameron explained how the majority vote came about in a letter to the *British Medical Journal* with Harry Keen and others.[2] The application would be conditional on a 'trust charter', incorporated in it, being accepted. The charter laid down a number of conditions, including priority for local residents' needs, community consultation and representation, and the protection of professional freedom of speech and conditions for research. There was some doubt in consultants' minds, however, as to whether this charter would be binding on the Health Secretary or on the hospital's eventual board of directors, and how it could possibly be enforced. And, as Harry Keen wrote to another journal, the vote 'was the expression of expediency, prompted by fear, spiced by temptation, all essentially uncomplicated by hard information'.[3]

Where consultant votes were taken in the acute hospitals applying, only at St Helier and the Royal Liverpool Children's Hospital were there higher-percentage votes for self-government than Guy's. Of the 27 hospitals whose vote was known, in only eight were even more than half the consultants in favour. At Guy's closest rival, St Thomas's, which applied for first-wave trust status but was later turned down, only a third of the consultants agreed, and this lack of support was backed up by a massive 93 per cent of local GPs against.[4]

The BMA spent September disseminating large numbers of leaflets and organizing ballots assessing the views of GPs whose local hospitals had applied to become self-governing. Eighty-three per cent were against such moves in the 22 districts studied. There was talk of sweeteners for such hospitals, about which Robin Cook and Kenneth Clarke had a rather inconclusive spat. It certainly seemed as if the hospitals finally chosen to be in the first wave might receive favourable financial treatment in some form. One means might be the way a hospital's initial debt was handled. The originating debt, arising from the assumption of ownership of its building, land, plant and equipment, was to be divided into two: a loan debt, on which interest would be paid, and public dividend capital, on which the dividend to be paid would be decided by government, and could be nil. Cook thought, as did the BMA, that this loophole might be used to give trust hospitals a financial leg-up *vis-à-vis* hospitals remaining under DHA control. Authority-managed hospitals were expected to provide a return of 6 per cent on the whole of their capital value. However, long-term interest rates were about 12 per cent at the time, so as a trust was only allowed to earn 6 per cent on its assets it could not be expected to compete if it paid interest on the full value of those assets. This was given as the reason why the government was dividing the originating debt, and why no dividends would have to be paid on the public dividend capital part of it until the 6 per cent interest had been earned. Early thoughts that trusts, once freed from health-authority control, could borrow at will either from the Treasury, or from other sources like banks, were soon dashed. Borrowing was still to be subject to limitations. Each trust would be given an external financing limit (EFL), which would indicate the money they could borrow or the money they could spend that they saved in their normal course of operation. The EFL could be negative as well as positive. A negative EFL would mean that trusts would have to reduce borrowing, either by repaying debt or increasing that part of their earnings that was invested. They could not fund new capital spending if they were given a negative EFL.

Many of the would-be first-wave trusts had submitted business plans in which financial projections were based on interest being paid on the lowest possible capital loan debt that the government might apply. It remained to be seen what decisions Clarke came to in respect of the various hospitals, but he had already intimated that the DoH would expect to use a third, a half or two-thirds of the capital loan debt as a basis for interest. Another criticism levelled at the woolly financial data provided by potential trusts related to inflation. Inflation at the time was running at over 10 per cent, which naturally the government wished to reduce, but the estimates of between 5 and 8 per cent provided by the first-wavers for 1991 seemed optimistic, and some applicants had ignored inflation altogether.

Further information about how applications by hospitals for trust status would be judged came in a letter from the Chief Medical Officer in England, Sir Donald Acheson, to Tony Grabham. They should 'demonstrate that [the application] carries a substantial commitment from consultants likely to be involved in [the hospital's] management.' This was a perceptible shift, but as only a minority of the consultants in any hospital would be involved in its management, and the general manager already had the power to select them from those whom he thought would be amenable, it was more cosmetic than reassuring. There was also to be an easing of the extent to which the guidance issued by the DoH had to be followed. Advice on contracting had been released in February,[5] and the consultants' committee was extremely sanguine about how much consultants would be involved in drawing up contracts. It looked to Paddy Ross, as he said at the JCC, that doctors' involvement would be simply that of employees whose services were to be bought and sold. At the same meeting, Paddy's long-term gamble paid off and he was elected to succeed Tony Grabham as chairman in October. At a meeting elsewhere Peter Griffiths, deputy chief executive of the NHS Management Executive, said, 'You cannot run an effective hospital without having consultants in key leadership positions and making decisions on resources,'[6] but it was difficult to see how they were going to be able to find the time without their numbers increasing faster than their average annual growth over the previous five years of 2.4 per cent. Consultants were already charged with the task of bringing down patient waiting lists, and the number of their junior medical staff was planned to fall along with an increase in their teaching commitment to those remaining. Many consultants felt the pressures bearing down on them were beginning to be unmeetable.

To make matters worse, in the summer the first news of likely swingeing cuts in London's hospital beds was leaked. Robin Cook, so often the recipient of leaks that he might have done good service as a bucket, released a confidential NHSME document. The content was alarming, predicting the closure of nearly 2400 beds as a result of the NHS reforms. The market would force hospitals in London to close beds because of their high cost, and this would start a chain reaction leading to more closures. Mr Cook typically scored off Mr Clarke by suggesting that rather than sending out leaflets as he had done at great expense, in effect acclaiming the reforms in the guise of explaining them, he should send copies of the NHSME document to Londoners so that they could be 'really informed about the impact of changes'. In fact, districts all over the country were already facing deficits typically of over £1 million each, and were closing beds to try and meet Sheila Masters' stern warnings that they must balance their books by April 1991. Managers were now very much between a rock and a hard place, especially painful now that many of them were on performance-related pay, because they had also been adjured to reduce waiting lists, which was difficult to achieve with fewer beds, increasingly discontented clinical staff and straitened finances.

Kenneth Clarke was also addressing meetings around the country trying to persuade GPs to sign up as first-wave fundholders by the 1 November deadline. He was offering to pay them up to £15,375 for computer hardware (twice as much as a non-fundholder could get), and all reasonable software costs, as well as a £16,000 start–up inducement, and £32,000 once fundholding began. This sounded generous but the greatly increased computerization and administrative costs of fundholding might absorb much more than he was offering. The real carrot would be in the savings which GPFHs might make from their budgets. It seemed to his audiences that it might be the early birds which caught the worms. To the more astute the risk was that, after a honeymoon year or two, budgets would begin to get tighter and tighter, so that ultimately any benefits of fundholding for GPs would come from what was becoming a fashionable NHS buzzword, empowerment, not from capital investment in their practices.

The day after I was elected chairman a meeting was arranged with the newish BMA secretary, Dr Ian Field. As I sat with him on the terrace of the Royal Bath Hotel in the brilliant Bournemouth sun-shine he briefed me about what I had taken on. There was the mandatory mobile phone, the fax machine, the secretary and the office in Tavistock Square; and the work of the BMA secretariat and who did what were explained. Although the post is unpaid, unlike the equivalent position in the American Medical Association whose occupant is rewarded with dollars well into six figures, some compensation can be paid to colleagues and employers for the mini-mum half of every week that the Council chairman needs to spend on BMA business. I was to discover that it would be more realistic for the Council chairman to take sabbatical leave from his medical post and work full-time at the BMA, but I never did this. It is something for which the BMA treasurer may have to find the money in future years. Unfortunately the cost will be much more than the equivalent arrangement that the National Union of Students, for instance, has had in place for a long time.

I spent very little of my time with Ian that day in talking about the medico-political situation. He was very much in the civil-servant mould and seldom got much involved in politics. He had, after an early career in the BMA secretariat after a short spell in general practice, reached under-secretary rank at the Department of Health and Social Security, rejoining the BMA in 1985 as deputy secretary. It seems remarkable to recall it but our conversation about my immi-nent first meeting with Kenneth Clarke, which Ian had arranged for me for 19 July, was largely about making sure I invited the Health Secretary to a dinner in the spring of 1991, and ensuring that I got some dates out of him. Ian's intimate knowledge of Whitehall and its ways was of course of inestimable value, and he always got the protocol right, which doctors are not usually very good at.

Ian had also organized a meeting for me with Sir Donald Acheson, a week before I was to meet Clarke. I was to discover later that Ian had regular private meetings with Acheson and his successor, and that he had channels discrete from those that BMA leaders had with the Department of Health to which I was not privy. This exactly paralleled the situation in Whitehall whence he came, where the senior civil servants of the various departments of state have their own network from which their political masters are excluded. The discovery came as something of a revelation to me, but it no doubt served a useful purpose. Even then, however, the Chief Medical Officer and the medical and other civil servants in the DoH were thought to be losing their influence with ministers. The impending move to a new managerially led health service could only weaken this further.

Indeed, when I met Donald Acheson he took the view that the reforms *per se* posed less of a threat to the health service than the managerialism that had started with Griffiths but was now coming into full flower. I agreed that this was true, but I believed that it was the reforms that would enable the management boom to grow like Jack's beanstalk. The giant to which it would lead would not be one of Beveridge's five, but Waste.

I asked Acheson whether Clarke would respond to a request to slow down and go for a very small number of trust hospitals and fundholding GPs to see how the system worked. I was thinking in terms of no more than 20 or so self-governing hospitals and 50 to 100 GPFHs at the most. He thought he might but did not sound too optimistic. I had a hunch that Clarke might not be long in his job. A possible result of the prolonged assault on him by the health service's staff, especially the BMA, and the public perception of a disaster overtaking the NHS engendered by this opposition, was that Margaret Thatcher might substitute a less abrasive minister who could come to terms with us. (It was a time-honoured prime ministerial dodge, and Mrs Thatcher had earlier put John McGregor into the Education Department to smooth teaching feathers ruffled by Kenneth Baker.) Acheson was as discreet as he could possibly be but I got a strong impression that he too thought Clarke was likely to move on soon. He advised me to adopt a friendly approach and felt there was a good chance that talking could restart. This confirmed my own impression and reinforced me in the view that I should risk being misunderstood by those I represented and seed my media interviews with expressions of hope that Clarke would seek our help in trying to make his new legislation work. I consistently took the line that although the government had got itself, and us, into a terrible mess by not asking for our advice before, we would not sit on our hands while the NHS got into a worse mess. I also included, for the benefit of my own side, the home truth that a discredited and weakened secretary of state is not much use to a health service, which desperately needs him to win battles against formidable competitors in Cabinet for a bigger slice of the government expenditure cake.

When I got to see Kenneth Clarke himself a week later I found he was, indeed, friendly. He expressed pleasure that a consultant had taken over from a GP as BMA chairman, which I wondered about. I did not probe him as to why this might be, although I could guess: he had taken a fearful pounding from the GPs over the limited drug list during his spell as a health minister in the early 1980s, on which he had a good case. He had taken a far heavier one from another GP, John Marks, throughout his time as Health Secretary. Clarke cultivates a popular image as an ordinary man – a lover of jazz, beer and football. Bird-watching is his hobby, and one more classless would be hard to imagine. And yet there is something in his manner that hints at the intellectual snob. Despite his bluff and jovial affect he is a more enigmatic politician than most.

He accepted that the BMA's campaign was going to continue despite the change in its leadership and I found that he was not going to discuss hospital trusts or GP fundholding. I was disappointed but thought this was reasonable at a first meeting. He did confirm that he would look very closely at all trust applications. This was in his own interest anyway, because if he was too lax the resultant financial failures would be very damaging to the government's case. He wanted to talk about other issues.

On medical staffing he agreed that there was a shortage of surgeons and of other consultants, and that consultant appointments should be made at a much younger age. The average age of appointment of consultants in the NHS has remained at 37 or 38 for as long as anyone can remember. With an efficient and non-exploitative training system, five years could easily be knocked off that, with, if anything, advantage to patients.

He wanted to know how the talks between the BMA junior doctors and his junior minister, Virginia Bottomley, were going. After meeting the juniors, Mrs Bottomley had delegated these to one of the deputy chief medical officers, Dr Diana Walford, rather than a lay civil servant, which was helpful in that someone who had once been a junior doctor herself would be able to grasp more quickly the matters in hand. Time was of the essence in view of the depth of junior anger over the issue of long hours and being treated like dogsbodies. I had gone with the juniors the previous month to see Dr Walford. Diana, who had been a haematologist before joining the DoH and is now director of the Public Health Laboratory Service, has a sharp mind and was obviously going to move matters along as fast as she could. She hoped to agree proposals to present to Mrs Bottomley by September, a tight schedule. She formed a technical subgroup to feed ideas to the main group, which was a sensible move. The juniors wanted financial penalties to be inflicted on hospitals which broke the reduced-hours rules agreed with the Department, perhaps by getting the doctors' pay-review body to devise a suitable mechanism. Dr Walford shied at that, but was happy to present 'general information' to the pay-review body, jointly with the juniors, in December. She was sceptical of being able to go to that body as early as September and was very cagey about actually presenting specific joint evidence in December. It had been an encouraging meeting with Walford but, as always, the sound of foot-dragging became deafening whenever solutions requiring money were broached. I formed the impression that Clarke thought Diana Walford might be a little too confident of progress than was likely to be the case, which disappointed me somewhat. I made sure he knew how angry junior doctors all over the country were about how they were expected to work. We talked about *Achieving a Balance*, which called for relatively fewer junior hospital doctors and more consultants. He expressed commitment to it and was aware that it was more than just a numbers game, and that the consultants were not going to take on the work of a junior doctor removed from their team, which their Royal Colleges would not wear either.

We talked for about an hour over a wide range of issues not directly concerned with the reforms, although general management cropped up. I tried to explain the feelings of consultants, who might be nearly 40 before they obtained their coveted consultant posts, after facing more than 20 years' very competitive struggle since achieving high A-level grades at school. They were then confronted with new general managers, who in medical terms were of about senior-registrar experience and seniority, who now seemed to have skipped ahead of them in power and influence. Clarke's response was to say that he did not think doctors were very keen on management. This was true, but in large part to do with what was on offer in terms of a career and the rewards then available, which his department had done very little, if anything, to correct.

I tried him on the huge deficit in the building and plant maintenance budgets over the years, which the National Audit Office had quantified at £2000 million in 1988 and to which the Commons Public Accounts Committee had drawn attention. He agreed it was a priority now and hoped that it could start to be dealt with over the next few years.

I remembered to ask him whether he would come to the spring dinner, to which he agreed, and I left Richmond House, if not very optimistic, at least confident that it ought to be possible to begin some serious discussions on the profession's concerns, not only over the NHS reforms but also with many other matters. He gave every impression that he thought he would remain as Health Secretary at least until the reforms went live in April the following year, although naturally we did not discuss his likely tenure. A few days later Mrs Thatcher reshuffled her ministers but he and his team were left unchanged.

On 25 July, I had an invitation to have dinner at Bentley's in Swallow Street with Dr Clive Froggatt. To me he was a grey and rather mysterious figure. I knew only that he was a leading member of the Conservative Medical Society, about which I knew very little, and that he had helped start the NHS Reform Group, which seemed to be a focus for what most of the doctors I knew thought of as quisling activity. He turned out to be a pleasant, prematurely balding man in his early 40s. He was younger than I had imagined, and was not even the senior partner in his general practice in Cheltenham. He made it very plain that he was acting as an intermediary for the government, but I was quite unable to decide precisely what status he had. No doubt, like a spy in a foreign country, he could be disowned if he compromised the government's position. He was by turns investigative and exhortatory: what would the BMA want, what could the government do?; the BMA should be positive, 'work the reforms', give a lead.

He told me that Mrs Thatcher was keen on making progress with the BMA, and that she was pleased that I had replaced John Marks as chairman. Then, and in subsequent meetings, he contrived to give me the impression that he had come hot-foot from No. 10. Froggatt said that Kenneth Clarke had thought the meeting I had had with him was 'useful'. He agreed that Clarke was a complicated man, and that he did bear some animus towards the medical profession, but that its origin was unknown. The government did not think my election was an accident of the unwritten tradition of consultant–GP alternation, about which he claimed to know; I was identified as a moderate, and there seemed to be a view that this represented some kind of sea-change in the BMA. If this truly was the government's belief, and not just a view that Clive had been selling to them, I was amazed at its poor intelligence sources. They must think the BMA very much more politically sophisticated than it was.

He claimed to lie towards the left wing of the Conservative Party, which convinced me that if I was thought to be a Conservative I must be off the pitch and somewhere in the stands. He did not agree with all that the DoH was doing, including that part of the new GP contract which offered payment for carrying out minor surgery, but he was strongly in favour of self-governing hospitals and GP fundholding. His views on the latter seemed to be related to the common feeling amongst GPs, quite unconnected with their politics, that hospitals, and particularly some consultants, had treated them like poor relations ever since 1948. The boot was now to be on the other foot, and they welcomed it.

When I told him of the extreme fury amongst consultants at the second overturning of the extra £1000 for those at the top of the scale, recommended twice by the pay-review body, he said that Mrs Thatcher had been in favour of paying it. Clarke also had been in favour, but the Cabinet had rejected it. As far as the trouble that Clarke had got himself into with the doctors was concerned, Froggatt blamed the bad advice he had got from the Civil Service for some of it, especially over the pitfalls in the new GP contract.

He was concerned about Labour influences in the Department of Health, and also in the BMA. Our brilliant head of public affairs, Pamela Taylor, was a bogeywoman to the Tories, a 'friend of Harriet Harman'. Dr John Dawson (a possible future secretary of the BMA who was tragically soon to die in his 40s from prostate cancer), with whom Pamela was associated, was another subversive influence. Clive was unflattering about John Marks, who he claimed was less than supportive of the BMA consultant leaders, although he had apparently never denigrated me.

I was intrigued by Clive Froggatt and made a mental note to be extremely careful in what I said to him. The impression I gained was that it would count very highly for him in the Tory circles in which he moved if he could claim to have softened the BMA's attitude by working on me. I believed myself to be totally immune to such an approach, and certainly no blandishments were ever offered.

He was collected from the restaurant by his own chauffeur-driven BMW for the journey back to Cheltenham, about which I was also curious. He told me that he received no financial help from the Conservative Party at all and that his weekly political trips to London to see ministers and to dine out with the likes of me were 'his hobby'. As far as the chauffeur was concerned, it did not cost much more to employ him once a week than the first-class return rail fare from Cheltenham, and he could get a lot more done in town with his own car. His logic was convincing; however there remained something odd about him, although I was not to discover his sad secret. He had been using controlled drugs for many years, which was eventually revealed when he was convicted in 1995 of offences under the Dangerous Drugs Act.

I also went to both the Labour and Conservative party conferences in October to host dinners for influential MPs interested in health. In Blackpool, Labour were confident that the health service controversy would be a major vote winner for them in the general election, which was thought to be coming sooner than it actually did. Harriet Harman appeared only briefly, but Lord Ennals, an ex-health secretary, was highly supportive of the BMA's stance. Two medical MPs, Lewis Moonie and the Glasgow neurosurgeon Sam Galbraith, and Alun Michael, demonstrated that the Labour Party had strength in depth on health issues, and it was a useful introduction to those with whom we might be dealing in the next year or so. The Tories in Bournemouth produced a less interested group as no ministers attended. Conservative ministers were reputed to be not particularly keen on attending annual party conferences: some secretaries of state tended to come down, deliver their party piece and return straight away to London.

I had gone down to Bournemouth immediately after chairing my first full Council meeting at Tavistock Square. What we discussed in London would not have pleased our dinner guests, and it was something of a rude awakening for me. Since the ARM at the end of June and the October Council meeting, the application of policy had been left with the Council's executive committee: we had agreed to maintain a slightly lower profile in order to see whether Clarke would respond. Council members had been disturbed by the relative silence and were not impressed with what little response there had been, certainly not publicly. It was to be the start of an alliance between my two predecessors as chairman, Tony Grabham and John Marks, which made my job even more difficult than it otherwise might have been. They were later seen as Ted Heath and Margaret Thatcher to my John Major, a comparison which flattered none of us. The upshot of a stormy debate was a motion proposed by Grabham and seconded by Marks that 'The grave concerns of the BMA regarding the reorganization of the NHS should continue to be expressed both nationally and locally,' which was passed with no dissenters. The 'nationally' was significant because we had recently switched the BMA campaign to local level, particularly targeting those places where trust hospitals were likely. My plea that we should be trying to ensure as few NHS trusts as possible came into being in six months' time and that 'a constant frontal assault will not achieve our objective' fell on deaf ears.

Some new members of the executive, including Ian Bogle, the GPs' new chairman, and John Chawner, who had taken over the consultants' committee from Paddy Ross, were more supportive, but both thought that adopting a lower profile did not mean neglecting the national stage.

That autumn I tried to meet as many different people associated with health as I could. Networking is vital to the BMA chairman, especially with those who might not be natural allies of the association. Quite early I received an invitation to lunch from a rather difficult to place public relations consultant named Hugh Elwell, who also invited Dr Marvin Goldberg, the head of AMI, which owned a large number of private hospitals in Britain. Elwell seemed well connected in Conservative circles, and certainly commanded one of the better tables in the Savoy Grill, where we met. As the conversation was mostly about the BMA's attitude to the government I was intrigued by Elwell's name and motives. In my lighter moments I wondered if he was related to Charles Elwell, the former head of MI5's 'F' branch, which dealt with domestic subversion. I ducked asking Hugh about it at this or a subsequent excellent lunch I had with him at the same table in December, but I remained slightly baffled by his invitations.

As with a later invitation to lunch at the Carlton Club from Sir Arnold Elton, a retired NHS surgeon, who was then chairman but subsequently president of the Conservative Medical Society, I very much got the impression that I was being inspected for possible Tory leanings and to establish whether the BMA really was changing its tune. Elton was also a long-serving member of the Conservative Party's National Executive and this was certainly his main interest. But it was not the *tune* I wished to alter. As I said in Council, it was on what instrument it should be played. Marks' trumpet had served its purpose, now was the time for something else – a dulcimer perhaps?

I also met Sir Robert Kilpatrick, the president of the General Medical Council, who was just starting his long, and ultimately successful, campaign to extend the GMC's powers in order to intervene earlier in a doctor's career if his pattern of performance showed signs of leading to medical disaster later. This was a very radical step and would require government legislation, as the GMC's rules are statutory and overseen by the Privy Council. I found myself immediately sympathetic to Sir Robert's ideas, but I knew there were some at the embattled BMA who would regard such changes as piling Pelion upon Ossa at a time when the profession viewed all change with suspicion, from whatever quarter it came.

The BMA remained in deep conflict with the government over the reforms, but all channels had to be kept open in the hope that other influences than our own might seep back to Mrs Thatcher and her colleagues. I therefore had many meetings with all kinds of bodies and individuals whose interests touched the NHS, however tangentially. To some in the BMA this heavy socializing by its chairman and other officers is often seen as frivolous fraternization, but it was actually extremely important. If it was not, why would every large organization, temporal and spiritual, go in for it? Surely not simply to enrich the caterers and cholesterolize the already cholesterolized.

Whatever effect the BMA's activities may have had, at the beginning of November the widely predicted reshuffle involving Kenneth Clarke occurred. He went to Education and Science and William Waldegrave, the cerebral second son of an earl, replaced him. Some believe that Mrs Thatcher sought to give the doctors and others in the health service a more emollient and compatible secretary of state, to try and move the noisy health debate off centre-stage before it further damaged the Conservatives' election chances. She herself says that she wanted Norman Tebbit to take on the Education brief but that he declined. Kenneth Clarke's bruising and brawling skills were the next best thing, so he was given the job. Waldegrave was recommended for office by the Chief Whip, Tim Renton, although he was not from her wing of the party.[7]

Very soon after Waldegrave's appointment, Deputy Prime Minister Sir Geoffrey Howe's resignation speech rocked Westminster. Margaret Thatcher was deposed and John Major replaced her as Prime Minister. Like Waldegrave's accession, this seemed a good omen for the health service. Although Major had been a member of Mrs Thatcher's review group, and was therefore intimately connected with the reforms, he very quickly staked his claim as a supporter of the health service. So keen was he to make this point that he said he had been looked after by the NHS since birth, which would have made him only 42 instead of the 47 he was, still the youngest prime minister this century. As Mr Waldegrave had supported Douglas Hurd, the Foreign Secretary, against John Major in the leadership struggle, we wondered if he might be the shortest-lived health secretary within memory. Mr Major, however, wisely kept him on, as he was without doubt the most suitable health secretary he had available at the time.

CHAPTER NINE

Waldegrave Replaces Clarke
November 1990–March 1991

The mill wheel turns, it turns for ever,
Though what is uppermost remains not so.
BERTOLT BRECHT, *Roundheads and Peakheads*, 1933

William Waldegrave was fortunate in the timing of his appointment. The pugnacious Kenneth Clarke had just concluded a hard battle with the Treasury for extra funding for the NHS in its testing first post-reform year, despite having part of his negotiating position revealed in yet another leak by Robin Cook. Clarke had obtained an extra £3000 million, which in cash terms was an increase of nearly 11 per cent. However, after likely health service inflation (always slightly greater than general inflation) was taken into account this was equivalent to only 2.2 per cent in real terms. Nevertheless it was one of the biggest annual rises the NHS had had, and only time would tell how much of it would be swallowed up by the new costs that the reforms would bring to the service.

Waldegrave had as ministers Virginia Bottomley and Stephen Dorrell, neither likely, it was thought, to ruffle the health professions' feathers in the way that their predecessors David Mellor and Edwina Currie had done from time to time. The BMA was encouraged by this switch, and I felt that my less confrontational stance was now more likely to be vindicated. However, my less realistic colleagues and the Council activists thought differently. From the hard time they gave me I could only assume they believed that Waldegrave would be much more vulnerable to shot and shell than Clarke had been, so why was I not rolling out the artillery?

The Labour Party's ammunition at this time included its latest health-policy document *A Fresh Start for Health*. If it was a possible health manifesto for the next general election, which Labour were increasingly confident that they would win, it was most encouraging. Robin Cook's introduction said that the health service was in crisis because of under-funding, and that dogmatic changes were being imposed by the government on an impossible timetable. Labour would reverse many of the reforms – abolishing trusts, fundholding and the internal market. They would spend more on the health service, and institute a system of regional health authorities allocating resources down the chain, based on agreed targets which would include some for health promotion and community services. A reserve would be retained to reward overperforming hospitals. Balm to the doctors was a pledge to honour pay-review body recommendations in full, which the Tories did only one year in five on average. As far as community care was concerned, Labour would ring-fence local authority grants and appoint a minister of state for community care, which is what Sir Roy Griffiths' 1988 report had suggested. The Labour document was very much in tune with what the BMA would have produced if, by some trick of fate, it had swapped places with the government's health department. There was even an undertaking to look again at the no-fault compensation for medical accidents which the BMA had advocated for many years but which successive governments had rejected. The adversarial system whereby negligence has to be proved in the courts is appallingly insensitive to those involved in medical tragedies, especially to patients and their relatives, but also to doctors and other clinical staff. The legal process is protracted and it can take many years of anguish on both sides before the resolution of a claim takes place. The necessity to prove negligence takes no account of the occasional and inevitable accidents of treatment without negligence that can affect patients severely, and the upshot has been that, of about £100 million awarded each year to plaintiffs in the early 1990s, about half went on legal expenses.

Unfortunately the cost of the improvements that Labour would make was not spelled out, beyond a statement that they would take at least the lifetime of a parliament to bring in. Nevertheless it did seem that if Labour got into government it would be willing to act with the health professions, as happened in neighbouring countries like Holland and Sweden, rather than against them. Labour put under-spending on the health service at about £4500 million, quite similar to other estimates, including that of the BMA which had calculated it at £5000 million or slightly more.

Waldegrave, of course, was not about to take Labour's advice. But I hoped that he might be persuaded to make a helpful political gesture by allowing only a very few of the applications for self-governing-trust status to go through. The number would indicate how keen he was to open a new chapter with the BMA. Twenty or less would enormously strengthen the position of those in the association like myself who were under great pressure from the implacables, to whom nothing short of surrender would do. William Waldegrave's reputation was that of a first-rate thinker but not a first-rate politician, and in my dealings with him over the years I am inclined to agree with that assessment, which many might think is to his credit. In the event he was not prepared to send a positive political signal to us over the trust applications. He accepted 56 of the 66 applications, which was a damaging blow to me at the time, and made it less likely that I could lessen the conflict between the doctors and the government much. However, only 30 of the 56 were district general hospitals, which was some consolation as this was where the worst risks to the NHS would occur. The 56 were to become 57 at the eleventh hour when the North Devon trust at Barnstaple which had earlier been rejected was allowed to join the pioneers at the end of January.

When he announced the successful first-wavers William Waldegrave said that a further 111 units had expressed an interest in being in the second wave. He called trusts the future 'natural model for . . . providing patient care'. He refused to be drawn on why the 10 applicants who were not going forward had been rejected, beyond hinting at management tasks that had not been completed.

I still believe that, in the honeymoon period enjoyed by any new health secretary, Waldegrave could have made better political progress with us by turning down many more of the trust applications than he did. A great number of the ones he accepted had produced very weak applications, as was underlined by a study of them under-taken by the management consultants Newchurch & Company. On adding up the planned capital expenditure of the 66 applicants over three years, Newchurch found that it totalled £1100 million. When this was set against the published government figures for capital expenditure for *all* the English health authorities in 1991–92 of only £1460 million, this looked remarkably optimistic. Few applicants had attempted to quantify the benefits that trust status would bring to their patients, and over half of them were simply aiming to main-tain their existing services.[1]

The BMA's analysis was very similar to Newchurch's. Errors and naïvety were common, and many applicants seemed driven more by thoughts of escape from health-authority control than of positively improving their patient services. My comment to the media at the time was: 'The figures do not add up. If they were the business plans of a management buyout they would get very short shrift from a merchant bank.' I had some knowledge of the stringency that is brought to bear when real (as opposed to government) money is at stake, because someone I knew had recently been involved in a management buyout of his company. Very few, if any, of the NHS trust business plans would have been given the time of day in the world of commerce which the new NHS was now supposed to emulate.

In addition to the acute hospitals included in the 56 trusts that were approved, there were three ambulance services, six mental-health and mental-handicap units and some community services. Every health region in England was to have at least one trust, but there were none in Scotland, Wales or Northern Ireland. Surprisingly the external financing limits of the successful applicants had not yet been set, which confirmed what an un-businesslike affair the launch was.

*

More and more, previously Conservative doctors began to change their political allegiance. William Waldegrave's scope for doing anything about this was limited. John Major was unlikely to support a re-examination of any of the basic principles of the soon-to-commence new health service, given his membership of Mrs Thatcher's original review group. And if modifying the reforms was ruled out, only major progress on junior doctors' hours of work or the GPs' unpopular new contract would give Waldegrave any leeway to lessen the hostility caused by Kenneth Clarke.

However Waldegrave did try. He was at pains to praise the clinical staff and to discourage the use of commercial language, and he did seem to be interested in the scientific and technical side of medicine rather than the purely managerial. In fact, when I first met him, at a small private meeting arranged by David Willetts, the first question he asked me, and which I was remiss in not being able to answer at the time, was 'Who was the last Briton to win the Nobel Prize for medicine?' The answer is actually Sir James Black (not to be confused with Sir Douglas), who won it with two Americans in 1988 for his work on beta-blockers and histamine antagonists that led to the development of two major new groups of drug. Waldegrave's general approach and interest in science was a breath of fresh air coming after Clarke's jaunty but closed approach. Willetts had actually organized the meeting for Clarke to attend, but events had overtaken him, and Waldegrave had only been in office just over a week when he came, so a deep discussion on policy was never going to have been possible. About a dozen people from different clinical disciplines attended including the Royal College of Anaesthetists' president, Michael Rosen, and Dr Michael Goldsmith, who like Froggatt and Willetts himself was connected with Mrs Thatcher's review.

I looked forward to meeting Waldegrave again when he was further up his NHS learning curve and I did so a fortnight later at a curious dinner at the Carlton Club, organized this time by Sir Arnold Elton. Again Clarke had originally been supposed to come, with his minister, with Sir Arnold presumably acting as midwife to a new rapport. After a short postponement caused by Mrs Thatcher's prime ministerial demise, Elton, Waldegrave, Virginia Bottomley and I sat down to dinner in one of the club's august private rooms, surrounded by dark red wallpaper and portraits of Tory premiers past.

After an initial discussion about the Cabinet moves, about which he and Mrs Bottomley were understandably upbeat, Waldegrave got on to the relationship between doctors and the government. He seemed keen to improve relations as long as this did not cost any money or radically change anything – a tall order. He had recently pleased the nurses by appointing the Chief Nursing Officer, Mrs Anne Poole, to the NHS Policy Board, thus removing the slight to the profession caused by her previous exclusion. Such gestures were unlikely to cut much ice with the BMA, who were looking for those of a more substantial nature.

(A more typical appointment to the Policy Board was made soon afterwards when Peter Gummer, whose brother John was the Agriculture Minister, replaced the estimable Sir Graham Day, the Rover Group chairman. Peter Gummer was the executive chairman of Shandwick, the world's largest public relations group, and had no known health experience, although there was little doubt that the higher echelons of the health service needed better public relations. Whatever the merits of the individual, it confirmed the impression yet again that friends of the government were taking over the health service.)

I explained the BMA's concern about having as few trusts as possible to start with, as Waldegrave had not at that time yet announced them. He accepted that there were risks but he was going to disappoint us. I put as delicately as I could that the fewer trusts there were the better relations with the BMA would be.

We had a long discussion about winners and losers and how, in my opinion, purchasers in the shape of health authorities would not operate a true market based on cost and quality, because some of the smaller trusts would not be able to compete with larger hospitals, whether they were trusts or directly managed. If a true market operated, the economy-of-scale advantage of the larger ones would cause the financial collapse of the smaller ones. This would jeopardize the healthcare of those in rural communities, like much of Dorset where I came from, because transport to distant large hospitals was difficult and expensive. They did not refute this, but Virginia, with her missionary zeal for trust hospitals, thought that the improvement in quality, even in small ones, would see to it that they survived. I thought other means would be needed to save them, involving tampering with the market by health-authority purchasers.

We talked about health service morale, which must be a very familiar theme to any health minister, as it is always mentioned when health service staff and ministers meet. I am sure Waldegrave and Bottomley became as sick of the subject as I did over the next three years, but it could not be ignored. Enoch Powell said when he was Health Minister that all doctors ever wanted to talk about was money. In recent years even this riveting topic has been driven into second place by morale. At the dinner Virginia Bottomley became animated by the idea that the new trust hospitals would galvanize the doctors and be very good for their morale.

In this she seemed to have been influenced by David Willetts and those who thought like him. Willetts had published a pamphlet, *Reforming the Health Service*, in 1989 in which he wrote,

> It is not good for an organisation to have such an incentive to self-denigration. It lowers the morale of staff and patients alike. The new internal market in the NHS will change all that because at last individual hospitals will want to show their best face to the public and to publicise their achievements. That will be the way in which they will win contracts to treat patients. It will boost staff morale and at last encourage a positive approach in the NHS.[2]

I knew and liked Willetts but his analysis seemed facile and his NHS seemed peopled by cardboard figures, or chess pieces on a board. He had been a member of a health authority, but it is not rare for members of these bodies to know very few of the clinical staff, and they are often in turn anonymous and remote figures to the majority of the staff. Willetts' optimism seemed wonkish, and based on wishful thinking like so much of the Conservative propaganda associated with the reforms.

Waldegrave was also interested in medical leadership and *esprit de corps*, and I was impressed that he had remembered something of the discussion at what had been a very wide-ranging meeting at the Centre for Policy Studies which we had both attended. It showed that he was a listener, and had not developed the deaf ears of some politicians who had been in office for a long time.

I was encouraged by his interest in where in their hospitals doctors talked about matters like trusts, and what in particular was discussed. He seemed to have a vision of dons chatting in their common rooms. I explained that very few hospital doctors had had anywhere like that since Richard Crossman's day, and we no longer had doctors' dining-rooms either. Virginia pressed me as to where hospital doctors did discuss things, and I had to say that in my district it tended to be at the private hospital after we had finished our health service work, because there we were treated as if we mattered and had somewhere to meet informally and often. A slightly cynical response, but it led to a discussion on reviving the symbiotic relationship between the private sector and the NHS, which had declined sharply ever since Barbara Castle's assault on private practice in the late 1970s. Waldegrave had been impressed by the private wings of major London teaching-hospitals like St Mary's and Guy's, and thought this model might usefully be encouraged elsewhere.

As an academic he was obviously reading widely as he eased himself into his new job, and was interested to know which health economists I rated. I mentioned Rudolph Klein, Chris Ham and Tony Culyer. I did not endorse Alan Maynard, who was a colleague of Culyer's at the University of York, the home of the quality-adjusted life year or QALY (see p. 213). I found Professor Culyer's more traditional approach to economics preferable to Professor Maynard's populist and provocative one. Whether Waldegrave took my advice I do not know. Health economists and social scientists seemed to be proliferating wildly in our newer universities and there were plenty more to choose from, some doubtless as good as the ones I had mentioned. (I hope he did look at Chris Ham's work. About two months later at a meeting attended by many top managers, Ham came out strongly against GP fundholding and correctly predicted that by introducing the changes throughout the health service at the same time the government was 'overloading the management agenda'. Nevertheless he thought there might be benefits from the purchaser–provider split. Alain Enthoven criticized fundholding at the same meeting.[3])

Waldegrave also wanted to know something of the structure of the BMA, a very sensible enquiry. 'Know thine enemy,' I thought. I had myself already got the BMA library searching for a copy of *The Binding of Leviathan*, a political book he had written in 1978 before entering Parliament, to help me discover what made *him* tick. A man's juvenilia may often provide clues. (Virginia knew quite a lot about the BMA, particularly the junior doctors to whom she had been talking about their hours of work.)

Waldegrave was leading the discussion we were having, but in comparison with Mrs Bottomley he was doing far more listening than talking. Even then I noticed that Virginia was inclined to push a view without necessarily listening to the reply. This was a long time before she became Health Secretary herself, but she showed signs of not welcoming criticism. Recently she had been on radio to defend the position of Watford General Hospital, which was being forced to close beds from Christmas until the new financial year in April. She claimed to have 'lost her rag' afterwards because she was only ever asked by the media to defend some enormity or other.

My overall impression was that Waldegrave was seeking a genuine rapprochement but that Mrs Bottomley was still giving off the reflected views of her previous boss, Clarke. I was further drawn to Waldegrave when Elton left the room for a moment. He turned to me and asked whether Sir Arnold was a friend of mine. When I said that I had only met him a couple of times before, and that he was a dignitary of the Conservative Medical Society, Waldegrave expressed his bafflement at the existence of such a group of political doctors. He remarked that when he was a minister in the Foreign Office he was not aware of there being a Conservative Foreign Affairs Society. Whatever Waldegrave thought about medical members of the Conservative supporters club, Sir Arnold had set up a useful meeting and I was to maintain my contacts with him for several years.

One feature of Waldegrave's approach, even in formal meetings with others present, was a willingness to explore matters in a non-ideological way quite unlike any of the other ministers with whom I have exchanged views. It may simply have reflected his confidence in his own intellectual agility in argument, but I always had the feeling that open discussion served a function for him too. He may have been aware that the same keen intellect that could lead him to apparently elegant solutions could also prove disastrous in political terms. His deep involvement in the poll-tax débâcle is one example. For my own part, my natural liking for Waldegrave may have been as damaging to me politically as his own openness and lack of aggression was to him. He struck me as a traditional, aristocratic, rather Whiggish Tory with a sense of public service who, unlike many others of his party, was not in politics for self-advancement or -aggrandizement. He was reputed to buy his wife Caroline's clothes, but I often thought she might have bought his with advantage, as he did not appear to care much about his own appearance. Less curly shirt collars and fewer drab ties, usually at half-mast, might have sharpened up his political image quite a bit. I wondered if Mrs Thatcher might have had a few words with him on the subject, as she was reputed to have done with Nigel Lawson on his need of a haircut.

About a week after our Carlton Club dinner, Waldegrave visited the BMA for the first time. He came to speak to the consultants' committee and had been provided with a list of topics about which questions were likely to be asked afterwards. This was at a time when the number of beds being closed and operating sessions being

cancelled was rising at an alarming rate, and the committee decided
to carry out another survey similar to the one in 1988 so that the
overall picture would be known. The GPs' committee, who were
visited by the Health Secretary later in December, estimated that
about 4000 beds were closed, 1000 of them in London. At that
meeting Waldegrave was more forthcoming than expected and
undertook to review their unpopular new contract immediately
and make changes if necessary.

Waldegrave was conciliatory when he arrived at the consultants'
committee. He was keen to dispel any notion that the changes were
paving the way to privatization and was at pains to say that the
market would be managed and not be allowed to test the purchaser–
provider split to destruction. He wanted consultants, as the leaders
of their hospitals, to join him so that morale would rise amongst all
groups. This was a bit much for his audience to stomach, as they
felt that one of the root causes of the drop in morale was that his
government had totally undermined consultants' leadership role by
introducing the new manager-dominated system. Duncan Nichol
had already had to write to all managers reminding them that 'successful contracting will depend on consultants and other professional
staff being closely involved in all stages of drawing up contracts'. This
was simply not happening in the hospitals. Managers had appointed
contract managers, many of whom were nurses but none doctors,
who were negotiating contracts without reference to the doctors
who would carry them out. Some contracts, for instance, offered
surgical procedures which had been superseded by better ones for
many years. In the unlikely event of a health authority or fundholding
GP purchasing such a procedure the clinicians would certainly not
carry it out.

The Health Secretary gave the impression of being cautious and
flexible, anxious to play down suggestions of business for profit, but
not giving an inch on the principal changes to be wrought by the
reforms. To questions about the postponement of the community
care part of the reforms he expressed concern but assured the committee that it would follow in due course. The consultants present

were much relieved at the change from Clarke but decided it was one more of style than of substance. I had heard a lot about changes of style and substance when I took over from my own predecessor, so the interpretation had a familiar ring.

One substantial development associated with William Waldegrave's move to the DoH was the settlement of the claim of more than 1000 haemophiliacs who had been infected by the NHS with the human immunodeficiency virus by the use of contaminated blood products. The government had been resisting their legal claims, as it seemed probable that proving negligence or a breach of duty by the NHS would have been difficult. However, there was a clear moral obligation for the government to come to these unfortunate patients' aid. More than 150 had already died, but up until then no financial help had been forthcoming. The £42 million eventually provided was not particularly generous, but it was welcome. Married men with children received £60,500, but single men only £23,500. Thirty or more cases where negligence was alleged were ultimately settled for higher amounts.

The next time I saw Waldegrave was at a memorial dinner at the Royal College of Surgeons of England in Lincoln's Inn Fields for Lord Trafford, who had died in September 1989. The dinner was attended by Lady Trafford and the medical establishment were there in force. In his speech the Health Secretary used the occasion to play down the commercialism that was overtaking the NHS. He went to some lengths to condemn the use of business language which was still rampant in the service, and which even Clarke, who had initially allowed it to spread, had throttled back before he went to Education. Unfortunately any good work that Waldegrave might have done was nullified by a speech from Norman Tebbit, who quite extraordinarily, considering that it was a memorial dinner, launched an attack on the medical profession over its resistance to the reforms, and extolled the new business approach to the heavens. I had never heard Tebbit speak in public before, and nor have I ever been to a dinner before or since when a decorated and dinner-jacketed audience came so near open mutiny. The *sotto voce* remarks and comments passed on Tebbit became less and less *sotto* as he dug a deeper and deeper hole for himself. The assembled medical dignitaries had very nearly reached the roll-throwing stage by the time he sat down.

As confrontational, but in a more serious way, was the announcement that the government was going to continue to press for the introduction of local pay bargaining. The new Act gave trusts the power to negotiate new contracts with their staff, outside national agreements, whether they were covered by pay-review bodies or not. The government's interference, for the ninth time in 11 years, with the recommendations of the doctors' pay-review body was another slap in the face. An average increase of 9.5 per cent was recommended, but government decided to pay only 7.5 per cent on 1 April, with the additional 2 per cent not arriving until the end of the year on 1 December. Consultants received 1 per cent more than the rest, partly as a sop to the two previous years' rejections. The GPs were justifiably incensed because, by jumping through the hoops of the new contract imposed on them by Clarke, they had earned about £3000 more per partner than the average target income set for them. It was announced that the money would therefore be clawed back. To make matters worse as far as the NHS and its dire financial problems were concerned, although the government would make £250 million available for the pay rises due to professional staff, this would leave a shortfall of £44 million which would have to be found by health authorities. Yet again the government was failing fully to fund pay rises which it had also 'phased', a euphemism for 'reduced'. Having climbed a few rungs of the ladder of improving relations, Waldegrave had immediately descended a familiar snake.

But at the end of January, Waldegrave announced that the junior doctors would retain their national terms and conditions of service. When asked for evidence, as I was repeatedly, that my quest for better relations with the government following John Marks' frontal assault had borne any fruit at all, this was the only change of any substance that I could plausibly attribute to dialogue and diplomacy. Waldegrave accepted the argument that junior doctors in training were a national resource; and that, as they needed to move frequently to new hospitals in their climb up the training ladder, they should not have to negotiate new and different contracts every time they moved. Having to do so might discourage them from pursuing what was already a highly competitive and difficult career, with the NHS being the loser. The BMA, the Royal Colleges, the medical schools and even NHS management had all asked for this departure from the White Paper and the NHS Act, but it was encouraging to see that a secretary of state could respond to reasoned argument rather than simply dismiss it.

This backsliding from Clarke's original wish to abolish nationally set pay scales, along with Waldegrave's charm offensive with the doctors, brought sniper fire from his own ranks. Stories were fed to the right-wing tabloid press, perhaps by Mrs Thatcher's acolytes the No Turning Back group, that Mr Major was dissatisfied with his Health Secretary's performance and that he would be reshuffled at the earliest opportunity. Waldegrave having only been in the job a few months, this rebounded on the credibility of the rumour-mongers, but it demonstrated the extreme political passions that the reforms aroused on both sides of the argument. The same type of attack was already being directed at me from within the BMA.

At the same time as he announced retaining national terms for junior doctors, Waldegrave introduced some more realism by announcing lower than expected external financing limits for the new trusts-to-be. Treasury caution had undoubtedly been involved. Thirty-seven of them received negative EFLs, although Guy's was cleared to borrow £8.5 million and Bradford £11.4 million, despite their existing debts. Trusts generally were allowed to spend on average £143,000 more on capital developments each than those hospitals remaining under health-authority management.

Other signs that harsh reality was breaking into his honeymoon with the NHS came with the release of a survey by the Labour Party showing that over 300,000 operations had been cancelled in the last three years, with most regions having a worse record in the latest year than in earlier ones. Many districts were only performing emergency and urgent operations until the new financial year – or, in the case of East Surrey, adjoining Mrs Bottomley's Surrey South West constituency, not until 'at least the beginning of May'. North East Thames RHA had a letter it had sent out leaked to the *Guardian*, which suggested that five 'minor procedures' would no longer be available on the NHS in that part of the metropolis. These were varicose vein operations, tattoo removal, asymptomatic wisdom tooth removal, the excision of benign lumps and *in vitro* fertilization. The letter had been written by the region's general manager and caused uproar amongst local doctors and outrage from patients' groups. As a sign of things to come it was not encouraging, however logical it might have seemed to managers in times of severe financial stringency; and murmurings of 'rationing is the only way' and 'prioritizing health care must be considered' were heard in fashionable non-clinical health circles.

Yet Waldegrave continued undaunted with his attempts to assuage the doctors' concerns. Mrs Bottomley's group had reported on the progress that had been made on junior doctors' hours of work; in announcing a unanimously agreed package Virginia Bottomley said, with the political triple rhetoric which she was to employ so often, that it was 'right for juniors, right for their education and right for patients'. The gist of the agreement was that no junior hospital doctors in hard-pressed posts should be required to be on duty for more than an average 83 hours a week, and that their educational needs could be met by a maximum average of 72 hours a week. There were to be maximum periods of total and continuous duty and minimum periods of off-duty. Ways would be found to relieve young doctors of tasks that could be done by less-qualified staff. Although many senior doctors thought that the introduction of shift-work by the agreement would have some retrograde effects, there seemed no alternative given the overall number of staff available. Medical shiftwork in hospitals leads to a loss of continuity of care, and the inevitable shortcomings of frequent handovers to a new team can lead to serious errors of omission.

Mrs Bottomley also promised a small amount of extra funds to provide for 200 new consultant posts and 50 staff-grade posts. The staff grade occupies limbo-land so far as a medical career is concerned. Staff-grade doctors exchange a place on the career ladder that should lead eventually to a consultant post for what amounts to jam today: slightly better pay, an established post and no insistence on a higher specialist qualification, but at the expense of a severely diminished chance of advancement. The BMA had an agreement that these posts would not be used to obtain specialists on the cheap by appointing staff doctors rather than consultants where the latter were needed. This was necessary because the NHS is to all intents and purposes a monopoly employer of doctors, and thus extremely powerful *vis-à-vis* the individual doctor, who could devote 10 to 15 years of his life to acquiring the necessary skills to be a consultant, only to find that only staff posts are on offer when he has completed them.

At a dinner held jointly by the BMA GPs' committee and the Royal College of General Practitioners Waldegrave also promised to have an early look at the GPs' new contract with a view to reducing the additional bureaucracy involved, and he announced several welcome adjustments. He also first floated the idea of a national strategy for health, in which he sought the co-operation of his audience of family doctors. This eventually saw the light of day as the *Health of the Nation* initiatives, which were to be the main epitaph of his spell at Health, even though they were introduced by his successor.

I was not at this occasion because I had gone to Helsinki to the forum of European national medical associations, organized regularly by the World Health Organization. I found there great interest in the brave new world of markets which was about to overtake our health service, particularly by those from the Scandinavian countries. The Swedes especially were watching events with interest, and all expressed surprise that our government had launched such a major reorganization without close consultation with the medical profession. I found that the BMA was held in very high regard as a model of what a national medical association should be, and received commiseration from a great many of the presidents and chairmen of the medical associations of our closest neighbours and partners in

Europe. After the hammering the BMA had taken from Clarke and his colleagues I returned to London in very much higher spirits than I had left.

Thus we continued to extend the hand of friendship to William Waldegrave and held a dinner for him and his ministers and senior officials in the Prince's Room at BMA House at the end of February. The Prince's Room is a very fine columned and chandeliered room, situated above the main entrance arch into the courtyard of the Lutyens-designed BMA House in Tavistock Square. It is not a large room and is ideal for dining up to about 30 guests. It has a curious echo effect caused by the high, domed ceiling, and visitors can be disconcerted by hearing conversations taking place 20 feet away coming to them loud and clear. It is as well to remember this if one's conversation could embarrass if allowed to travel beyond its intended recipient. The room is quite lavish and is sometimes called in evidence by certain sections of the press when they wish to accuse the BMA of high living, and thus other rarefied and arrogant tendencies. The dinner further cemented the improving relations with Waldegrave and his colleagues, although the BMA's best claret (whose vintage might have disappointed our press critics) was wasted on him because it turned out that he always forswore alcohol during Lent. The chairmen of all the BMA's major committees attended and it was a useful opportunity for an exchange of views in non-adversarial circumstances.

Taking stock next day it seemed remarkable that changes that would turn the NHS upside-down were only just over a month away, and a good deal of the detail, as predicted, had still not been filled in. True separation of the purchasers and providers was not going to take place; GPs who hoped to be fundholders had not yet received confirmation; hospitals in many cases had not priced the procedures they were to offer, and those that had showed enormous variations; and the new capitation-based funding system had been bowdlerized in order to protect London's higher RAWP-based funding from the catastrophic turbulence that a true market would bring. But at least now we had a health secretary who would think, rather than bluster, when things went wrong.

Waldegrave had given an extensive interview to the editor of the *British Medical Journal*, Richard Smith, in which he had ably shown that he was now fully in touch with doctors' feelings about the changes, even if he was going ahead with them.[4] He hoped he would still be Health Secretary in two years' time when considerable changes would have taken place, and he recognized that the reforms would highlight the special problems of London, whose cure had been postponed for too long. The main benefits of the reforms would lie in better information on what we were doing – about what we could get for our money and about 'how much things cost', and there were 'real gains [to be had from] devolved management'. He thought that the NHS had been so difficult to manage because of confusion between the separate roles of producing a public-health strategy on the one hand and running hospitals and other units on the other. The reforms would make matters explicit. He had obviously been mugging up on other countries' healthcare systems and thought that our radical new internal market would be copied by some of them. He knew that the changes would force him to take some tough decisions, which he welcomed. Smith made the telling point that while he was extolling the virtues of the reforms in encouraging a bottom-up approach from those who provided the service, why was it that the reforms themselves were imposed in such a 'terribly top down' way? Waldegrave clung to the ropes with the excuse that he did not know 'whether the personalities then about were actually in the business of real consultation or of just trying to stop everything'. Of course the medical 'personalities then about' (presumably John Marks and his supporters) would have been delighted to have been consulted and were by no means Luddite. It was the *government* personality, Mrs Thatcher, who went ahead without them. He interestingly acknowledged a recent statement by David, now Lord, Owen, who said that he should emulate Iain Macleod, who followed Aneurin Bevan and wanted to be the first health minister to pass no legislation and just run the health service.

He accepted that fundholding by GPs would produce an uneven

movement towards improvement but thought this would be a spur for others to catch up. The market would also have to be managed, and the managers would have to be leaders. When taxed on the likely increase in bureaucracy, he fenced by saying that 'one man's bureaucrat is another man's leader', a good quote, but not one with which many in the health service would agree.

On devolution of pay-setting for consultants to their local hospitals he gave plenty of examples from industry and academe, where he thought it worked, but he was utopian when asked to explain what advantages it would have for the health service. Questioned on waiting lists, he was optimistic that the new system would reduce them, but tacitly accepted that John Yates, the DoH's adviser on waiting lists who had just resigned, was right when he warned that simplistically operating on those who had waited longest might prejudice the chances of those whose needs were more urgent.

To the inevitable question about Britain's low spending on healthcare as a proportion of national wealth, he skilfully inserted the 'irritating example of Japan spending less and having better health' than us. He dismissed the high-spending American system as 'a shambles and wasting money hand over fist'. Here at least was a health minister who had done his homework. Japan indeed remains an anomaly, but, as Waldegrave was well aware, at least some of the reasons why the Japanese appear healthier than we are probably lie with their healthier lifestyle, about which the NHS can do little or nothing, despite the health-promotion aspects of the GPs' contract.

London, he thought, was 'an extreme case of how the present system doesn't work', and that now some decisions would be forced 'out of us cowardly politicians'. He assured Richard Smith that community care would not be forgotten, and that the missing part of the new Act would not be allowed to slip further. It would be a priority.

On tobacco he went as far as he could go without committing the government to banning advertising, and he was sound on alcohol. He trailed his forthcoming *Health of the Nation*, and did not sidestep questions on rationing and resource allocation, which he thought should be more explicit and a matter for the public, politicians and clinicians – an answer difficult to fault.

I have summarized this long interview relatively fully because it demonstrates what a formidably well-informed minister Waldegrave was. It may also go some way towards explaining why he had much more success with the medical profession than his predecessor. Not only was he well-informed, he was unusually frank and open for a politician, and had an instinctive compatibility with doctors. Whether this made my task in opposing the reforms easier or more difficult is open to question.

Despite our much better relations with Waldegrave than with Clarke, the BMA Council decided that a direct approach to the Prime Minister should be made. Therefore on 15 March, a fortnight before R-day, I wrote a letter to John Major in the following terms:

Dear Prime Minister
The British Medical Association is receiving information from all over the country about the serious crises occurring in the National Health Service.

Problems include bed closures, the freezing of staff and equipment replacement, lengthening waiting lists and a huge hospital maintenance backlog. The Audit Commission recently put the latter at £2 billion.

Despite the increased monies made available by the Government in the last decade, all of us believe that the underlying cause remains an insufficiency of resources.

A poll taken in Ribble Valley at the time of the recent bye-election is reported to have shown that the NHS came second in public concern only to the Community Charge, and my Council shares this grave concern.

I would like to have an opportunity to meet you to express this concern personally because we feel that, despite the considerable and much appreciated efforts made by Mr Waldegrave to meet with and listen to members of the medical profession, this is a matter of overall Government policy on the funding of what is, or should be, the jewel in the crown of British public service.

It was acknowledged by his private secretary, Barry Potter, three days later, but no reply came from Mr Major until 22 April. In it he defended the government's record on the NHS, saying that the priority given to it had increased 'so that it now stands second only to the Social Security budget in terms of public spending', and that spending was at an 'all time high, which represents an increase in funding of 50 per cent in real terms since 1979'.

He recognized the stresses and strains in the service, especially in London and some inner cities, but denied that crisis or disintegration of the health service was evident. He went on to say that 'the problem is not one of insufficient resources but rather one of organiz-ation', and that his government's reforms and the increased resources put in would make the NHS more effective. He doubted 'whether a general meeting on NHS funding would be particularly helpful at this stage' but he had asked William Waldegrave to get in touch to discuss any specific concerns we might have. However, unlike Mrs Thatcher with my predecessor, he did offer to meet me later in the year about the reforms.

On the face of it, it was a not unreasonable reply even if it had been unnecessarily tardy. However by sticking to the government's line that the NHS's problems were organizational rather than finan-cial he lit the blue touchpaper with my Council. I therefore replied that they were not able to accept his view but that we would be meeting Mr Waldegrave on 9 May, and hoped to meet him soon as well. Council also decided that the BMA should launch a campaign immediately to highlight the underfunding of the NHS and to draw attention to the damage that the reforms would do.

Just a fortnight before the reforms would start the names of the 1720 family doctor fundholders in 306 general practices were announced. Their average practice budget would be £1.2 million, which was about £100 for every patient registered. There were another 350 practices interested in becoming fundholding the following year. When Mr Waldegrave released the details in the House of Commons he went to some lengths to praise the new fundholders for their desire to improve their service to patients, but he would not be drawn into attacking the BMA for its opposition. He knew by then that the most almighty row was simmering in the GPs' committee about fundholding, and he must have judged that undermining Ian Bogle by using the occasion for an assault would seriously compromise the tender flower of conciliation that was just visible beneath the frost still lingering from the last traumatic year.

CHAPTER TEN

The First Six Months
April–October 1991

We trained hard, but every time we formed up into teams,
we would be reorganized. I was to learn later in life that we
tend to meet any new situation by reorganizing – and a
wonderful method it can be for creating the illusion of progress
while producing inefficiency and demoralization.
PETRONIUS, *c.* AD 60

There were rumblings right at the start that inequity was going to be
an issue. The Christie cancer hospital in Manchester announced that
it would open a ward for the priority treatment of cancer patients if
the 26 health authorities it approached would pay. The idea that cancer
therapy, of all treatments, could be prioritized by the ability to pay
caused a furore, and William Waldegrave's response that the Christie
was using the new freedom offered by the reforms to fund a new ward
failed to quell the deep unease caused by the announcement. Dr John
Roylance from Bristol, Waldegrave's constituency city, and one of the
very few medically qualified general managers, did nothing to douse
the flames by telling local fundholders that if they had the money their
patients could be treated straight away. He omitted to say when the
displaced patients of non-fundholding GPs would be treated.[1]

However, as was hoped by government the reformed health service entered the new era without a bang. The intended quiet start
was brought about largely by there being little change in the planned
number of patients to be treated, where they would be treated and
which hospitals would receive the resultant income. In every region
block contracts to achieve this were the norm, even those entered

into by the more entrepreneurial GP fundholders. There was not enough reliable information on costs for it to be otherwise; the price lists for operations published by the hospitals showed this. The farcical variations commented on in the national press confirmed that very few hospitals indeed were ready to 'play shops', as I dubbed it at the time. In the West Midlands, confusion amongst the GP fundholders was extreme when they found, for example, that an artificial hip replacement would cost £7485 in the Sandwell district general hospital but only £1996 in Mid-Staffordshire, with an average cost in the region of £4145. One of the hospitals, Walsall's Manor Hospital, was so alarmed it cut its prices dramatically, claiming the traditional computer error for its original high prices.

The large differences in the prices quoted by adjacent hospitals were also responsible for great disparities in the budgets fundholding GPs were given. A Sutton Coldfield practice with 12,000 patients was allotted £1.4 million, nearly one and a half times as much as a similar-sized practice in nearby Chelmsley Wood. When the local MP, Terry Davis, complained that the needs of patients served by the less well-funded practice were at least as great if not greater than those in more affluent Sutton Coldfield, he was told by the regional health authority that budgets were calculated on the price charged by the local hospitals and on historic prescription costs, a clear negation of the vaunted internal market.[2]

The West Midlands prices for hip replacement were themselves very high. In the north, Blackburn Royal Infirmary was quoting only £1027, and even London teaching-hospitals were cheaper than most Midlands prices, Guy's offering to do the operation for £1596 and Charing Cross & Westminster for £2566. It seemed very clear that those hospitals quoting the lowest figures were either aping the loss-leader idea employed by their local supermarkets (a dodge which had been forbidden by the Management Executive) or displaying serious financial incompetence. The highest quotes suggested that close attention should be given to the functioning of those hospitals' finance and contracts departments, or just possibly that their overall manning levels were considerably above the average.

Elsewhere some health authorities and hospitals were unable to provide any prices at all. In Wales, the South Glamorgan Health Authority said it was 12 months away from providing family doctors with detailed price lists, and fundholding practices were having to have countless meetings with business and contract managers to establish the cost of what they wanted.[3]

In the hospitals themselves, doctors felt they were being marginalized. I described doctors at the time to Sheila Masters as feeling like 'pilots in an airline run by deskbound managers'. Although the pilots knew how to fly the planes, which the managers did not, they did not know what tickets their passengers had been sold or to where they had bought them.

The managers, whose numbers were increasing dramatically, like swans were paddling desperately beneath the water. At my instigation, Dr Andrew Vallance-Owen, a senior member of the BMA's medical staff, had investigated this increase, which was inevitable given the huge extra administrative load the reforms had placed on the health service. The survey was a simple one. Almost all the senior managerial posts in the NHS are advertised in the *Health Service Journal*, the managers' weekly reading. Between May and October 1990, nearly 1800 new posts related to the NHS changes were advertised in the journal, carrying an annual salary bill of £41 million. The cost of the advertisements alone would have been at least £600,000 and it was estimated that, over a whole year, an extra £80 million for the new managerial and administrative salaries would have to come out of the NHS budget.[4] Few if any clinicians believed that £80 million would be saved in efficiency as a result.

As well as increasing the managerial time needed to run a new health service the reforms caused an enormous proliferation in the amount of paper circulating. The two increases were connected. A consultant I knew, who was a clinical director at the time, found that he was receiving 30 management letters and 13 reports every week – 300 sheets of A4 paper to read in all. To make matters worse his access to a secretary was shared with eight other doctors and he had no office. He therefore carried all the paperwork around with him and used the boot of his car as a filing cabinet. He bought his own word processor, and he and his colleagues clubbed together to buy his department a photocopier. He, and others like him, were extremely irked by both the increasing bureaucracy brought about by the reforms and its cost.

Disquiet was also being expressed about the make-up of the boards of the new self-governing hospitals. Robin Cook had conducted a survey on behalf of the Labour Party and had found that property development was the largest single business interest of board members. His statement 'Is the NHS safe in the hands of the estate agents?' achieved wide coverage. Waldegrave defended the heavy bias towards business among trust directors by claiming that they were there to ensure that taxpayers got value for their money. In the past, members of NHS authorities had been unpaid. Now trust chairmen were to receive up to £20,000 and non-executive directors £5000 annually – relatively small sums when compared to remuneration in the business world, but a new departure for the health service, where such people had always given their services free.

Another survey, this time of 82 district health authorities in England (40 per cent of the total), revealed that of the 410 non-executive seats, 164 were occupied by businessmen and accountants, 51 by doctors and 31 by local councillors. The rest came from a variety of non-medical occupations. The change of emphasis from health to business was well illustrated by what happened in Macclesfield. Before the reforms the DHA was made up of four local councillors, three doctors, a nurse and eight others from backgrounds in the social services, teaching and business. The new much smaller authority included an industrial manager, a management consultant, another businessman, a journalist and a social worker. There was no one from the health professions.[5] Medical input to the new authorities came from directors of public health, who were salaried officers and rarely had any detailed knowledge of specialist hospital medicine or general practice.

There were also early signs that the public-health directors at the health authorities were going to be faced with some very difficult problems, for which they had not been trained. In the pre-reform days, if a doctor thought that a patient required the services of a particular consultant or specialized service outside his district there was usually nothing to stop him referring the patient there, beyond acceptance by the receiving consultant. In this way rare conditions could be treated by experts who had built up their experience and reputation in a specialized field. It is true that in the past some GPs would refer patients to consultants at their old Alma Mater or to other prestigious hospitals unnecessarily. This was sometimes at the behest of a patient, often affluent, who felt there was some cachet in having their hip replaced on the NHS by the eminent Mr Sawbones at St Elsewhere's who had seen their sister in Harley Street, but in most parts of the country the system worked well and was not abused.

Many local district hospitals, although providing a good general range of treatments, did not offer procedures in fields which were undergoing rapid advance like transplantation or *in vitro* fertilization. Patients requiring these treatments were referred to special centres, usually in teaching-hospitals. The problem was that after 1 April the district health authority in whose area the patient lived would have to pay. Robin Cook was able to cause considerable political damage by quoting examples where authorities refused to pay. 'One of my constituents', he said in the Commons, 'has been on the waiting list for *in vitro* fertilization at Guy's Hospital and was expecting to be treated in April. She was told last month that her local health authority, the Lothian Health Board, will not now pay for it.' Stephen Dorrell, a junior health minister at the time, accused him of resorting to attack by anecdote, but it was a telling blow. There were many such cases reported, especially around London, where it had been the practice for years for patients from Kent and Sussex to be referred to Guy's or St Thomas's for quite routine procedures and consultations, rather than to their local district hospitals, which were much less well-funded than these centres of excellence in the metropolis. What seemed doubly unfair in the Cook case was that the patient had already waited in the queue, only to have the door closed in her face on reaching the head of it because the system had changed. As someone aptly commented, it was rather like waiting in the checkout queue at Sainsbury's for some time, only for the till to be closed on reaching it, and being told to go to Tesco and start queuing again.

It fell to the public-health directors to try and sort out the mess. What should have happened in the Scottish woman's case was that the Lothian Health Board should have had a contract for IVF with a specialist unit, probably in Scotland, to which she could have gone. Her doctor however had referred her, some time before the reforms arrived, to Guy's. This may have been because he was familiar with the quality on offer there, or because his patient had a particular reason for going there, quite likely relating to previous treatment or investigation over many years for the condition which had rendered her infertile, or for some other good reason. Unfortunately for her, some health authorities were now refusing to pay for IVF at all, and others had strict criteria for doing so.

In addition, many health authorities had set aside very little of their budgets for these extra-contractual referrals, or ECRs, hoping in this way to effect a crude form of healthcare rationing. The Director of Public Health for Preston, Dr Stuart Horner, who was also chairman of the BMA's ethical committee, said that his own authority in Lancashire had allocated only £200,000 of its £45 million budget for ECRs and that one patient alone might need £30,000 of it. An example might have been bone-marrow transplantation for leukaemia, which was to prove so controversial later when the father of 'Child B' (Jaymee Bowen) sued the Cambridge health authority. The authority had refused to pay for a second procedure after the little girl had relapsed following a previous transplant, although they maintained throughout that the reason was medical not financial. In 1991 the cost of a bone-marrow transplant was between £30,000 and £40,000.

In a thorough review of ECRs, the Public Health Director for Richmond, Twickenham and Roehampton HA examined 235 requests for extra-contractual referral of patients submitted to his authority in the first three months of the new NHS.[6] Seventy-nine requests were for emergency care and 156 were for planned treatments. Initially 61 were refused, of which 20 were because the authority was not liable to pay. Deciding on an authority's liability in itself could be extremely time-consuming, as it meant establishing first that the patient was entitled to NHS care, i.e. was not a foreign national in the case of planned care, and then that his or her main residence was within the health authority's area, which was often not coterminous with that of the local authority. Of the remaining 41 patients entitled, 17 were accepted after appeal. This still left 24 patients, about 10 per cent of the applications, for whom Richmond would not pay. The difficulties and the protracted wrangling which this new task brought to the public-health directors can be imagined. It is not hard either to envisage the huge extension of bureaucracy that ECRs brought in train, or to appreciate the immense dissatisfaction of rejected patients and their doctors.

Early on, some consultants became incandescent with rage when, on seeing a patient in their hospital who clearly required the specialist services of a colleague in another hospital, they were told that they could not simply get on the telephone as of old and transfer the patient. First they had to notify the contracts department of their hospital or authority to find out whether a contract existed; then, if not, the ECR procedure had to be gone through, with extensive paperwork. Next, permission had to be obtained for the ECR to proceed. The whole affair could take several days and this was quite unacceptable. Eventually some of the red tape *was* cut and consultants were allowed to arrange the transfer or referral first, and complete the administrative paperwork later – still a time-consuming and tiresome arrangement.

As if the mechanics of the new way of working were not bad enough, very soon news of serious upheavals in some of the most prominent new trust hospitals began to emerge. At the end of April, less than one month into the new service, the flagship Guy's and Lewisham Trust announced that it would have to cut 600 jobs, 10 per cent of its workforce, in order to save £12.8 million from its

£90 million staff budget. The new chief executive, Peter Griffiths, had recently moved from his post as deputy chief executive of the NHS Management Executive to take up his £90,0000-a-year job at Guy's. He said that the first year would be difficult for the trust because it needed to clear its £6.8 million debt from the previous year, when it had been forced to close over 100 beds.

The news from Guy's caused a frisson of alarm to run through the other London teaching-hospitals. Their higher metropolitan labour costs and capital charges implied that they might have to charge 40 per cent more for their services than hospitals just outside the inner-London ring, and purchasers would not be funded sufficiently to buy their more routine offerings. Not only would this be catastrophic financially, but it could seriously prejudice their vital role of teaching medical students, who needed to see common conditions, not just exotic ones. A study by the York University's Centre for Health Economics suggested that just leaving the inner-London hospitals to the market would be unacceptable, and that planned running-down and closure of some of them would have to be carried out. This idea was to gain ground steadily and culminated in the King's Fund and Tomlinson reports which raised so much controversy, and ultimately led to the closure of Bart's and the emasculation of Guy's.

The announcement of massive cuts at Guy's was followed by a similar tale from Bradford, where 300 jobs were to be lost. The political timing could not have been worse so soon into the new market era. The Health Secretary's admission that he had not known that Guy's planned to make 600 staff redundant when he approved the hospital's application for trust status was met with incredulity. He was soon questioned again about the Coopers & Lybrand report he had commissioned, which had said that only 12 of the 57 first-wave trusts were financially secure.

News of the looming financial catastrophes at Guy's and Bradford, and rumours of further troubles to come at other leading hospitals, cast a shadow over a new initiative timed to take the spotlight off the reforms in their difficult early stages. This was a new Green

Paper on a health strategy for England. It had been intended to publish it about two weeks before the Guy's story broke but it was delayed, ostensibly for further changes. Once again Robin Cook was able to leak the contents of a yet-to-be-published government document. He picked out salient omissions which he knew would puncture the government's apparent good intentions, in particular its silence on the connection between poverty and ill-health, a sensitive area for the Conservatives ever since Patrick Jenkin had tried to muffle the impact of the Black report in 1980.

John Major made a gesture to the profession by inviting about 20 leading doctors and others involved in healthcare to Chequers to discuss the paper, which was to be called *The Health of the Nation*. I was slightly piqued at not being invited, but assumed this snub was probably because I had recently publicly criticized the reforms more strongly, at the behest of my Council. Nevertheless the BMA's president, Dame Rosemary Rue, was invited and, as a public-health specialist and recent ex-regional medical officer and general manager, she was particularly well able to comment on the state of the nation's health as well as its health service. Paddy Ross also went, as did the juniors' chairman, Stephen Hunter, and Dame Margaret Turner-Warwick and Colin Warne from the Royal Colleges of Physicians and General Practitioners respectively. Rosemary came away encouraged that the government now at last seemed to be prepared to listen to those in the health service, who could provide much-needed advice about both health and long-term planning.

However, when John Chawner, Ian Bogle and I met William Waldegrave on 9 May there was no semblance of an accord. Waldegrave showed that he was wedded to the market ideology of the reforms. We even offered to stop our campaign of opposition to the existing first-wave changes while they were properly assessed, if he would agree to halt further extension of trust hospitals and fundholding GPs. This was a very big step for us given the depth of feeling in the association, but he would not agree.

After the meeting Waldegrave announced that John Major would see us 'soon', despite putting us off only a fortnight before. Presumably he must have cleared this with the Prime Minister, but it took me another four months actually to see Mr Major. This delay seemed to show either indecision, or an attempt to take the steam out of the situation for as long as possible by keeping the date on hold. It appears to be a characteristic of the Major government for early refusals or denials to be eventually overtaken by *force majeure* or a change of mind – notable examples include Britain's leaving the European Exchange Rate Mechanism, the sacking of David Mellor and the handling of the BSE in beef affair. This on-again, off-again course was also pursued with the Joint Consultants Committee. Paddy Ross had first sought a meeting in early 1991, asked formally for one in October, when they were asked to be patient, and then in December was promised one as soon as Major could find time. The meeting was finally arranged for March 1992 but cancelled by the Prime Minister at the last minute.

The long wait did not fill us with confidence in Mr Major over the ensuing months in which we hammered home the funding deficiencies of the health service. I was using a shortfall figure of £6,000 million at the time, which was the amount the health service would gain if the proportion of the country's gross national product devoted to healthcare was brought up to the average percentage of our European neighbours. Actually the latest figures from the Organization for Economic Co-operation and Development showed that, in the five years from 1985 to 1989, the UK's spend on health had actually fallen from 6 per cent to 5.8 per cent of GNP. Of the 24 developed countries in the period considered by the OECD, only Greece spent a smaller proportion than us. In written evidence to the Parliamentary Health Select Committee the BMA included in addition to these sombre figures the fact that between 1982 and 1989, while activity in terms of patients treated increased by 16 per cent, the real resources to carry it out went up by only 3 per cent.

Ten days later I went on a Sunday to see William Waldegrave privately at his London house in Kensington. As always he was very friendly and straightforward, and was quite happy to discuss 'what if' questions off the government's own agenda. 'Supposing several billion pounds more were available for healthcare, how would you spend it?' he asked me. This question was usually asked rhetorically by Tory sympathizers, in the media and elsewhere, and then answered themselves in the trade-union vein that, as 70 per cent of the NHS's funds went on staff costs, what we were really after was more pay. Waldegrave did not ask the question in this way, but I could think of 1001 things on which the extra money could be well spent, depending on whether it was capital or revenue, or a mixture of both. I had to admit that prioritization was a more difficult question.

My meeting with him was pleasant and friendly, and for all I know he may have used it to judge how far the BMA was prepared to go in making it hot for the government up to the next election, which might have been only a few months off. Certainly the press the government was getting was unremittingly bad, and he had accused the BMA in a speech the week before of forming an unholy alliance with Labour.

Another blow for the Tories was their loss in the Monmouth by-election of a relatively safe seat to Labour. After this heavy defeat Major must have put all thoughts of a 1991 election from his mind, especially as his Chancellor, Norman Lamont, was also not promising much in the way of an economic recovery before the end of the year. Major began to defend the reforms in his own speeches and reversed the earlier promise of meeting the BMA 'soon'.

Waldegrave was now coming under serious fire from his own party for not standing up to Robin Cook's parliamentary attacks effectively enough, and his career was on a knife edge. Therefore I was surprised when he agreed to take part in a debate with me arranged by the *Daily Telegraph*. Maurice Weaver, the journalist who had set up the meeting, placed a newly bought microphone and tape recorder between us on the Health Secretary's large oval table, which successive occupants of the post used as a desk, and left us to get on with it with minimum interruption. Neither of us was at our best after long and tiring days. I had driven the 120 miles from my hospital in Dorset and William had had a terrible couple of weeks.

We rehearsed the differences between us in a non-partisan and civilized way. I went for better funding and William, predictably, went for better organization. I used an engineering analogy to question the government's idea of a service run by managers and accountants; Waldegrave countered with the need for professional managers whether in engineering or health. I was sceptical that the increased overheads of the new system were going to be retrieved in terms of greater efficiency. Waldegrave's response was that he was 'astounded at the low level of information technology within the NHS' that was going to need a lot of money to rectify in the short term – not a very adequate answer. He did however fill in a bit of my case by putting it to himself, which was very civil of him. As Weaver wrote in the resultant article, there was hardly a meeting of minds, but we parted amicably enough.[7]

It seemed to me that if Waldegrave had been himself a medical consultant, which was not all that far-fetched, he might have argued the BMA's case very well. In his book *The Binding of Leviathan*, published in 1978, he opines that liberalism is 'a splendid philosophy for opposition, as is anarchism or extreme socialism, since it enables you to support all the pressure groups which are resisting the government of the day'.[8] He made it sound rather attractive, and he painted Thatcherism as an 'amoral liberalism' attempting to fill 'the vacuum left by Social Democracy and Keynesian Conservatism'. However he nailed his colours to the mast on the health service by also writing in 1978:

> let us apply the conservative approach to some areas which we have predicted will face us with increasingly desperate problems in the years ahead: the problems of incomes policy, of industrial dereliction and of the cities. There are plenty of others, such as the question of how to manage, or replace, the nearly collapsing bureaucracy of the National Health Service.

Unfortunately, in the book he chose to discuss only the first two, incomes policy and industrial and urban dereliction, so he left no hostages to fortune for us. His predictive powers were actually very good. He foresaw the collapse of the Soviet Union from the centre at the end of the 20th century as 'it is difficult to make an ideology which is simple enough to be useful for running the imperial bureaucracy down to its lowest levels, also interesting enough to maintain the allegiance of the outstanding men of action or the subtle thinkers'. It may have been difficult, I thought when I read it, and it may not have been an ideology precisely, but the old imperial NHS bureaucracy kept the allegiance of the surgical men of action and the subtle physicianly thinkers for over forty years.

At the beginning of June, the delayed Green paper on a health strategy for England appeared. This was welcome for several reasons. First of all, *The Health of the Nation* was about improving *health*, rather than simply about healthcare. Second, it recognized the need to select targets, and, most importantly, to measure whether these goals were reached: a strong contrast to the way the reforms were introduced without effective means to check any accruing benefits in terms of quality or amount of healthcare against new expenditure. Third, it offered consultation on its contents. It was all *Working for Patients* was not, and it was tantalizing to imagine what might have been if the NHS reforms had been put forward by Major and Waldegrave rather than Thatcher and Clarke. It was difficult to imagine Margaret Thatcher or Kenneth Clarke writing in the foreword to the consultative document, as William Waldegrave did, 'We are clear about one thing: a strategy imposed by the Government which takes no heed of the views of those who will have to implement it, including the people themselves, is valueless.' Another well received inclusion was the recognition, *pace* the Black report, that the physical and social environment, and social class, have a considerable influence on health, morbidity and mortality. The document was not before time, because the government had endorsed the World Health Organization's similar strategy of *Health for All* as far back as 1981,[9] but it was nevertheless well received by those involved, who had almost given up hope that a Thatcherite government could do anything sensible on health.

The Health of the Nation identified 16 possible areas for improvement falling into five groups. Under 'Causes of Substantial Mortality' were coronary heart disease, stroke, cancers and accidents. Examples of 'Causes of Substantial Ill Health' were mental illness, diabetes and asthma. 'Factors Contributing to Mortality, Ill Health and Healthy Living' were smoking, diet and alcohol, and physical exercise; and 'Areas with Clear Scope for Improvement' included the health of pregnant women, infants and children, rehabilitation services for people with a physical disability and environmental quality. Finally, 'Areas with Great Potential for Harm' identified HIV/AIDS, other communicable diseases and food safety. From this long list the government hoped to agree a smaller number of targets for particular attention. There were omissions: no specific reference was made to poverty *per se*, for instance; and some complacency was shown when comparing Britain's progress towards hitting the 38 *Health for All* targets for Europe, but at least some genuine dialogue was now going to take place over the five months offered for consultation.

The *Health of the Nation* targets were eventually published as a White Paper a year later, in July 1992, by Virginia Bottomley, who succeeded William Waldegrave after the general election. The five key areas finally chosen were coronary heart disease and stroke, cancers, HIV/AIDS and sexual health, mental illness and accidents. Coronary heart disease is both the single largest cause of death and the single main cause of premature death, and accounts for about a quarter of all deaths, in England. Strokes cause about 12 per cent of all deaths. The targets for both CHD and stroke were to reduce the death rate in those under 65 by at least 40 per cent by the year 2000, and for older people by 30 per cent for CHD and 40 per cent for stroke. Many of the other targets were equally tough.

An important risk factor for CHD, stroke and cancer is cigarette-smoking, and doctors remain dismayed that the government have so far failed to bite the bullet and ban advertising and sports promotion by the tobacco companies. The *Health of the Nation* initiative gave them a golden opportunity to follow our neighbours in Europe and in Canada, Australia and New Zealand in banning tobacco advertising. The document set targets to reduce cigarette-smoking in men and women of 16 and over to no more than 20 per cent by the year 2000. The figures then for smoking by men and women were nearly the same, at 31 and 28 per cent respectively. It seemed to us that using solely the fiscal measure of increasing tax on tobacco every year was quite insufficient to achieve this goal, and smoking incidence continues to bear this out. Every year while in office I led a small delegation to the Treasury to ask for heavier taxes on tobacco. Our highly knowledgeable team that year included the eminent now-retired Hammersmith Hospital physician Professor John Goodwin, and David Pollock, the director of Action on Smoking and Health. We were always courteously received by one of the junior Treasury ministers like Richard Ryder or Gillian Shephard at the time, and tobacco tax was nearly always increased, sometimes sharply. But we knew that this would not be anywhere near as effective as reducing the appeal and glamour of smoking to the young, most of whom once hooked would be customers for life, by reducing their all-pervasive exposure to advertising. Studies in other countries confirmed our view, and the DoH-commissioned study from its own chief economist, the Smee report, pointed the same way.

In her foreword to the final strategy, Mrs Bottomley set out the government's commitment to improving the health of the population, but although she announced the setting-up of a new cabinet committee to co-ordinate the strategy's implementation, as the targets could not be the concern of the DoH alone, much of it rang hollow when compared to the actions that had actually been taken so far.

At my first BMA annual representative meeting as its Council chairman, held in Inverness in July 1991, I had to account for my stewardship of the BMA's public affairs over the previous year. In May I had had to deal with an angry Council as a result of the Prime

Minister's letter to me of 22 April, claiming that the NHS's problem was not one of insufficient resources. Calls for my resignation had already been made after a misunderstanding of a remark about tactics I had made at the GPs' committee. One particularly fiery member of that committee, who was also a member of Council, had circulated a letter to all members claiming that I was, in effect, a closet Conservative who therefore did not wish to embarrass the government. What I had said at the time of the meeting was that then was not the best moment to launch a high-profile attack on the reforms because the poll tax was currently occupying centre-stage in the media, and the impact of anything we had to say about the NHS would be lessened. My opponents falsely took it to mean that I did not want to add to the government's troubles with the poll tax by piling the NHS on top.

In my opening speech I decided to use a nautical analogy. The reforms had been launched on a sea of troubles, and the doctors had seen that there were two classes of cabin: first-class and second-class. Was a two-tier service intentional? I scorned the new business jargon then rife, and the softening of some of the original market words used, and pointed out that soft words could hide harsh realities. I encouraged medical involvement in management and quoted Sir Roy Griffiths' idea that doctors should be 'T-shaped managers', where the downstroke represented their in-depth professionalism and the crosspiece its accompanying broadening of management experience.

I urged the profession to get involved, but I lamented the huge extra cost of the new system, which had recently been extensively examined by the American economist Professor Donald Light. The best estimate seemed to be an initial cost of as much as £2000 million, followed by annual operating costs of around £500 million. I gave examples of what this sort of money would buy if spent directly on healthcare: £370 million would have cleared the orthopaedic waiting list in England and Wales, £44 million the cardiothoracic and £76 million the ophthalmic – surely a better use of £490 million.

I explained the basic conflict between those who care and those who fund. The Treasury's approach is, 'Take this money and see what you can do with it, as it's all you are getting'; doctors see it as 'What do we need to provide and how can we obtain the money to provide it?'

It was not a bad speech, I was told, but it should have been delivered with a lot more *hwyl*. Whatever my abilities as a platform speaker, and I was to receive some professional tuition later in the year, the majority who attended had come to hear another lambasting of an intransigent government, which they would have got from my predecessor. However there were signs that Waldegrave was doing something on his side to lessen the tension and I was anxious not to pour too much paraquat on what might be emerging green shoots. He had condemned two-tierism and agreed a way of combating its worst excesses (although the market broke through this very quickly) and was due to sit down with the GPs to look at fundholding in depth.

Nevertheless consultant morale was very low, as a recent *BMA News Review* survey had starkly revealed. Three-quarters felt less valued by the government than five years before, and 40 per cent contemplated taking early retirement, with 41 per cent of these saying they would 'go tomorrow, if a full pension could be guaranteed'. The GPs were still fuming over their contract and the junior doctors had become very disillusioned again by the time it was taking to reduce their hours of work to something more reasonable.

My attempts at lifting the heads of my profession were a failure, and at the Council meeting at the end of the representative meeting I faced one of the most determined attempts to unseat its chairman that the BMA had ever experienced. Most serious for me was that among its ringleaders were my two predecessors, John Marks and Sir Tony Grabham. Fortunately the chairmen of the major craft committees and some of their most influential members gave me their support, and after a long debate in which I asked every Council member to give me their views, a vote of confidence was substituted for an impending one of no confidence and carried unanimously.

It was a very unpleasant three hours for me and a time of great trauma for the BMA. Ian Field was so aghast at events that he told me afterwards that he would have resigned if my opponents had succeeded in unseating me. I hope that on sober reflection he would not have, as loyalty to politicians by their civil servants should never extend as far as their jobs, unless they have been responsible for the disaster, which Ian was not. I left Inverness seriously shaken in my belief that I could do anything at all to help the health service and make my members happy.

The interval between the representative meeting in early July and the first Council meeting in the first week of October is normally a quiet period for the BMA. I used it to continue to meet those who might be influential with the government and try and extract some tangible benefit from the more conciliatory attitude that had nearly cost me my chair. I saw William Waldegrave again with Colin Smith, the chairman of the BMA's medical academics' committee, who was very concerned at the way medical schools were being squeezed by their parent universities. Medical academics did their clinical work in the NHS, but the universities claimed not to be able to afford the rates of pay agreed by the NHS, because medical salaries were higher than those of most other dons. If failure to implement these pay rates became the rule, academics would leave the medical schools to work wholly in the NHS, and the education of future doctors would be jeopardized. Waldegrave was sympathetic but the problem rumbles on to this day. And after what seemed like an interminable delay, on the last day of September, two days before the first BMA Council meeting of the new session, I was invited to breakfast with the Prime Minister, along with Ian Field.

Ian and I duly turned up at No. 10 Downing Street shortly before our 8.30 a.m. appointment and were ushered through the unexpectedly bright scarlet ante-rooms to the waiting-room on the ground floor. There were six of us for breakfast. John Major was accompanied at the table by his private secretary Barry Potter on his right, with Carolyn Sinclair, an adviser from the No. 10 Policy Unit, on his left. I sat opposite Major, with Ian on my left and William Waldegrave on my right. John Major was informal and courteous, acting as host himself in inviting us to help ourselves to bacon and eggs from a side table in the small wood-panelled breakfast room on the first floor.

I was allowed to open the exchange by expressing our prime concern of underfunding. I rehearsed the usual arguments about our low GNP-percentage spend, and suggested that the money allocated to the NHS might be based on a fixed proportion of GNP. Major replied that the NHS might get less money as the GNP could fall as well as rise – it was lower in 1991 than the year before. He told us that Helmut Kohl and the Dutch premier were both worried about their countries' health spending, but as their countries spent so much more than us I was not surprised. Kohl was apparently another subscriber to the bottomless-pit argument. I explained the basis of our view that £6000 million more annually should be allocated to the NHS, and said that, although it was a somewhat rough and ready calculation, using the average GNP-percentage health spend of countries comparable to our own as a yardstick seemed as good as any other way of arriving at the shortfall, which we knew from our daily work existed. Our health spend would not reach German or Dutch proportions even if we did spend another £6000 million a year more, because both countries spent well above the European average.

Major was anxious to dispel any idea that the reforms were intended to pave the way to privatization, to which I replied that I had never personally accused the government of that intention, which he agreed. I was keen that doctors in general and the BMA in particular were not seen as riding pillion on the Labour opposition's bicycle. Major seemed very pleased with a recent article in the *Economist* attacking Robin Cook, that I thought was rather right-wing and unobjective. Ian said that although we did have some political left-wingers on our Council, and mentioned Sam Everington, who was an adviser to Robin Cook, we were not a political body – just doctors who cared about the health service. Both Major and Waldegrave agreed that we had some able members too who were not pursuing a political agenda, and mentioned Stephen Hunter.

Family doctors were accepting fundholding, according to John Major, and while not disagreeing with him that some were, I explained that their independent-contractor status was very important to them, and that to some fundholding seemed the best way of keeping it. He believed that consultants were fully involved in management and the contracting process, which we informed him they were not, and he asked Waldegrave what he thought about this. Major expressed a strong belief in the devolution of management to the local level and in cutting bureaucracy, but it did not seem to us that he had been briefed on the reasons why hospital consultants wanted their employment contracts to stay at the regional level, rather than be devolved to hospital managers. Waldegrave was aware of this, and the other reasons why consultants felt that regional health authorities should not be abolished. Major's experience of hospitals and GPs came from his own constituency, where he thought there was enthusiasm for the changes.

I raised the question of the scruffy appearance, poor eating and common-room facilities for staff and the general run-down nature of our hospitals. Clinical staff did not appreciate having to queue up with visitors in their staff canteens, which were now run on commercial lines, when they often had only a brief time in which to snatch lunch. And doctors necessarily used lunch to make vital contacts about patients and their treatment, and could not do so cheek-by-jowl with those, like visitors and some staff, who were not party to medical confidentiality. Richard Crossman's vision of general dining-rooms for all, similar to those in Japanese factories, was not an ideal model for hospitals, and damaged *esprit de corps* rather than enhanced it, I said. Major agreed that such a factory that he had visited was indeed rather soulless, a somewhat oblique response to the point I was making.

He also said, which was generally true, that patients praised the NHS – when they got in. What was complained of were waiting lists and times, and poor premises. He believed that the reforms would improve all these things. Unfortunately the good will of the clinical staff has been largely lost in the process of skewed priorities, inequities and increased bureaucracy, and the financial position is even worse now than it was then.

The meeting overran by 10 minutes, and although his next meeting was pressing, John Major escorted Ian and me to the stairs with great charm and expressed a wish to have further meetings with us. We walked down the stairs with their rather ugly metal balustrades, past the black and white portraits of his predecessors (James Callaghan's is said to be in colour but I did not notice it), favourably impressed by Major himself but wondering what if any use would come from the meeting. We had to be in Brighton that evening to host a dinner at the Labour Party conference for their health spokesmen and interested leading backbenchers. I had met most of them before and got on well with them but I was beginning to suffer from a surfeit of politicians of all parties. Unless they had worked in the NHS, few politicians seemed able to really understand what those in the health professions feel about the NHS and how it is run.

CHAPTER ELEVEN

The Tory Victory Means the Reforms Continue
November 1991–March 1993

Elections are won by men and women chiefly because most
people vote against somebody, rather than for somebody.
FRANKLIN ADAMS, *Nods and Becks*, 1944

At the rowdy Council meeting in May I had felt like a sleigh-driver pursued by wolves. Throwing some meat off the back in the shape of a promised health-strategy document enabled me to make my escape. I had anyway long wanted to set up a think-tank to consider the problems of the NHS. The loud and relentless confrontation between the government and the BMA was beginning to deafen even our own side. We were in danger of being widely seen as purely negative, and ultimately the genuine strength of our case would be diluted by satiating the public with tales of doom and gloom.

At the meeting 'a manifesto for the future of the NHS with the intention of informing the public debate and providing a yardstick against which the promises of all political parties may be judged' was proposed by Tony Stanton, deputy chairman of the GPs' committee. The idea was approved by Council and seized on with enthusiasm by me. Stanton was one of our wiser heads and he too could see the danger of ranting on about the defects of the reforms without putting forward any positive ideas of our own.

I set up a working party to produce such a document. Fortunately the Council had not tied my hands by demanding to choose its members. I chose Dame Rosemary Rue, our immediate past-president, who had given me such expert and welcome support in my first year as chairman; Richard Smith, the sparky and well-informed new editor of the *British Medical Journal*; Chris Ham, the highly respected healthcare academic, who at that time was a fellow in health policy management at the King's Fund College; and Tony Stanton himself. The working party's leg-man and secretary was Andrew Vallance-Owen, a senior member of the BMA's medical staff. Andrew was given the task of interviewing anyone and everyone who might have useful views that could be brought back to the working party. He eventually interviewed about 60 people, including influential reform supporters like Lord McColl and Baroness Cumberlege, and strong opponents like Professor Harry Keen and Dr Julian Tudor Hart. He also obtained interviews from old health service combatants like Enoch Powell and Renee Short, and diligently sought out health economists, sociologists, patients' representatives, managers, MPs and health-authority chairmen, as well as nurses and doctors. His very thorough research led to the separate publication of a book containing edited versions of 45 of his interviews.[1]

The working party met many times between May and October, when our report *Leading for Health* was published.[2] The report was expertly written by Richard Smith, who has a great facility for gathering complex and rather disorganized material together. The first of the report's three parts considered the 'philosophy of improving health', the second looked at ways of organizing systems for improving health, and the third examined the provision of the necessary resources. We reviewed the healthcare systems of 10 other OECD countries, and reproduced in six appendices some comparative health data tables from the latest OECD survey from 1987.

Richard kept it very short, 32 pages in all, and it was distributed widely – including a copy for every BMA member. It was generally well received by adversaries and supporters alike. William Waldegrave thought it constructive, and John Major received a copy. We had decided that we could do no more than raise the questions that needed to be answered, after first setting out the problems as we saw them. This questioning format was not what my opponents on

Council had been hoping for, but they themselves had not gone beyond attacking what the government had done, which was easy. We offered four models of delivering care. The first was a development of the old NHS; the other three were variants of the purchaser–provider model. We called the report an 'agenda for health' as that is what it was. After the section containing the four model systems, some of the questions we asked were: 'Is it advantageous to separate the purchaser and provider functions? Or could the old planned healthcare system be improved to a point where it worked much better than such a system? What are the relative merits of the two systems? If a purchaser–provider system is preferred which model would work best? How can community care best be fitted into such a system?'

Whatever its political impact, *Leading for Health* was popular with the schools of healthcare policy springing up in the newer universities everywhere. I received several requests for copies to use in teaching students in these establishments.

Meanwhile the government was hatching another initiative of its own. John Major had earlier produced the Citizen's Charter and announced that there would be further developments of this 'big idea', including its extension to the health service. At the end of October I went down to Richmond House to see Waldegrave, pending the imminent release of the Patient's Charter. In the preceding discussions the main worries of the professions had been that political promises would be made on behalf of the health service that we would not be able to deliver for lack of the wherewithal. I confirmed this to Mr Waldegrave. The public already had seven established NHS rights: to receive healthcare on the basis of clinical need, regardless of ability to pay; to be registered with a GP; to receive emergency medical care at any time; to be referred to a consultant when needed, and to have a second opinion; to have any proposed treatment explained, including any risks and alternatives, before agreeing to it; for health records to be confidential and for patients to have access to them; and to accept or reject participation in medical research and student training. The Patient's Charter added three more: to be given detailed information on local health services, including maximum waiting times; to be guaranteed admission for treatment by a specific date within two years; and to have any complaint investigated, with a full and prompt written reply.

As well as these 10 rights that patients now had, there were to be nine national charter standards which the NHS would aim to meet. These specified waiting times for assessment in accident and emergency, to see the doctor in outpatient departments, and for ambulances; what should happen if operations were cancelled; having a named nurse; reasonable arrangements for hospital discharge, the use of services, and information for relatives and friends; and a respect for privacy, dignity and religious and cultural beliefs. In addition to the national standards, health authorities were exhorted to set local charter standards too, on matters including waiting times for first outpatient appointments and for treatment in accident and emergency departments.

It was all very laudable, some said sub-utopian. Robin Cook justifiably, if carpingly, concentrated on the absence of sanctions if targets were not achieved and called it 'toothless'. The realists, among whom were doctors, could see that meeting some of the more rigid standards might lead to deficiencies simply being transferred elsewhere in their hospitals and departments, and this indeed has happened.

Many in the NHS predicted that accident and emergency departments would now employ triage nurses to assess patients on arrival, thus meeting the standard, but that unless more doctors could be found (and afforded) waits for treatment might continue to become longer. In many hospitals this also has happened. I have personal experience of a relative, whose scalp was badly lacerated and bruised by a fall, being seen by a nurse almost immediately in one of London's largest casualty departments, but then waiting, still bleeding and caked in blood, for nearly five hours before receiving medical attention and suturing. This scene is played out daily in hospitals all over the country, and in countless cases the injuries are far more serious. A piece of elastic can be stretched only so far, and Canute-like directives can no more resolve the underlying staffing and resource shortfalls in the health service than monarchs can stem tides.

As with successive waiting-list initiatives for planned operations, concentrating on those who have waited longest may lead to eyes being taken off the more important matter of treating first those whose need is most acute. Healthcare is a qualitative matter before ever it can be a quantitative one. In addition patients repeatedly confirm that, while waiting can be very irksome, all would prefer to wait and then receive first-class attention than receive immediate but hurried or less optimal treatment. As you can only have a chole-cystectomy once, there being only one gall bladder in all of us, operations are not like cans of beans to be bought where the queue is shortest.

The number of patients waiting more than two years for treatment was down to 20,500 by early 1992, and Waldegrave claimed that the Patient's Charter target of none would be reached during the next year. Unfortunately, he did not dwell on the fact that the number waiting up to one year had increased, and doctors were becoming increasingly restive about minor operations taking precedence over more urgent work just to meet politically set deadlines.

Apart from the pie-in-the-sky aspects of parts of the Patient's Charter, its politically driven, and above all centrist, nature caused despondency in those who had believed that the government really did intend to do what it said its reforms were designed to do – devolve responsibility to local level. Should not such detailed charters be the proper province of local hospitals and general practice management, or at the least should not the exhortations come from the NHS Management Executive rather than from government politicians?

Confusion between policy and operational concerns was not all one-way. There had recently been a row over a *Daily Mail* interview with Duncan Nichol which led to him being accused of meddling in politics. He had dismissed Labour's accusations that the government was intent on privatizing the health service, and there had been calls for Sir Robin Butler, the head of the Civil Service, to reprimand him. This politicization of the NHS was deprecated by nearly everyone but few could resist getting in their two-pennyworth in what proved to be a long pre-election period.

William Waldegrave now set out to attack Harry Keen's NHS Support Federation, which had been making public-relations headway, by accusing it of being simply a left-wing political organization. Keen forced a score-draw by agreeing to ask its leading members to disclose their political affiliations if Waldegrave published those of every trust and shadow trust board chairman.

Waldegrave also sought to draw an international cloak of acceptability around Britain's reforms at a conference on healthcare organized by the *Financial Times*. He said that countries with market systems, by which he meant insurance-based ones, were moving towards greater regulation and planning, and those using central direction were looking for more competition. The Conservatives always liked to claim that our health service was the envy of the world; most recently Waldegrave had used the phrase in his foreword to the Patient's Charter. It seemed that we were now the envy of the world because we had introduced an internal market. I spoke at the same conference on whether the reforms posed ethical problems. My underlying theme was that here we do not regard medicine as a business, and I used as an example not to follow the United States, where to a large extent it is. In some parts of America a quarter of all television advertising concerns medical products and services, and because of supplier-induced demand unnecessary or inappropriate treatment can be high – up to a quarter or even more for some procedures. I thought that the marketing outside the NHS of non-clinical hospital-based services like laundry, which was already happening, would lead eventually to the clinical threshold being crossed. We are much closer to this now, with some NHS trust hospitals seeking to offer insurance schemes for private medical care. The Private Finance Initiative, which forces trusts to seek private capital to fund improvements, also looks likely to lead to the quasi-privatization of the health service.

Despite, or because of, the imminent general election, John Major invited Ian Field and me to another breakfast meeting just before

Christmas. We started without William Waldegrave on this occasion because he had been delayed on the rail journey from his Bristol constituency by a bomb near Clapham Junction station. Carolyn Sinclair was again there but Major's private secretary this time was William Chapman, who took notes. We again went over the familiar ground of the UK's low health spending as a proportion of the country's wealth compared to other European countries like Germany and Holland. Major would not accept the gross national product argument. It is true that there are technical reasons why comparing in GNP terms the health expenditure of different countries using different healthcare systems is less than perfect, but the discrepancy between the UK and other countries is far too great to be dismissed in this way. He wanted to stress that the NHS's financial allocation that year had been a good one, which we acknowledged but thought, 'When is it not in an election year?' He said that 'The Chancellor of the Exchequer thinks it a lot,' which may either have meant 'but I don't really', or that Norman Lamont had had to have it dragged out of him. And like John Moore back in the late 1980s he used the familiar 'output' defence: it is not how much money you put in, it is what you get out that matters. Irrefutable, but, like the old saw about paranoia – being paranoid does not mean that someone is *not* actually out to get you – not mutually exclusive. It is axiomatic that more money devoted to the NHS would ensure better and more healthcare whatever the efficiency levels are, and they are in fact very high. To illustrate the problem I used again the figures showing that health service activity had increased much faster than the available funds, which was equally irrefutable. Given this increased productivity more funds would be even better used now, and were essential if the problems presented by an ageing population, higher expectations and new medical capabilities were to be solved.

Major felt that the 'false fears' aroused by the reforms were being dispelled, and the changes introduced would now show where the huge sums of money spent on the health service were going. From personal experience I said that my hospital was under stronger financial pressures than ever before, and that the staff were having to cut corners to get everything done. What went first were internal communications, record-keeping and documentation. Carolyn Sinclair agreed that greater through-put meant greater demands on staff and resources, which was self-evident.

I then raised the question of the shortage of particular staff. We had half as many surgeons per head of population than France, for instance, and junior doctors were very disillusioned with their career prospects. Medicine was actually declining in popularity as a career. In the last 10 years applications for medical-school places from those who had the necessary A-level results had fallen from three for every place to two, and the increasing number of women doctors (now more than half the medical intake) who needed to take time out of their careers to have their families meant that medical staffing problems would increase. In response, John Major could offer only a full acceptance of the pay-review body's recommendations, which would be announced that afternoon. He was surprised there was still a career blockage for juniors qualified to become consultants, but I explained that most employers had not got the money to appoint more consultants.

Ian told the Prime Minister that if the government had talked to the profession before introducing its reforms much trouble could have been avoided. This seemed to be stating the obvious, but Major agreed that further talks at least would be useful, and we accepted that his Health Secretary and the Chief Medical Officer were consulting much more widely than had been the case in Thatcher's day.

William Waldegrave arrived moments before Major had to leave and we heard the full details of the review-body report from him after Major's departure. We warned him of the junior doctors' likely unfavourable response, although we thought we had persuaded them not to hold their planned demonstration in Whitehall later in the week. The BMA juniors had just elected a new and militant chairman, Edwin Borman, a South African-born anaesthetist. Waldegrave agreed to my bringing him to see him soon.

After this second meeting, Ian and I thought that despite the cordiality nothing much had been achieved. With hindsight the net political gain, such as it was, went to the Prime Minister as no discernible benefit to the health service or to its staff came from the two meetings. I never felt the need to ask for a further meeting with him, although I was of course to have many more with William Waldegrave.

The general election year of 1992 started for the health service with an up-beat review of the first six months of the reforms by the Management Executive. Duncan Nichol again sailed close to the political wind in the way he extolled the reforms' 'really good start'. He gave no hint that the extra quarter of a million patients who were expected to have been treated in the year to April, and the more balanced financial position, might be due to the injection of more cash in a pre-election year, harder work by clinicians, better management following the Griffiths report, and Sheila Masters' toughness on financial management failings. As far as government was concerned, NHS reform was the responsible chicken and the improved performance was this particular chicken's egg and had nothing to do with any other chickens. They had certainly resisted putting in place any measures to establish which birds were actually laying, because theirs was a political fowl, and was bound to be a layer.

Soon after, William Waldegrave extended what GP fundholders could buy beyond hospital services. From April 1993 they would be able to purchase district nursing and health visiting from community trusts, and also the services of dieticians and chiropodists. He also announced a second wave of 1400 fundholders to join the existing 1700, bringing the proportion of the population served by them up to 14 per cent, or 6.7 million people.

A major survey of all GPs, carried out by Electoral Reform Ballot Services for the BMA GPs' committee, to which over 70 per cent (25,000 of the 35,000) responded showed that although three-quarters of the first-wave fundholders favoured fundholding, 13 per cent opposed it, and only a third of the third wave favoured it, with 40 per cent against. The second-wave fundholders were intermediate in both respects between the first and the third waves. Waldegrave was not winning hearts and minds amongst the family doctors. The second wave of hospital trusts, 99 in all, also came into being eight days before the general election, bringing the total to 156.

A fortnight before the election, the BMA held its long-scheduled special representative meeting, which had been planned in October to discuss *Leading for Health* and the reforms. Long before the date of the meeting arrived it had been realized that it would take place very close to an election. The Council was fairly evenly split as to whether it should be cancelled, but legal advice was taken which confirmed that as long as the BMA itself did not take up an overtly party political stance, or provide a platform for those who did, there was nothing to stop it holding the meeting. More than 400 doctors attended and it provided a useful overview of medical opinion on the reforms after a year in operation. Motions were passed calling on the BMA to increase its criticism and to monitor the reforms' effect on patients, but to seek continuous dialogue with government rather than confrontation, which was some encouragement to me. I had taken the precaution this time of coming with facts to counter the inevitable criticism from some quarters that the BMA was not doing enough to keep our concerns about the reforms in the fore-front of the public's mind. A motion to that effect was defeated, though only by 30 votes, after I put on record that BMA leaders including myself had undertaken 82 media interviews, provided 54 press statements and had achieved 290 quotes in the media since Inverness in July the previous year. That was hardly sitting on our hands. Much of the debate was taken up by the reforms, and *Leading for Health* did not form the basis for discussion that it should have done. I decided, rightly or wrongly, to leave it on the table to be picked up as and when an opportunity arose. In many ways it had served its purpose.

What the meeting did show, which was one of the reasons some had wanted it to be cancelled, was that there was a politically embarrassing divide developing between the consultants and the GPs over the purchaser–provider split. Quite a lot of the GPs were now in favour of the split, but the consultants were mostly against. As Judy Gilley, one of the GPs' committee executive, pointed out, the split seemed destined to be retained in some form whoever formed the next government, and several other GP speakers supported the new power it gave them to try and improve hospital services for their patients. The internal divisions caused by fundholding were still threatening the stability of the GPs' committee too, and its leaders were acutely aware of the dangers this presented them. Ultimately the meeting stuck to its guns and opposed separating the purchasers from the providers in an internal market, but a separate debate on rationing healthcare concluded that this was inevitable. The health service debate that day that was to have a much greater impact on the general election did not take place at the BMA's meeting. It was the 'War of Jennifer's Ear', which reached a climax at a press conference elsewhere.

In an election broadcast a few days before, the Labour Party had highlighted the inequities in the NHS by contrasting the case of a little girl who had waited nearly a year for an ear operation with another child's similar treatment, which she received privately. The comparison was not well chosen because it did not show two-tierism actually within the NHS, but it was based on a real case, and perhaps inevitably the media tracked down the protagonists. It turned out that Jennifer Bennett's long wait was said by her consultant to have been due to an administrative error, although he had earlier written to her parents saying the unacceptable delay was caused by a shortage of nurses due to inadequate funding. The furore was maintained for days by Tory accusations that Robin Cook was exploiting patients' distress, and Labour's counter-claims that Waldegrave or the Tories had unethically revealed Jennifer's identity. The mud stuck to both sides, but Waldegrave's upright image was dented more than that of the street-fighter Cook. There seemed little doubt that Labour were ahead in the health debate by the time the election came, and surveys of doctors' voting intentions showed that they certainly had switched in large numbers to Labour from their more traditional Conservative stance.[3] Conservative support among doctors had dropped from 51 per cent to 28 per cent, and those who intended voting Liberal Democrat had risen from 24 per cent (for the old Alliance) to 33 per cent. This reflected continuing hostility to the reforms, particularly by GPs, 78 per cent of whom said that the changes had not made the NHS more efficient, and even more thought that hospital trusts and fundholding were not improving patient care.

One of the last throws of the dice just before the election was Labour's assertion in national newspaper advertisements that the 'election is a referendum on the National Health Service'. They promised to invest an extra £1000 million in the modernization of the NHS, a return to free dental checks and eye tests, the scrapping of tax relief on private health insurance for the over-60s (the money from which would go towards improving cancer services) and the banning of tobacco advertising. The Conservatives pledged to continue to reduce long waiting times, to increase resources for the NHS 'year by year', and to increase the number of trust hospitals and fundholding general practices. The Liberal Democrats, who had no chance of gaining power, allowed themselves to go a little further than Labour in reversing the government's reforms, and proposed a new national inspectorate for health to ensure a better health service.

On the night of the general election on 9 April I was at one of the biggest medical dinners of the year, that of the Association of the British Pharmaceutical Industry, at Grosvenor House. Ironically, as I had had to come to London the day before I was unable to vote in the election, although at least this meant that if asked (as I surely would be) whether I had voted Conservative, or for any other party, I could truthfully reply, 'No.' After the dinner I joined Pamela Taylor and many other diners in one of the hospitality suites upstairs to watch the election results coming in on the television sets installed. It was with mixed feelings that, long before the small hours, I realized along with everyone else that Labour were not going to win. On health, Labour's policies were infinitely preferable to anyone who believed in Bevan's original concept of a health service. But the soundness of a government led by Neil Kinnock left serious doubts in my mind. I was not particularly looking forward to dealing with

Robin Cook as Health Secretary either, although it is possible that he would have got a more senior job anyway. Cook was extremely good at the dispatch box and regularly made mincemeat of William Waldegrave and others in debate, but he had the aura of the revolutionary about him, and I felt the BMA might ultimately regret leaving the Waldegrave frying pan, then on a temperate heat, for the fire of Cook's kitchen.

The Tory victory meant a government reshuffle, and William Waldegrave was transplanted to the Duchy of Lancaster, where he exchanged his interest in medical science for that of the whole of science as its minister, and expanded his responsibility for the Patient's Charter to its progenitor, the Citizen's Charter. He was not too sad to leave Health, although he could probably have persuaded John Major to leave him there, as despite his mauling over Jennifer's ear and his often poor media showing he had carried forward the reforms in a less fevered atmosphere than his predecessor.

John Major brought two women into his cabinet for the first time, Gillian Shephard and Virginia Bottomley. As Waldegrave's deputy, Mrs Bottomley had the merit of knowing the job. She had also been a psychiatric social worker for eight years and thus knew something of the NHS at ground level. She had the reputation of being a frenetic worker, continually mopping up the information her civil servants put before her, and being regularly late for everything because she got so involved with what she was doing. No doubt Major thought she would charm the public, and, with luck, the health service. Nevertheless there were rumours that she was some way to the right of Mr Waldegrave politically, which was worrying. But in her first public statement on taking office she said she wanted to take the politics out of the NHS, to which I responded that if so I thought we could do business with her – echoing Mrs Thatcher's comment about Mikhail Gorbachev, because I was under no illusions about the ideology she represented, however attractively she attempted to package it. Her new deputy as Minister for Health was Dr Brian Mawhinney, a saturnine Ulsterman whose doctorate was not in medicine but in medical physics. He had been a senior lecturer at the Royal Free Hospital, so also knew something about the inner workings of the health service. He soon gained the reputation of having a short fuse, but doctorates in physics command respect amongst medicos, who are usually glad to leave the subject behind at A level, and he was an able man. The junior ministers were also replaced and were increased from two to three: another earl's son, Tom Sackville, the short-lived-in-office Tim Yeo and Baroness Cumberlege in the Lords.

Now that the Conservatives had won another four or five years in office, the BMA realized that as far as the NHS reforms were concerned it would be more of the same. Funding, although pledged to increase year by year, would not increase by much – probably not enough even to accommodate the increasing demographic and technological demands. The *Health of the Nation* White Paper was acceptable as a strategy, although it did not go far enough, particularly on tobacco. Given the financial circumstances, some form of healthcare rationing was inevitable. In the old health service this was achieved by hospital waiting lists, and individual patients were prioritized by doctors. The government had jettisoned this method, because long waiting lists were politically embarrassing and showed up the shortage of resources, but had not provided a satisfactory alternative. In the new NHS, rationing was called 'prioritization' and was largely in the hands of managers and non-elected health authorities. Thus the public had the worst of both worlds, as surveys show that it trusts doctors to decide on who should be treated and what treatment they should receive far more than managers and politicians.

Experiments in America and elsewhere have cast serious doubts on the feasibility of the public itself deciding priorities. The most famous was in Oregon in the USA, where the State President was a doctor, John Kitzhaber. A health services commission of 11 members, five of whom were doctors, was set up to provide a list of conditions and treatments which would be provided under the state's medical programme, which provides medical care for the elderly, the disabled and most, but not all, poor people. The first version of the list was universally rejected, after coming up with some bizarre priorities, so it was decided to extend consultation to the public. Nearly a year later, after about 60 public meetings, attended by about 600 citizens, and a telephone survey of 1000 more, a new list ranking 709 items in order of medical priority was published in 1991.

The items were costed and the legislature discovered that, after extending the scheme to all poor people, an omission previously heavily criticized, the money it had allocated to Medicaid would only allow the first 587 items to be funded. The new list itself was more rational, having at its head the treatment of pneumonia, followed by tuberculosis. The lowest priorities were given to babies born without a brain (anencephaly) and those of such low birthweight that, in the unlikely event of their surviving long, they would be handicapped. These, along with over 100 other conditions, would not be paid for. While this list was less controversial, there were intense moral qualms at what amounted to rationing healthcare for the poor, voted for largely by the rest of the population who carried health insurance and thus did not need state care. In addition, over half of those who had come to the public meetings were healthcare workers, so was the public, as such, really fully involved? Apart from the moral dilemma, the technical one remained. Although enormously difficult, a decision on which conditions to treat might be made, but *how* to treat them is much more difficult. And while the prognosis for one patient treated for a condition may be very good, the chances of survival of another with the same condition may be very poor. The very mechanistic approach put forward in Oregon was eventually blocked by the national Bush administration in the run-up to the presidential election of 1992 after representations from disabled and right-to-life groups. However the scheme was later approved by President Clinton, even though only 83 per cent of treatments remain funded.

Another controversial way of deciding priorities is the quality-adjusted life year (QALY) system produced by Maynard, Culyer and their colleagues at the University of York. In the QALY approach, deciding to treat is based on the intervention's impact on life expectancy and its quality. A complete cure, returning the patient to a normal life expectancy with no diminution in its quality, ranks highest; minimal survival with great suffering ranks lowest. As its prime purpose is economic, the QALY is intended to be costed, so that for instance the cost per QALY was (at 1983 prices) £240 for a benign brain tumour and £69,000 for a malignant brain tumour.[4] The QALY is intrinsically more flexible than the Oregon list, but measuring the quality of life is so subjective, and prognosis is such an inexact science, that this unit is never going to find acceptance as more than a rough guide by doctors, who have been applying the same kind of principles in an informal way since Hippocrates.

Another huge problem for rationing is that the greatest costs for the health service come at the extremes of life. Our first year of life is the most expensive: £1666 on average, according to the Office of Health Economics Compendium of Health Statistics 1995. But 80 per cent of our hospital costs come in our last few years. While children only cost £178 a year between the ages of five and 15, by the age of 75 we need £1637 annually. Given these facts, if rationing is to be decided by public debate, how would the age of the debaters influence the result?

The Cambridge & Huntingdon Health Commission, well known for its 1995 refusal to fund a second bone-marrow transplant for Child B, has responded to the opprobrium it received by setting up a 'citizen's jury' to consider health service priorities.[5] Again it was found that the public prefers to leave the ultimate decisions to doctors and other health service staff, but it wants to have a national framework for priorities, with guidelines which would be flexibly applied according to the circumstances. This is probably about as far as public participation can go, and the convening of such juries itself consumes vital resources (up to £20,000 in Cambridge & Huntingdon's case). And, rather like the case for and against capital punishment, perceived public opinion may not necessarily be morally right. An interesting sideline on the second Oregon list is that, while liver transplantation for cirrhosis not involving alcohol was ranked

366th, that for alcoholic cirrhosis was only 690th, meaning it would not be carried out. This despite the fact that the outcome of transplantation for the latter is at least as good if not better than the former.

As 1992 was not going to see the end of the internal market as was hoped, the BMA focused its attention on making the best of what could be done to improve the NHS within its constraints. At the annual representative meeting in Nottingham in July, rationing became the dominant theme. As an issue it had the merit, for those embittered by the Tory reforms, of putting the government on the spot; and, for those prepared to see some good in parts of the reforms, one on which unity could be maintained.

I had taken Pamela Taylor's advice and commissioned a writer and coach for my ARM speech, after the disaster at Inverness. She recruited Harvey Thomas, one of the very best, who had provided his services to countless industrialists and politicians including Margaret Thatcher. He was quite closely identified with the Conservatives and right-leaning captains of industry, so I was not anxious for his recruitment to be widely known, but in the event I found that even if he was a Conservative he did not bring his politics to work. He had been much involved in earlier years with Billy Graham and his evangelistic tours of Britain, and was a committed Christian: charismatic in all senses of the word. Having agreed the content of the speech he produced numerous drafts, typed in a very large font with the syllables and words needing the heaviest stress underlined. The text never went below the upper half of each page – a device which helps the speaker to hold his audience by not needing to drop his head to see it. In several coaching sessions he improved my delivery enormously, and he even came up to Nottingham to rehearse me in the conference hall on the Sunday before my speech the next day. I remain very grateful to Harvey, a great bear of a Welshman who in an earlier incarnation would have made a mesmeric preacher in valley chapels. My speech was received warmly, if not perhaps as rapturously as it would have been had Harvey delivered it himself. Its theme was that the BMA had to be constructive, which did not mean dropping our opposition to the changes. I made an appeal to the warring factions to stop bickering, but in this I was not successful.

We decided to take the rationing issue further with a major conference, to which leading proponents from around the world, including Oregon's Dr Kitzhaber, would be invited. The date of this was eventually set for March 1993, and the BMA and the *British Medical Journal* were joined by the King's Fund and the Patients Association in setting it up. I was only able to get Mrs Bottomley to participate by substituting 'Priority Setting' for 'Rationing' in its title. I knew agreeing to this change would lead to criticism from John Marks and his followers, which it did because to them 'rationing' was a stick with which to beat the government. Virginia Bottomley was of course not going to present them or anyone else with this weapon, and I did not think the distinction was sufficiently important to make a fuss about – we all knew that we were talking about rationing. She actually said at the conference, 'The NHS is not . . . rushing towards some sort of rationing Armageddon.' She wanted the process carried out locally, by purchasers, who would toe the party line on national priorities, and would use public consultation and evidence on effectiveness sifted by professional advice. She did not explain how national priorities would be set and by whom, and what would happen if local decisions ran counter to them. Of the speakers, Dr Kitzhaber still remained optimistic that consensus on what should be covered and what should not would be achieved, but others were more sanguine. Dr R. L. Scheerder, Holland's Deputy Director of Health, regarded the task as belonging to the community and not the individual, and defined priorities by assessing necessity, efficacy and efficiency. Controversially, he argued that *in vitro* fertilization should be excluded because it was not necessary, homoeopathy because it was not effective, and adult dental care because it was an individual rather than a community responsibility. However in Holland nothing had been decided on because of the political difficulties involved, so the Dutch were not much further down the Oregon trail than ourselves.

At the end of the meeting none of the basic questions had been resolved, and no generally accepted method of rationing healthcare has yet been found. At the moment, the ideas of Ronald Dworkin, a law professor in Oxford and New York and a leading ethicist, are fashionable.[6] He proposes a 'prudent insurance principle', which depends on the notion that few people would insure themselves for life-saving treatment beyond the age of 85, which they might not reach anyway. The employment of such a principle by the state rather than the individual would lead either to various packages being on offer, perhaps involving different levels of national insurance contribution, or a basic package for all, with individuals being invited to buy enhancements over and above this. Such systems are quite close to the present American situation where employers provide health insurance for their employees. However the idea of anyone of 85 or over, because they had not contributed to an 'enhanced' scheme, being ineligible for a life-saving procedure would be anathema to most, and unacceptable to the caring professions.

The NHS reforms have nevertheless made the whole question of rationing explicit, and have hoisted the politicians who instituted them with their own petards. Previously, doctors accepted that it was their duty to take these difficult and often agonizing decisions on their own shoulders. It is now becoming increasingly hard to do so, although GP fundholders can often act in an independent way, and politicians are trying hard to keep the problem at arm's length by calling the district health purchasers in aid. This cannot work for long because the public has had no say in the appointment of the health-authority members, and they are in any case sometimes too closely identified with government. Whatever the proffered solutions, the issue of healthcare rationing will not go away.

At the end of 1992 and early in 1993, I had several meetings with David Blunkett, then the Labour Shadow Health Secretary. Apart from the obviously exceptional determination it must have taken for someone who is blind to rise from being a councillor, then leader of the council in Sheffield, to becoming a leading Labour MP and ultimately a member of the shadow cabinet, David possesses great integrity and strength of purpose. At a dinner with him, his researcher and his guidedog, Offa, at L'Amico, a favourite political waterhole in Horseferry Road, I also became aware of how desperate for office he and his Labour colleagues are. Although he himself had only been in the House for five years, remaining in opposition for at least another four years irked him greatly. He is currently Shadow Education Secretary, but I found myself more in tune with him and his approach to the problems of the health service than those of his successor, Harriet Harman, whose surgeon grandfather was actually a leading light in the BMA in the 1930s. In 1996, now that Ms Harman has been replaced by Chris Smith, it remains to be seen whether Labour health policy will regain Blunkett's pragmatic clarity.

Meanwhile, frequent meetings with Virginia Bottomley were raising doubts in my mind as to whether she had the vision to take the right decisions on many of the difficult problems that were facing her, much as I liked her personally. In public she was becoming unpopular for her constant regurgitation of figures which were often not directly related to the issues with which she was supposed to be dealing. It was rumoured that the BBC current-affairs programmes wanted to institute Bottomley-free airtime if they could get away with it, as she was maddening to interview. In contrast she was greeted rapturously on the stump by the rank and file of Tory supporters, and by managerial staff and directors when she visited hospitals and other health establishments. Her effect was often compared to that of the Princess of Wales, which must have irritated her greatly, because she has a slightly diffident, girlish charm which, coupled with her striking prettiness and general eagerness, has bowled over many a non-believer along with her fans.

A great test for her came with the publication of the Tomlinson report on London's healthcare in October 1992.[7] A long-standing criticism of governments was that they gave undue precedence to events in London to the exclusion of other parts of the country. Crises on Westminster's doorstep always hurt the most, probably because that was where the nation's media were most concentrated.

Reports of huge impending cash deficits in some of London's most famous hospitals had been crashing around William Waldegrave's ears by the autumn of 1991, and he was forced to rule out awarding trust status to some of them because of it. In the end he took the usual governmental way out: he appointed a special adviser to come up with a solution to London's looming problems and gave him a year to do it. He chose Sir Bernard Tomlinson, a former professor of neuropathology who had been the chairman of the NHS's Northern region. Tomlinson had many qualities. He had been a skilled chairman of the Joint Professional Advisory Committee, which had been given the Sisyphean task of trying to match the supply of specialists in training in the health service to the changing needs for trained consultants in different specialties. The job was of course impossible but he had made a better fist of it than most would have predicted. Tomlinson, as an RHA chairman, was also known to be onside as far as the reforms went, and had the supreme merit (or demerit depending on which side of the argument you were) of having no connections with London nor knowledge of the intricacies of its healthcare provision. His report struck London's health service like an artillery shell.

Sir Bernard's terms of reference had been 'to advise the Secretaries of State for Health and [for] Education and Science on how the relevant statutory authorities [were] addressing the position of healthcare in inner London, working within the framework of the reformed NHS'. His team, which included Mollie McBride, a leading GP, had to consider the balance of primary health services, and the organization and provision of undergraduate medical teaching, postgraduate medical education and research and development. They had to take account of both the resident and the daytime population (inner London's resident population of about two and a half million people is swelled on weekdays by about another 1.3 million commuters, and over the course of a year altogether eight million tourists visit the capital). They also had to consider health-authority purchasing plans and their impact on inner-London hospitals; future developments in acute and primary care; and the need to maintain high-quality patient care and its underpinning equivalent standards of medical teaching, research and development. A crucial omission from their brief was the need to consider also the balance between general acute beds and supportive and rehabilitative services like care of the elderly and mentally ill, although psychiatry was mentioned in the report. The task was thus something of a poisoned chalice on this account alone, quite apart from the likely fury which would descend from any hospitals recommended for merger or closure as happened with Guy's and Bart's. Tomlinson predicted that the number of inpatient beds needed in inner London would fall by 2000–7000 by the end of the 1990s, because the reforms would force purchasers to buy from cheaper local services rather than the inevitably more expensive teaching-hospitals.

The report drew attention to the fact that general practitioner and other primary and community services in London were 'comparatively underdeveloped', and wanted the hoped-for savings from mergers and closures channelled into primary care. Tomlinson thought that £140 million would be needed to improve primary care, which was a very low estimate compared to the £250 million thought to be necessary by the much more comprehensive King's Fund report on London which had preceded his study. (The King's Fund report ran to 13 volumes, and contained a mass of factual information as well as analysis. Interestingly, it drew attention to 17 earlier reports on London's healthcare problems, dating from as far back as 1892, much of whose content had been successively ignored by those to whom they were addressed.[8])

On this occasion the Health Secretary, as adjured by William Waldegrave when he commissioned Tomlinson's work the year before, would act. The report provided some ready targets for closure by including a league table of hospitals most vulnerable by virtue of the new market forces unleashed by the reforms, the size of their dependent populations, their costs and the state of their buildings. The most at risk was the already merged Middlesex & University College Hospital, but the latter was recommended for saving by virtue of its high research reputation and its conveniently situated accident and emergency department. Bart's had maintained its proud independence, despite its small size, and had not undertaken any attempts at integration with its nearest neighbour, the Royal London. It was recommended that it should not continue unchanged on its historic 900-year-old Smithfield site. St Thomas's and Guy's were urged to amalgamate on one site, the choice of which was 'finely balanced'. The historic rivalry between the two hospitals was eventually to be resolved in favour of St Thomas's – an ironic twist given that after Guy's was founded in 1725, opposite its older rival in the eponymous St Thomas's Street, Thomas's had decamped to its present position on the other side of the Thames from the Houses of Parliament. There was less controversy about most of the other detailed recommendations, including the merging of eight of London's nine medical schools into four.

Mrs Bottomley allowed until January for consultation, and the criticisms poured in. Major concerns were the human problems and huge expense that would arise from the very large number of redundancies that would result. Any rejoicing from those outside the capital, who had always resented London's greater share of the funding cake, was short-lived when it was realized that what was to happen to London could with equal force be applied to other large metropolitan cities. Birmingham was ripe for review, and in Scotland, Glasgow was a target.

A particular criticism of Tomlinson's approach from the BMA was the way in which catchment areas of the hospitals had been defined in order to detect overlapping and thus overprovision. Isochrones had been used, in which a line is drawn on a map through the points from which it is thought to take the same time to reach a particular place. The report contained a map showing the 10-minute isochrones calculated for inner London's main hospitals, but the journey time was calculated only for road transport outside peak rush-hour periods. This seemed to us too crude a measure, knowing the problems the London Ambulance Service had in reaching the major accident and emergency units, and the difficulties the resident population, much of which was socially deprived, had in getting to hospital by public transport. We disagreed strongly, for instance, that patients who would normally use the accident and emergency department at Bart's (due for closure) could easily get to Guy's or Thomas's, one of whose departments would also close. The outrage in the City when this recommendation became known was considerable. And as Brian Jarman, Professor of General Practice at St Mary's Hospital, was later to point out, the existing distribution of hospitals in inner London fitted quite well with the availability of public transport, and it is much easier to travel radially in London than across town. Jarman also disputed the large number of bed closures suggested by Tomlinson and drew attention to the relative dearth of residential-home places for elderly people, amongst other trenchant criticisms.[9]

However, by and large, the main thrust of the report, that some rationalization had to occur, was not disputed. Many felt that a start should be made by amalgamating some of the smaller, often highly specialized, units like St Mark's, the Hospital for Tropical Diseases, the Samaritan Hospital for Women and Moorfields Eye Hospital, with appropriate larger ones. There was little support for the closure of Bart's and the emasculation of Guy's or Thomas's. Such major disruptions seemed enormously wasteful of first-class services built up over centuries, and the cost was likely to be excessive even in money terms. And while it was indisputable that more resources should be put into London's primary care, Tomlinson's estimate was almost certainly too low and it would take far too long for any savings to be realized from the mergers and closures proposed.

However in February 1993 Mrs Bottomley grasped the nettle, initially rather gently, by announcing a London Implementation Group to be chaired by Tim Chessells, recent chairman of the South-East Thames RHA, later knighted for his services.[10] Bart's was offered three alternatives: closure, merger with the Royal London or contraction into a small specialist hospital. It chose merger with a heavy heart, and the fate of its wonderful old buildings and state-of-the-art new theatre block has still not been decided. Either Guy's or Thomas's would cease to be a comprehensive hospital on its existing site. The bitterness which now pervades Guy's like a pall reveals that they lost. They had embraced the reforms, admittedly after much dissent; they rightly regarded themselves as one of the most renowned hospitals in the world; their Professor of Surgery was an architect of the reforms and now a Health Minister in the Lords and PPS to the Prime Minister; their dean was a member of the NHS board; and their pre-merger chief executive had been deputy chief executive of the NHS. Their main benefactor was Sir Philip Harris, the carpet tycoon, and he was furious that the enormous sum of money he had given to construct the new building named after him looked like being wasted. After he later helped to rescue the Conservative Party from its crippling debts he was mollified maybe with a peerage. Strenuous efforts to rescue the hospital from being salami-sliced to extinction continue.

The blow to Guy's has perhaps received less publicity than that to Bart's, but the feelings of betrayal by government are no less deep. A letter in *The Times* by Dr Robert Knight, chairman of Guy's medical staff, highlights this. Writing just after the Tories lost the Staffordshire South East by-election in April 1996, he says, 'Three hundred years ago the Tories lost the seat at Tamworth, Staffordshire, to Thomas Guy. One would like to think that Mr Guy, who sat as the Whig MP from 1695 to 1707, is looking down with satisfaction at the by-election result. He would certainly be very angry with the present Government, which is trying to destroy the hospital he founded and endowed'.[11]

Doubtless the monk Rahere, who founded Bart's in 1123, would have joined him.

CHAPTER TWELVE

Five Years and Beyond
April 1993–May 1996

Wood may remain ten years in the water, but it will never become a crocodile.　　　　　Congolese proverb

The final brick in the wall of the NHS reforms, the reorganization of community care, was put into place on 1 April 1993. The defining NHS Act of 1990 had largely followed the 1988 Griffiths report on community care, but the implementation of this part of the Act had been delayed by William Waldegrave, who left this to his successor. Many thought the change was an even bigger leap in the dark than the rest of the reforms. The whole success, or otherwise, of the scheme depended on the robustness of the shared-care plans agreed between the health authorities and the social services departments of the local authorities. These plans aimed to provide comprehensive agreements between the two on how the potential recipients of care in the community would be assessed, how their needs would be catered for, and by whom. However there was widespread concern about the pass-the-parcel scenario so graphically illustrated by the Rubber Windmill study three years before. The difficulties that would arise when hospitals were ready to discharge patients before the community services were able to accommodate them remained unresolved. In fact the situation was likely to become increasingly worse because of the internal-market pressures on hospitals. In order to fulfil contracts and make so-called efficiency savings, hospitals were shortening patients' stays dramatically, and it was feared that services in the community could not cope with this increased turnover. It was estimated that up to 15 per cent of acute hospital beds might be blocked by patients awaiting discharge, with dire consequences for some hospitals' financial viability, and this has now happened.

A key problem remained the grey area between nursing care and social care. Would long-stay residential care now fall entirely to local authorities, and, if not, when was it the responsibility of health authorities? Both were extremely short of money, and circumstances could easily be foreseen when the necessary co-operation would break down. Nor could the realization by patients and their relatives that staying in the NHS was entirely free, but that residential care for most people was not, be ignored. Disputes could also arise between doctors who considered that continuing care in the NHS was necessary for their patients, and managers who were desperate to offload the financial burden they represented. After complaints, in 1996 the Health Ombudsman commented unfavourably on events at Basingstoke's Park Prewett Hospital, where the judgement of the consultant psychiatrists looking after a number of infirm elderly patients was overridden by management. The patients were discharged to nursing homes against the wishes and advice of their consultants, and several died soon afterwards.

After two years, in February 1995, the Department of Health published further guidance on the health service's responsibilities for long-term healthcare needs.[1] In it all health authorities were instructed to produce their overall policies for consultation, including the criteria on who would be eligible for such care. These plans were to be finalized by April 1996. Unfortunately, in many places the boundaries between health- and local-authority responsibilities remain blurred, and effective formal arbitration procedures to deal with inter-authority disputes have not yet been set up. In addition a very important departure from a 'free' NHS lies buried in the document. The call for health authorities to define eligibility criteria represents the first central directive to institute rationing within the health service.

In the 1970s about a quarter of all elderly people in long-term care were looked after free by the NHS. Now only about 10 per cent are. The remaining 90 per cent are means-tested before they can get funding, which now comes from local authorities. More than half a million elderly people now live in nursing and residential-care homes, most of which are privately run, and this number will continue to rise. Some bodies, like Age Concern, believe that the setting of criteria for long-term care should not have been entrusted to local health authorities. They believe it should be the responsibility of central government to define such potentially controversial matters. However in practice the detailed guidance in the DoH's documents has been closely followed by nearly all health authorities, so this has more or less been achieved, although Age Concern's principle has not. Unfortunately, while the criteria themselves tend to be very similar around the country, the success in meeting them varies widely. This is because few health authorities are prepared or able to allocate sufficient resources to apply them fully.[2]

At the outset in 1993, local authorities received £565 million to fund the scheme, but an investigation by the Commons Health Select Committee found that despite this a fifth of them would still find themselves unable to meet the financial consequences of the new arrangements. There was a £135 million gap between what the town halls thought they needed and what they were being offered.[3] Community care remains the health service's distant relative.

In the service itself, it was becoming evident that the purchasers were proving to be the weak link in the new internal market. Horse laughs could be heard from opponents of the purchaser–provider split: could it be that market forces were creaming off the best managerial staff into the providing sector, where they were paid more and had much more of a chance to make their mark? Brian Mawhinney made a series of three speeches about strengthening purchasing in the spring. He called them a 'trilogy', which seemed a trifle overblown, but it showed the seriousness with which the Department was taking the imbalance. He might have better spent his time studying a report by health economists from the University of York for the Institute of Health Service Management and the Royal College of Nursing, that criticized the secrecy surrounding the DoH's annual bids to the Treasury for funds to run the health service.[4] The methods used to calculate the bids were crude, and relied too much on assumptions that present levels of funding were 'right' and only needed increasing for numerical factors such as demographic change. More people aged 65 and over simply triggered an increase in spending on this age group proportional to their larger number. Whether existing allocations remained sufficient per head was not generally examined. Nor was the impact of fundamental changes like community care, the London healthcare review and the internal market itself properly costed.

The burden of my keynote speech at the BMA's annual representative meeting in Torquay at the end of June was that the reforms were causing widespread disaffection among those who delivered the service. Despite the changes the health service was still grinding to a halt every winter, with surgery in many hospitals being confined to emergencies for anything up to four months before the new financial year in April produced more funds. I used an analogy of the Royal Mail accepting only letters and not parcels for several months every year to point out the absurdity of the situation. There had recently been a landslip in Scarborough on the north-east coast and a prominent hotel had gradually crumbled away and fallen into the sea. The health service seemed to me to be doing the same thing – free eye tests had gone, NHS dentistry was on the way, and so was long-term NHS care of the elderly. The apparent governmental intention to encourage the private sector to take as much work as possible from the state should be resisted, I said. In an effort not to be seen as entirely negative I advocated that, because funding rather than organization and management was the prime aetiology of the NHS's difficulties, other methods of financing it, like an earmarked tax or social insurance, should be seriously re-examined.

I also challenged the government's spending priorities. Between 1990 and 1992, spending on managers had increased by 109 per cent, while that on doctors and nurses had only increased by 10 per cent and 2.5 per cent respectively. Between £50 and £100 million had also been spent on external management consultants in 1992, and the £400 million spent so far on simply introducing the reforms could have been much better spent on direct care for the NHS's patients. It was probably the strongest speech attacking the government and its changes that I had made, but I thought that we now knew enough about the effects the reforms were having to make it, and my patience was wearing thin. I knew that public rhetoric will seldom fail for being too loud, and is all the more effective if the loudness follows a quieter passage. I was also determined to dispel the idea, which had been most damaging to me during my chairmanship, that I was 'soft on the reforms', because I very much wanted to continue as Council chairman. I felt I had laid the groundwork. I had spent three years trying to reason with the government, without reaching for my trumpet too often like John Marks, and I could by no stretch of the imagination be described as a militant or a politically driven left-winger. I now wanted to try and capitalize on that position, which had been enormously strengthened on the GP side by the patience and hard work of Ian Bogle and his negotiators.

As at the meeting a year before, I ended by making a plea for unity within the profession, as I was concerned that the continuing unhappiness within the GPs' committee over fundholding might yet again break out in a damaging public split. Ironically, it was the split within the Council itself which was to lead to my own nemesis as its chairman. Sandy Macara, a public-health academic from Bristol and a successful previous chairman of the Representative Body, had long coveted the post. He was certainly eligible and, although he did not know it, several months before I had stood myself I had suggested him as a possible candidate to John Marks. In the event Macara was proposed and seconded by two of Council's medico-political left-wingers, Ruth Gilbert and Christopher Tiarks, and easily carried the vote. I was proposed and seconded by Ian Bogle, the GPs' leader, and Brian Lewis from the hospital side, whose influence had begun to wane despite his unparalleled experience. When the votes were counted I could only muster 17 members against Macara's

35 – a comprehensive win for the forces of reaction that surprised many of my supporters as much as it surprised me. I had imagined it would be close. In the claustrophobic mid-summer afternoon heat of the basement room at the Imperial Hotel, I made a short valedictory speech pledging Sandy my support and urging that unity should prevail. I left unsaid any thoughts of '*Et tu, Brute*' that I might have had. I felt a certain fellow-feeling for John Major at that moment, or perhaps for Dickie Bird, who on making 181 not out for Yorkshire was told he would be batting for the second eleven next week. On the other hand I had had one of the most interesting, albeit difficult, three-year terms of any recent BMA chairman, and there had been many good times as well as bad.

In the next few days, Macara seemed to be taking exactly the same line as I had, even to the extent of using my Scarborough analogy on one occasion, which gave me a certain amount of morbid satisfaction.

Many had been predicting that, like me, Virginia Bottomley would soon be relieved of her post. But in July, soon after I ceased to be the BMA's chairman, when John Major reshuffled his ministers, she remained. Brian Mawhinney was promoted to the Cabinet as Transport Secretary, and the ambitious Gerry Malone replaced him as Health Minister. Tarred by some as a Scottish carpet-bagger when he took over the Winchester seat from the discredited John Browne in 1992, Malone is an eager operator and a smooth talker but has not so far won the trust of those who work in the health service. His wife, Anne Blythe, is a consultant anaesthetist and his friends include James Johnson, the present chairman of the BMA consultants' committee, and Andrew Neil, the flamboyant ex-editor of the *Sunday Times*, of which Malone was once Scottish editor. He therefore should at least be well informed. He seems particularly keen on performance-related pay, soon transmuted to 'locally determined pay' as a less inflammatory way of describing the same thing. In this the government is totally at odds with the health professions, who see the idea as discredited (many industrial concerns, and public services and utilities like the Inland Revenue and British Telecom, have already abandoned it), divisive (the health service depends on teamwork between different staff and professions) and inequitable (who decides who should get more and who less in a team-working situation?), as well as time-wasting and costly. One of the prime tasks of the health pay-review bodies is to decide on differentials within and between the various professions but the 1994 report on doctors' and dentists' pay lost much credibility by accepting the government's edict that local pay would be introduced.

In 1995 consultants were moving towards sanctions against the government if Mrs Bottomley secured an enabling clause in Parliament to allow individual trusts to pay hospital doctors locally decided salaries. She drew back at the last minute, and the consultants' threats to treat patients on clinical need only, ignoring the two-tier system created by the priority being given to GP fundholders' patients, and to give up any work not strictly defined in their contracts, were withdrawn. Nevertheless the row still causes a nasty taste. Hospital doctors should not allow themselves to be involved in a two-tier system anyway, and that it could be a sanction against their employer to stop doing so is unpalatable to say the least.

The nurses have been antagonized by their pay body even more than the doctors, as theirs recommended a low national percentage increase which could be topped up locally, an extreme course which was not followed by the doctors' body. Such was the nurses' anger that the Royal College of Nursing eventually voted to rescind its no-strike policy in protest, which action was met by a threat, not so far carried out, to abolish their pay-review body. One of the reasons given by Mrs Thatcher for refusing to include NHS hospital technical staff like laboratory workers in the pay-review body system for other professions allied to medicine was they had once gone on strike.

After a correspondence with Gerry Malone and Virginia Bottomley about local pay I was offered a meeting with them at Richmond House. It was my case that doctors were so disenchanted with the way the NHS was going already that to force local pay on them was an unnecessary diversion and a needless provocation. The economic argument for such schemes was looking increasingly threadbare, and there was at least as much evidence against its effectiveness in industry as there was in its favour. The annual running cost of all the health service's pay-review bodies and General Whitley Council systems was estimated at about £600,000, while that of local pay bargaining would be at least £2 million. As far as doctors' arrangements were concerned the ratio was even more adverse, and in any case hospital personnel departments, despite their great increase in size and costs since the reforms, could not hope to obtain sufficient expertise quickly enough to institute acceptable pay systems across the whole range of different staff who work in hospitals. Both Mrs Bottomley and Mr Malone seemed to be under the impression that the consultants' distinction-award system was tantamount to performance-related pay, and so professed surprise at our violent reaction to the government's wishes.

I pointed out to them the crucial differences between awards and performance pay. Above all, awards were superannuable, and normally permanent. Their role was to reward long-term excellence and the wait to a first award was long. The higher awards maintained some comparability with leaders of other professions, and peer review by doctors was important because they were best able to assess the medical distinction of the colleagues with whom they worked. Finally, awards were more akin to financial medals than bonuses. Decisions on performance pay were clearly going to be managerial and that was quite a different animal. If local managers wanted to reward doctors for achieving management targets they no doubt could do so in some other way, if they could find the extra money from somewhere, but distinction awards had been instituted at the inception of the health service for something else. Whatever the criticisms of the system, consultants would not agree to awards being turned into local pay. So far this has not happened. The recent DoH review of the award system carried out by the then Scottish Chief Medical Officer, Dr Robert Kendell, has however resulted in changes: a further increase in the input of managers, and the replacement of the lowest, 'C', awards by five discretionary salary increments awarded at trust level, using nationally accepted criteria similar to the awards replaced, have been introduced.

Murmurs are however coming from the hospitals that greater managerial involvement is leading to the preferment of consultants who take on managerial roles, like clinical directorships, rather than those most skilled at their primary, medical, task. About 15 per cent of consultants now have some form of local pay, but the profession's pay-review body has not yet ceased to recommend national pay scales for all grades and types of NHS doctor. Nevertheless the present chairman, Brandon Gough, an accountant who until recently was chairman of Coopers & Lybrand and is now chairman of the controversial privatized utility Yorkshire Water, looks to be on a collision course with the general practitioners over the way their remuneration is calculated. The GPs want a 'core contract' priced, so that the increasing burdens placed on them by burgeoning night calls can be separately valued. It may be that Mrs Bottomley's successor Stephen Dorrell's current re-examination of the way GPs are employed will avert a clash with the review body. Only time will tell.

The latest, some might hope the last, health service reorganization under the present administration sprang from the report of a management review set up by Virginia Bottomley. It was led by Kate Jenkins, who was well-known for her involvement in the proposals for governmental 'next steps' agencies,[5] and who was now on the NHS Policy Board. From April 1994 the NHS has been managed and run from its new headquarters, Quarry House in Leeds. The NHS Management Executive, which has contracted its title to the NHS Executive, now rules through eight regional offices, which replaced the six so-called management outposts and 14 English regions. A parliamentary Bill was necessary to abolish the regional health authorities and to merge the district health authorities with the family health service authorities administering general practice, and this was passed in late 1994. The regional health authorities finally ceased to exist in April 1996, and their remaining functions were transferred to the eight regional offices. There are now some 80 or 90 merged district health authorities in England. The changes have resulted in a large number of posts being shed: over 3000 in the regions and about 700 in Leeds and Whitehall. The cost of the resultant redundancies has been considerable, as has been the cost of setting up the new NHS headquarters. Any real savings resulting from the latter move will not be seen for several years.

Along with the management reorganization came changes in the formula allocating NHS funds to the new English health authorities. Weighted capitation was retained but the new formula takes less account of age and more of socio-economic factors like poverty and deprivation. The new system was based on work commissioned by the NHS from the Centre for Health Economics at the University of York, which used sophisticated mathematical analysis to confirm again that more resources should be distributed to poorer areas of the country.[6] The move to the new arrangements has been introduced gradually, especially as money previously held centrally for the specialist postgraduate teaching hospitals in London will now go to the regions, and the stability of London's health service remains under severe threat.

Another recent development that will, if carried forward, have enormous significance for the health service is the Private Finance Initiative. In 1992 the then Chancellor of the Exchequer, Norman Lamont, desperate to find ways of reducing state spending on capital projects within the public sector, hit on the idea of inviting in private finance. At first this initiative had little effect on the NHS, but in 1995 Treasury rules were introduced forcing NHS trusts to show that they had sought private finance for capital developments before government funding could be considered. In addition private finance could now be used not only for buildings but also for the services associated with them. Thus a whole hospital could be built with private money and the company providing the finance could in theory run it afterwards, right down to employing the clinical staff. Such a company would at the very minimum wish to safeguard its investment by taking a very close interest in the management of any establishment built under the PFI. The implications for the health service are immense, as it is not difficult to see parts of it becoming private in all but name.

Whether health ministers are as keen on the idea as the Treasury is not known but it appears to be a case of *force majeure*. In the November 1995 Budget, Chancellor Kenneth Clarke, in announcing increased funding for the NHS of £1300 million, cut spending on its capital programme by 16.9 per cent. This means that at least some of the shortfall will have to be met by private finance. Expectations are that this might amount to about £165 million in 1996–97.

Plans have been announced for major new hospitals to be built in Norwich and at Stonehaven in Scotland, as well as the rebuilding of one at Swindon. However the road to completion looks to be stony. After the first rush of enthusiasm for the idea by entrepreneurial companies and hospital managements, doubts have arisen. A major worry for private companies would be that their investment could be lost by the failure of the hospital in the internal market environment. There has always been the possibility that an NHS trust will be dissolved: what can happen to Bart's can certainly happen to Loamshire General. In order to protect private investors from this possibility, Stephen Dorrell is trying to push a National Health Service (Residual Liabilities) Bill through Parliament that will guarantee compensation for any debts resulting from such a dissolution. This guarantee is highly controversial because it appears to give private companies a unique opportunity for risk-free investment at the expense of the taxpayer.

The true benefits of PFI for the NHS in the long term are hard to see. Borrowing private money in this way is bound to be more expensive than borrowing it at the Treasury rate, and that the gap can be made up by more efficient building and running of the resultant plant is conjectural at best. There are also signs that some of the biggest companies involved in the PFI are getting cold feet, despite the new Bill. John Laing Construction, who have formed a consortium with General Healthcare Group to build the new £170 million hospital from scratch at Norwich, have pulled out of a similar larger project in East London.[7] This scheme to build a new Royal

London Hospital for £260 million is associated with the closing of Bart's, so it is politically highly sensitive in the City as well as elsewhere. Laing's explanation is that it found that financing the contract, including the hospital's design, building and management, too involved. The cost of bidding for such large contracts is itself very high – £500,000 for Laing in the case of east London – and the delays and bureaucracy involved are discouraging other potential bidders. Another two companies, Trafalgar House and W. S. Atkins, have just pulled out of the bidding for a PFI scheme worth £25 million to renovate and expand two hospitals in Sheffield because of the cost of the process.[8] The legal contract for the rebuilding of Walsgrave Hospital, Coventry under the PFI, drawn up by NHS managers, runs to 17,000 pages,[9] so it is not surprising that construction firms are losing interest. Such bureaucracy also calls into question the NHS management costs that must be involved. The Parliamentary Treasury Select Committee expressed doubts in 1995 about the suitability of the PFI's application in the health service for other reasons. The committee thought it would inevitably lead to interference in the planning of services by NHS trusts.[10]

As always in the health service its problems can be traced back to its financing and the methods used to overcome them. A shortage of money for necessary capital development is at the root of the dangerous flirtation with the Private Finance Initiative, and it is behind the continuing shortage of intensive-care beds, especially for children, which led to Mrs Thatcher's initiation of the NHS reforms. The cost of a paediatric intensive-care bed is now put at about £250,000 a year, and because such beds tend to be fully filled in the winter months, and because not enough money has been spent on training sufficient specialist nurses to care for them, tragedies continue to occur. Matters came full-circle in May 1996 when the Health Secretary, after yet another investigation caused by public dissatisfaction at more highly publicized shortages, announced that health authorities would purchase 30 more such beds by the winter, with 25 more to follow over the next two years. £2 million would be found to train 225 more intensive-care nurses, but no more money would be provided for the beds; so Peter would yet again be robbed to pay Paul. This assumes that the new market system allows Peter to be so robbed. It is a flaw of the internal market that when a national or regional deficiency needs to be remedied like this, the power of the Health Secretary is much reduced unless he can accompany his edicts with new finance.

Another factor in the health service's struggle from crisis to crisis is the largely unexplained rise in emergency admissions to hospital. This rise in acute admissions is medical rather than surgical and, apart from particular rises in self-poisonings and childhood asthma, is general across the board. Responsible factors may be many, of which rising patient expectations, decreasing support at home for the elderly, and social deprivation may be important, but the trend has been visible for over forty years; it is just rising more sharply now. Only a small proportion seems to be due to population ageing *per se*, although older patients are more prominent. There are worries too that faster patient turnover may be leading to more frequent readmission. In the flashy healthcare argot of the United States, 'sicker and quicker' discharge may lead to the 'revolving-door syndrome'. Whatever the cause, the combination of a 5 per cent increase in emergency admissions with only a 1 per cent increase in planned admissions, and mandatory 3 per cent 'efficiency savings' imposed by government, have forced many leading hospitals towards technical bankruptcy. Deficits of £5 million and more within a month of the start of the 1996 financial year have been reported by large and efficient hospitals from around the country, which can only be rectified by health authorities raiding contingency funds.

Towards the end of 1994 my disillusion with the culture change in the service and the wanton disregard of the views and knowledge of the clinicians who worked in it by the government was such that I did not wish to stay. I had just reached the earliest pensionable age of 60, so I decided to retire from the NHS. I announced this at a meeting of the BMA Council. The editor of the *BMA News Review*, Mark Jessop, was present and asked me to write an article about it for his next issue, due to be published at the end of January. The

BMA is as incontinent a vessel as the government and the contents of the article were leaked to the medical editor of the *Independent* at the time, Celia Hall, before it appeared. She ran a piece under the headline, 'Consultant quits over "Tory dogma"' on 19 January, and Margaret Beckett, the Shadow Health Secretary, immediately issued a press release calling my resignation 'truly sensational news'. A characteristic spin common to all political press offices was added, to the effect that I had 'made no secret of the fact that [I had] been a long-term supporter of the Tory party' and had 'never voted Labour'. It will not escape the logical that because someone has never voted Labour it does not mean they are a long-term supporter of the Conservatives. Nevertheless the gist of both pieces was correct – I had had enough. The *BMA News Review* was besieged by journalists wishing to have the full text of my article and Jessop decided to release it for information under the usual publication embargo, as it was to be the lead 'exclusive' for his own journal in a few days' time. He was very angry next day when the *Independent* published it in full without his or my permission.

As events would show, the unplanned way in which the article first saw the light of day probably heightened its impact. Journalists are understandably attracted by anything which is leaked or which they come by covertly, and I was inundated with requests for interviews and quotes by the news media. I later discovered that 10 Downing Street rang the chief executive of my hospital, presumably seeking any information that would help to refute my criticisms, but it was not my hospital I was complaining about, and I had not mentioned it.[11] Gerry Malone did his best in his own press statement in response. He had checked the situation, and said, 'I would alert him to the fact that the number of consultants in [his] hospital from March 1993–94 has increased by a fifth, which doesn't seem to indicate this is a service which is finding it difficult to meet the needs of its patients.' What he perhaps did not realize was that an increase of this size might also indicate something else: a hospital trying desperately to keep up with the increasing demands being made on it. The whole affair was a nine-days wonder, but I was delighted that I had not wasted the last shot in my locker, which had achieved a direct hit on its target, the doctrinaire eroders of the NHS, to which I had devoted my career. As Gerry Malone knew following my meeting with him and Virginia Bottomley, the last straw for me had been their intention to substitute national pay for hospital doctors by local pay bargaining without any evidence that a better health service would result. In his statement he called my outburst 'a curious contribution to the debate for somebody who is so close to the issue and I am rather surprised that he has got it so wrong. One of the things that clearly exercises him is the question of introducing performance-related pay across the board. He may use his own words, but that is not the government's policy and never has been.' Who was kidding whom?

Later in the week I was pleased to be invited by the *News of the World* to have another bite at the cherry in their invitation leader slot, which I was interested to discover had been turned down by Virginia Bottomley. And the *Daily Telegraph* also asked me to write a piece for them, which I was told caused Mrs Bottomley's office to be on to them six times that day. Of the large number of letters I received, the favourable ones exceeded the unfavourable by a ratio of 10 to one, and included one from the redoubtable Sir Douglas Black. He enclosed a paper, which I had not previously read, containing similar views to mine in a more academic form which he had written for a medical journal. I thanked him and enclosed a copy of my *News of the World* article, a paper I expected he for his part had not read.

It was also time for a change of scene for Virginia Bottomley. In July, another Cabinet reshuffle brought in Stephen Dorrell to replace her in a straight job swap, she taking over from him as National Heritage Secretary.

Mrs Bottomley made a particularly poignant remark when she left the Health Department. Sound-biting to the last, she said, 'Most of us don't deserve our appointments and we do not deserve our disappointments.' What the latter were can only be guessed at, but political office is no bed of roses, and I had always thought that although she was prefectorial in temperament, the commercial ethos generated by the reforms was surely as foreign to her beliefs about public service as it was to mine. A particularly caustic ex-president of a medical Royal College once said to me of Mrs Bottomley, 'She would make a splendid ward sister, but Secretary of State, no.' This criticism is too harsh as she was by no means the worst Health secretary we have had, but very few leave with the plaudits of the health professions ringing in their ears.

The change was welcomed because Dorrell had the reputation of being a listener and had previous experience of Health as a junior minister. It was noticeable how from the beginning he avoided the bandying-about of figures as far as possible, and he made particularly strong attempts to improve relations with family doctors, who were in near-revolt about their increasing workload, especially that due to out-of-hours work. However the growing fashion of talking of a primary-care-led NHS has made many of them uneasy. This was a trend that had started in 1994, as it had dawned on the Health Department that general practitioner care is much cheaper than the high technology and expensive overheads of the hospitals.[12] In this they were perhaps taking a leaf out of the World Health Organization's book in their 'health for all' policies which had been the basis for *The Health of the Nation.*

The dominance of primary care might massage GP egos but it presumably also meant the transfer of care to them from the hospitals. One reason for their increased workload already was the speedier discharge of patients from hospitals back to their care, which often involved them in aspects of aftercare just short of acute which many thought reasonably should not be their job. The increase in day surgery added to this, and a feeling was growing that they were being 'dumped on'. Dorrell made a series of speeches in which he praised general practice, including calling it 'the jewel in the crown of the NHS' at the Conservative Party conference in October 1995. Another mixed blessing for the GPs was Dorrell's expressed belief that their greater involvement in emergency care would take some of the load off accident and emergency departments around the country, which were being overwhelmed by minor-injury and other work. He was also keen on GPs taking on more work in mental illness and in disease prevention. As recruitment to general practice was falling there were wry faces in the BMA GPs' committee when they heard the message that their enthusiastic new overlord was retailing. They were also uneasy about what the new unified health authorities would expect of them in April 1996 and how knowledgeable about general practice the latter would be. There seemed every evidence that the familiar FSHA component of these bodies would be dominated by district health authority staff and ideas. Dorrell did his best to reassure them that the new combined authorities would increase the influence of non-fundholding GPs on commissioning healthcare from the hospitals, but they were not convinced.

Dorrell seemed not fully hardened by the political process. At 43 he was extremely young for such a demanding post, but he gave every sign of thinking problems through before rushing to the media. That is until the bovine spongiform encephalopathy and Creutzfeldt-Jakob Disease débâcle, when by sheltering behind the rather tentative advice of scientists he alarmed rather than reassured the nation.

He had previously stirred up the managers with his announcement of a reduction in bureaucracy that would threaten many jobs. At the party conference he announced a reduction of 5 per cent in NHS management in order to release £140 million for direct patient care. Mrs Bottomley had tried to find out what the health service's management costs were some time before, and a study showed huge local variations. In some NHS trusts management costs were as low as 2 per cent of their income, while in others it reached 11 per cent. In health authorities, administrative spending varied from £3.50 to £10.50 per head of the population they covered.[13] In another survey, the Audit Commission costed the total amount spent on senior management in NHS trusts in England and Wales in 1993–94 as about £900 million, or 4 per cent of their income. This figure included the cost of work done by clinical directors, but not that of administrative and clerical staff, who brought the figure up to 10.5 per cent. The commission did however warn the Health Department that reducing management, while politically popular, could be dangerous.[14]

Clinicians were as anxious as anyone to see managerial and administrative costs come down, but held the government's reforms responsible for their remarkable escalation and not the managers. A useful spin-off from the Audit Commission's study was that their methods could be used in subsequent years to follow the progress achieved in cutting administrative costs. Dorrell added another objective: that of reducing the amount of paperwork required of GPs, which was singled out as one of the most significant factors in their disaffection, and continues to be so.

It is only the dedication and professionalism of all the NHS's staff that is maintaining the excellent standards of care that still remain, but the thin multi-hued line in their brightly coloured post-reform uniforms is wearing increasingly thin. The US cavalry in the form of Alain Enthoven's ideas for an internal market have come over the hill but they were not the reinforcements that were needed. What is required is finding a way to finance the service better.

CHAPTER THIRTEEN

Failings and Solutions

There is no failure except in no longer trying.
ELBERT HUBBARD, *The Note Book*, 1927

I wrote in my resignation article in the BMA's news magazine in January 1995, and I still believe, that

> doctors will have to recognize that their traditional conservatism and their professional ethos is at greater threat from a Conservative than from a Labour government. The window-dressing from ministers about involving doctors in management is largely tinsel. Lions led by donkeys have a habit of eating the donkeys in the end and John Major would do well to remember this.[1]

It was no doubt the first sentence of this paragraph that most led to the subsequent parliamentary excitement, but the last drew a furious letter from a local health authority chairman whom I knew. His letter crystallized the yawning gap between the professional and the manager or director. He took strong exception to my 'comment that the Boards put over you are donkeys'. In fairness he had not read the article, but only a report of it in his newspaper, the *Daily Telegraph*, but in context I thought it was fairly clear that it was the Prime Minister whom I was casting as Earl Haig and not health service boards and managers. Nevertheless his reaction illustrated well that many appointed chairmen believe that they have been 'put over' the doctors. Unfortunately, NHS doctors do not accept that they are working 'under' anyone outside the profession, only within the managerial framework of a public service and the professional constraints laid on them by the General Medical Council. They work for patients.

The nearest to a true profession in Britain is probably the Church, but judges and doctors come fairly close. None answer directly to politicians or employers outside their profession for their professional actions, and that is what makes their calling a profession. An incompetent or wayward parson or judge is called to account by his peers, as is the doctor. This does not mean that transgression cannot lead to executive action involving his remuneration or employment, nor that his parishioners, defendants or patients cannot call him to account, but this is quite a separate matter.

It seems to many in the medical profession that just as the present Home Secretary is seeking to influence the independence of judges in laying down mandatory minimum sentencing for defined offences, there is a growing threat to medical independence that is not merely organizational or resource-based. As an aside, it is worth making the point that the chairman or chief executive who is in the habit of speaking of 'my doctors' and 'my nurses' is unlikely to be as successful as one who understands health service relationships better. Even in the armed services, where a commanding officer speaks legitimately in the possessive of his non-combatant professionals, be they doctors or padres, there is no question as to where these individuals' first professional loyalties lie – to their patients and their flock.

In the new NHS the imported business culture is leading to greater and greater misunderstanding of the principle of professional independence. It may seem a far cry from the NHS trust surgeon instructed to operate on GP fundholders' patients first irrespective of clinical priority, to the Iraqi doctor ordered to amputate a hand under shariah law, or a psychiatrist in the old Soviet Union forced to certify and treat a dissident as mentally ill because of his political opposition. But the slope is a slippery one and any system which tolerates such faltering first steps must be rejected.

There can be no doubt now that the NHS reforms are intrinsically inequitable on a scale far beyond what was unintentionally present before. At the heart of this inequity is GP fundholding. About half of all patients are now registered with a fundholding family doctor. Many will not even be aware of the fact until they need a planned operation, or some other NHS service which falls within the 20 per cent of hospital and community healthcare for which the typical fundholder has a budget. Then if they are lucky enough to have a fundholding doctor they may well leap over the queue of other patients whose care is bought by their local health authority.

It has been the plea of successive health secretaries that fundholders are the pathfinders to a better service for all, and thus presumably if all GPs were fundholders the health service would be better for everyone. Unfortunately there is no evidence for this, and there are serious doubts as to whether the high cost of fundholding has done other than switch money from one underfunded part of the health service to another. Up to the end of the 1994–95 financial year the administrative costs of introducing fundholding have been £232 million, but the efficiency savings produced by the experiment have been only £206 million.[2] Not only have the savings been less than the cost of the staff, equipment and computers needed to manage fundholding itself, but the scheme has imposed greatly increased costs on health authorities, and on providers like hospitals. To make the overall financial benefits to the NHS of fundholding even more dubious, the fundholders have been allowed to retain the £206 million savings made under the scheme to spend on improvements to their practices, but any losses in previous years are not subtracted from the savings. About a fifth of fundholders make losses every year.

These practice improvements are supposed to be approved by FHSAs (since April 1996 by the new combined health authorities), but about half of the fundholding practices examined in the Audit Commission's wide-ranging 1996 study did not have savings plans which the FHSAs could agree.[3] It seemed therefore that many of the improvements paid for have not been scrutinized by the authorities. On average, 60 per cent of the money has gone into improvements in premises, office furnishings and equipment. Many GPs benefit personally from capital investment in the premises which they own and this is where a large proportion of the money has actually gone. During 1994–95 only 16 per cent of the savings made went into extra hospital and community care. There is nothing necessarily wrong with this, as better premises do benefit patients as well as doctors, but in a time of great financial stringency for the NHS it has to be shown that all money spent is well spent. Some fundholding practices avoid the criticism of feathering their own nests with the savings they make by placing all assets funded by them in trust, so that retiring partners do not benefit personally when they leave. Others believe that there should be some benefit accruing to them for the extra work fundholding brings, and see nothing wrong in increasing their capital investment in this way. The Audit Commission study shows that while many fundholders have achieved some improvements for their patients, only a minority have achieved more than a small proportion of the benefits the commission believes to be potentially available. They put this down largely to insufficient management development, and they were disappointed with the primitive level of budget management in many practices. Less than half of the budget managers who were using computer spreadsheets to monitor expenditure, for instance, were looking at changes to waiting lists, commitment forecasts and average prices achieved, or used graphics.

Before the health service invests more money in better management of fundholding it should look very hard at the downside. For a trust hospital, and nearly all NHS hospitals are now trusts, the work involved in dealing with a multiplicity of small purchasers, the fundholders, is enormous. Some trusts now derive as much as 20 per cent of their income from fundholders, but the average fundholder's budget is only £1.7 million, of which about 78 per cent, or £1.3 million, will be spent on hospital care spread over several hospitals. Even if a practice spends £1 million at one hospital, this will probably be divided into a large number of smaller contracts for different specialties and services and will be administratively complex to set up, cost and charge for. Trusts have to invoice fundholders within six weeks of the patient being seen or treated or they may not get paid. This is not as easy as might be imagined. The patient must be identified as one who should be charged for; and what precisely has been done, and whether the procedure carried out was covered by a contract (emergency surgery would not be, for instance), must be checked. Some GPs have a patient turnover as high as 12 per cent every year, and 5 per cent of patients may move their address but stay with the same GP, which adds further difficulty.[4] Without expensive and sophisticated information technology, hospitals can find it very difficult to keep track of what is owed to them. In one case, a single fundholder legitimately retained £500,000 from a trust which failed to meet its invoice deadlines.[5]

Thus the transactional costs of fundholding are very high. Even if fundholding were to be abolished, as the Labour Party has said it will do if elected, retention of the internal market will also be too costly. It is true that if a provider like a hospital did the majority of its contracting and billing with one commissioning authority and this included all its services, not just the 20 per cent currently bought by most of the fundholders, the cost would come down. However this would still leave hospital and community trusts with too high an administrative overhead, and a difficult-to-quantify involvement by consultants and other professional staff, who would be better employed confining themselves to their clinical work.

The other main plank in the NHS reforms is the NHS trust – mostly acute hospitals, community hospitals and ambulance services. Here, devolution of responsibility has brought some benefit, but the democratic deficit must be corrected. In the old NHS, the hospitals were run by the district health authorities, who in turn were monitored by the regional health authorities, who reported to the Health Secretary and the Department of Health. This structure, on the whole, worked very well, although it did mean that innovation at the level of patients and the hospital could be difficult and slow. Hospital managers were often frustrated by the dead weight, as it seemed to them, of the chain of command above, but for the brighter ones there was a promotional career path ahead of them, via the district to region. Hospital consultants were responsible to the regional medical officer, so that this individual had considerable power. An exceptional RMO like John Revans in Wessex or Rosemary Rue in Oxford had enormous influence in the planning of hospital services, right down to the appointment of extra consultants, the development and distribution of new services and the necessary capital investment.

Consultants frustrated by the failure to provide them with the resources that they thought necessary to develop their departments and their specialty could always go and see the RMO about it. If he or she thought that particular consultant was worth supporting, means would be found. This was the NHS which I found when I was appointed as the first consultant haematologist in Dorset in 1969. I spent five years labouring single-handed in the vineyard before going to see Dr Revans with my plans and demands. He listened and more medical staff and resources were provided. When I left the NHS there were six consultant haematologists in the district to which I was appointed 27 years ago, and their workload was if anything higher than mine in the early 1970s. Mine is a specialty which has expanded very fast. There are a few fields, such as tuberculosis, which have contracted equally fast. Planning ahead is vital in such a changing field as medicine and the NHS reforms show every sign of not providing a satisfactory substitute for the regions' planning role. The new, fewer, relatively tiny regional offices of the NHS Executive cannot possibly fulfil the tasks undertaken by the old regional health authorities which, in addition to planning and providing numerous advisory services, employed hospital doctors and oversaw the distribution and training of the junior ones.

The fragmentation of the health service into competing trusts and multiple small fundholding businesses has destroyed not only much of the ordered planning of the NHS but has damaged its immensely valuable medical networking systems. No longer can doctors in different hospitals freely help each other out with information and second opinions, and even with staff and equipment loans on occasion. They now work in competing 'companies' in which some of the information which used to be exchanged is now deemed to be commercially sensitive.

One benefit which trust status *has* brought to hospitals has been that capital for new developments and refurbishments has become easier to find. That is not to say that the interest charges may not cause financial problems in the future, but the old and disastrous one-year Treasury-driven financial cycle has been ameliorated. This annual reckoning was largely responsible for the extremely slow building of new hospitals and other major capital projects, which almost always had to be phased over many years, leading to long-continuing inefficiencies and frustrations.

The jury remains out on whether the new trust boards – made up as they are of government-appointed chairmen of politically approved views, appointed non-executive directors of often similar views and full-time hospital executives – are better than what went before. The new guidelines from Lord Nolan's 1995 report on standards in public life will no doubt help to ensure that earlier suspicions of political correctness being the prime requirement for such posts are dispelled; but, if trusts in some form are to continue, some way of ensuring a voice for the public and input from the hospital staff will have to be found. Hospital boards in the 1970s often contained much dead wood, but they included many members from local authorities who gave freely of their time and energies in the knowledge that they had some legitimacy by virtue of their election to the local council. They were appreciated all the more for donating their services. The National Association of Hospitals and Trusts has recently complained that the amount of work required of non-executive directors has increased so much that more than the current £5000 a year should be paid to them. It is certainly true that the workload of conscientious non-executives has risen markedly in recent years, particularly in regard to their involvement in the rocketing number of complaint investigations. But the NHS is a public service and work on trust boards should also be just that. Any remuneration should remain as a nominal amount, and not form part of a portfolio of the sort of directorships collected by the financially ambitious.

The introduction of NHS trusts has forced much greater responsibility on management. While predating the reforms, general management has become so strongly associated with them that it can no longer be entirely disentangled. Managers have also assumed much greater power in other parts of the health service, except in general practice where doctors are still in charge on the ground. Some form of accommodation must be found between managers and doctors. Individually, many managers are very able and well-motivated. The hospital manager is by no means the first to leave the hospital at the end of the day, and his or her workload often equates with some of the hardest-working consultants (although he is seldom recalled at night or at weekends). Doctors are unavoidably élitist. They have been used to being amongst the brightest in their schools, they have had to work longer and harder while at university – no long vacations for them, and in many cases they have had to take highly competitive examinations into their 30s. The lot of a junior hospital doctor is a hard one, and it does not get much easier during the rest of a medical career, whether in hospital or general practice. From this point of view, the path to chief executive of a trust hospital, on a salary equal to or higher than that of a consultant with at least a 'B' merit award (which only 10 per cent of consultants have), looks much easier. If the truth were told it probably is, but then so is the path to many other jobs in the public and private sectors that pay as much or more.

What doctors have to recompense them is, still, public esteem; an enormously satisfying job – when face to face with patients at least; and, until quite recently, job security. In addition, relatively few doctors actually want to be managers.

What would help to bring the two sides together, and I use the word 'sides' intentionally, would be to integrate the training of managers with that of doctors at some stage in their careers. I once had lunch in the Savoy Grill with William Waldegrave and Kenneth Calman, the Chief Medical Officer, at Waldegrave's invitation, at which I floated the idea of an NHS staff college. In the Royal Air Force, in which I served for eight years, officers singled out as high flyers in their respective branches were brought together at the RAF Staff College for several months. The *raison d'être* and long-term strategy of the service was taught and discussed by all, whether they were pilots, navigators, electronics officers or doctors. Officers on the course tended to be in their 30s or early 40s, which might be a little late for the NHS, but a great deal of *esprit de corps* and sense of purpose was instilled in those who would later rise to the highest ranks. A suitable stage in the health service would probably be at the registrar level for doctors, and deputy chief executive for managers, and attendance would be by selection. Waldegrave seemed quite interested in the idea but so far nothing has been done about it. The intention would not be to turn doctors into managers or vice versa, but simply to familiarize each group with the other's priorities, skills and problems faced, and help to achieve better teamwork and thus a better health service.

The changes that I would like the NHS to adopt are set out below.

First the transactional costs of the internal market should be removed. Their huge expense of around £1500 million a year is not justified by the results, and the money swallowed up could be put to much better use. The abolition of the internal market removes the rationale for fundholding general practices but it does not remove the need for the more efficient management demonstrated by the best fundholders. (I have no doubt that strong practice management is also found in the best of the non-fundholding practices, but the 1996 Audit Commission study did not examine these, nor compare fundholders with non-fundholders.) Fundholding provided a useful impetus to general practice, and gave it a welcome and necessary involvement in the services which GPs and their patients should get from hospitals. A way must be found so that this impetus is not lost. Commissioning of hospital care by health authorities, in which general practitioners are deeply involved, but which does not involve the transactional costs of contracting, is such a way. Health authorities must have strong public-health medicine departments which should work with general practitioners and hospital consultants to plan and fund the right services for the district's patients. Authorities would retain the power to switch the allocation of funds away from under-performing hospitals, but at the same time they would work with those hospitals to correct their failings in rather the same way that concerns like Marks & Spencer work with their suppliers. The only form of individual payment that should remain is for patients crossing health-authority boundaries, either for tertiary or specialized care such as neurosurgery and transplantation, or when patients are treated away from their district of residence. In such cases fees corresponding to nationally agreed (or in some instances special) rates should operate. Health authorities should maintain contingency funds to pay the costs of such eventualities, and should monitor referrals closely.

Hospitals should retain their management boards, but the clinical directors should join the main board, and not remain at a level below this as at present. The number of clinical directorates in a hospital should be reduced so that the main board does not have a membership exceeding about 15. The clinical members of the board should equal the number of the non-clinical, excluding the chairman. The medical and nursing directors, the finance director and the chief executive must be members of the main board. A case could be made for the personnel director also, although he or she should not be called the 'director of human resources', an appalling import from the world of business. Non-executive directors should be appointed from those who have applied via open advertisement and from those nominated by local bodies. The local bodies would include local authorities, businesses and companies and professional practices – with the proviso that any nominees must live or work within the catchment area of the hospital. The selection process for non-executive directors for hospital and similar boards should be run by the district health authority.

Members of the DHA board should be appointed from those applying and being nominated in the same way, and their medical and any other clinical non-executive members should be sought from the local professions at large. Both boards would nominate their own chairmen but the Secretary of State for Health should retain the power of approving their appointment.

The rules of appointment would give guidance as to the qualities and skills required for the respective boards – they would not be the same for hospitals and health authorities. The procedure for appointing regional health authorities would be similar but the Chief Medical Officer and the Permanent Secretary of the DoH would have a role in appointments. RHA membership would include the reinstated regional medical and nursing officers, the regional chief executive and the finance and personnel directors. Other medical members would include the regional medical postgraduate dean, who would have a specific responsibility for doctors in training. Parallel structures would operate in Scotland, Wales and Northern Ireland.

If this structure looks similar to the NHS of 1970 it is no accident. The planned health service of that era was very cheap and effective administratively. What was lacking was the much better financial management and the greater responsiveness to patients of today's NHS. We now also have the Health Service Ombudsman, the Audit Commission, the King's Fund accreditation scheme for hospitals and a host of other important developments which help to monitor the efficient working of the system. The Department of Health used to run the health service without the aid of an NHS executive and I would abolish the NHSE. If health secretaries wish to appoint an advisory board that is up to them, but the NHS would be quite safe in the hands of the DoH and the two-tiered health authority structure I have outlined.

The NHS reforms were the damaging answer to the wrong question. The most important question that should have been asked was, how does a modern state pay for the healthcare of its citizens in order to satisfy their reasonable expectations? Margaret Thatcher's prime ministerial review which led to the present reforms was triggered by public opprobrium over the tragic circumstances of two small children in Birmingham whom the NHS failed. That such events are still occurring in the heart of Britain despite the most traumatic upheaval in its healthcare system for nearly 50 years is disappointing in the extreme. It shows that the health service's reorganization along market lines was not the answer. By fragmenting the health service and substituting competition for co-operation it makes such events more likely rather than less likely to happen.

The root of the health service's problems is that it receives insufficient money to do what can be done for patients at the end of the 20th century. What is more, the media age in which we now live ensures that everyone knows this. Our Conservative government consistently maintains that the nation cannot afford to pay any more, despite apportioning less of the country's wealth to healthcare than just about every other comparable country on the planet. On every occasion that the BMA or any other body has gone Oliver Twist-like to government to ask for more, the tired old argument about the potentially 'bottomless pit' of healthcare is recited. It is a characteristic trick of politicians to distort the case of supplicants or opponents. If John Major were the Beadle he would say to the shivering Oliver not that he wants another helping but that he is wickedly asking for the whole cauldron. It would be very informative if, instead of commissioning interminable management studies and public-relations exercises, the Health Department applied Oregon's list of procedures to the UK and found out at what point on the list our health budget would run out. If a smallish state in the USA with a population less than one-twentieth of ours can do this, why cannot we? It may be that the cut-off point would be so embarrassing that the government would not want it known. I do not believe the Oregon scheme, or anything like it, should be used in Britain, but as a research exercise it would be very valuable.

Anyone with any awareness of economics would agree that there must be an optimum level for public spending, and most, if not all, economists would agree that inflation should be squeezed out of the system as far as possible. However, surveys have shown repeatedly that in the public mind health takes first priority for extra spending.

The government should note that if the people were given a choice between the three options of (i) reduced taxes and less health spending, (ii) keeping both the same, or (iii) increasing both, the third option of increasing both tax and spending has now overtaken the status quo middle option, which was the most popular in the early 80s.[6] The public want their NHS to be much better funded, but as the government refuses to will the means, the obvious answer is to resort to the ballot box. However, general elections are not won and lost on single issues, however near to the hearts of voters, and therein lies the dilemma for those who would like to vote for more money for the NHS.

Until now paying for healthcare in Britain out of general taxation has not been widely questioned. The UK set up the first national health service in the world and it seemed best at the time to pay for it out of total government receipts. This method was simple, equitable (assuming that the tax system itself was fair), easily administered and under total governmental control. The fact that no other comparable country has chosen to follow us does not seem to have occasioned surprise.

The cost of the NHS in relation to tax receipts is really very large. In 1992–93 our gross NHS expenditure of £36,100 million was very similar to total VAT receipts of £37,246 million, and as a proportion of income tax it would have accounted for very nearly two-thirds.[7] Because of the size of this expenditure in relation to all government outgoings it has never seemed very attractive to the Treasury to allow it to be hived off to any other body or mechanism. Unlike the BBC, whose licence pays for its services, a National Health Corporation funded by licences or subscriptions would be an order of magnitude larger. Removing such a huge slice of the nation's money from the Chancellor of the Exchequer could severely constrain his endeavours, not always successful, to manage the economy.

However, earmarking tax for health has many attractions. Politically, such hypothecation would take much of the pressure off the government of the day. A straight question could be put to the electorate at any time as to whether health tax should be increased or not. The increasing demand for public participation would also be met. Nevertheless there are drawbacks. A flat-rate health tax for all would be severely regressive, that is, it would fall most heavily proportionately on the poorest. This would clearly be unacceptable, as the poll tax showed, and would lead amongst other things to widespread evasion in the same way. Hypothecation could be banded or graduated depending on wealth or income. A health tax could be collected at the local level like council tax, at least in part as it is in Sweden. Thus local taxpayers would have an input into the funding and, via local elections, the running of their health service. Local collection would have the additional advantage that those well enough off to have more than one home would contribute to their medical treatment wherever they were living when they became ill. Because the amount of tax collected locally would be less in socially deprived areas, where healthcare needs are greater, part of the health tax would have to be collected centrally and distributed in a similar way to rate support grant and other governmental funds.

A simpler method of applying a health tax would be to link it to income-tax coding and assign its collection to the Inland Revenue. The important distinction is that hypothecation means that the amount of any earmarked tax paid is separately and clearly identified, and it can be raised and lowered independently of income tax or any other taxes.

Another mechanism for raising hypothecated taxes is to link them with specific goods and services like VAT. It would be attractive, for instance, to place a swingeing health tax on consumer goods like tobacco, the consumption of which leads to greater use of the health service. Others such as some sports equipment might attract lower or even no health tax because greater use might diminish users' demands on the NHS. Considerable research would have to be done before setting these rates because it might be found that wearers of football boots, for instance, cost the health service much more than those of hiking boots by virtue of footballers' common attendance at accident and emergency departments on Saturday evenings. Such consumer health taxes are almost certainly too complicated to be practical or to gain public support.

A disadvantage of hypothecated taxes in general is that they are inflexible. As Aneurin Bevan found out, the idea that a health service would so raise the standard of health in this country that demand would eventually fall was demolished very early on. However, it is conceivable that a greater proportion of the available money might be better spent on the prevention of ill-health in the hope that less would have to be spent on illness. Unless a health tax paid for measures to improve health and discourage ill-health it could fail by reasons of its rigidity. As *The Health of the Nation* demonstrates, many ways of improving health do not fall within the power of the Health Department and nor would they all be eligible for funding by a health tax.

Linking hypothecation with the gross national product would be possible, but it is true, as John Major said to me when I met him, that the GNP can fall as well as rise. A falling GNP is certain to increase healthcare demand as well as pressure on the Social Services budget. Nevertheless if the linkage were set at a GNP proportion not lower than the average percentage GNP health spend of a group of similar countries, it would almost certainly satisfy the public as being reasonable. This would carry significant political advantage, and is worth looking at for this reason alone. The proportionate GNP spend of the OECD countries actually varies quite widely both in terms of its total and in its breakdown into private and state contributions. In Norway, 99 per cent of the health spend is public; in the USA it is only about 40 per cent, with the rest being made up by private sources such as insurance. In Britain a little over 85 per cent of our health expenditure is by the state. Private healthcare provision is growing slowly in this country, but because private medical insurance is heavily biased towards paying for elective surgery – rather than funding the long-term treatment of chronic conditions – it does not provide a true alternative to the health service. Nevertheless it is becoming more and more urgent to re-examine what the NHS should provide free, and what should be its core services.

The government was forced to introduce co-payments for spectacles and dentures less than two years after the NHS started, but the whole question of charging within the health service needs a thorough-going review. In particular, the imposition of charges must always be carefully weighed against the cost of collection.

The present situation in relation to prescription charges is extremely unsatisfactory and its overhaul is long overdue. Exemption is allowed for patients suffering from some chronic conditions, but not for others which may place just as severe financial burdens on sufferers. In many parts of the country NHS dentistry is almost impossible to obtain, and, when it is, the charges made seriously stretch the ability to pay of some patients who fall just outside the safety net. The incidence of eye-testing has fallen following the introduction of charges, and consequently the adventitious detection of the potentially blinding condition glaucoma is likely to drop. Such co-payments as we have are not necessarily the most appropriate. It astonishes the victims of road accidents that they may be liable to pay for their attendance at the accident and emergency department. If their car insurance pays for this they may be content, but all casualties may not be covered by such insurance.

Patient attendance at general practitioners' surgeries is rising steadily, as are requests for night visits. In Sweden attendances are charged up to an annual maximum, and patients are also charged a daily rate while in hospital. Here some form of usage-based charging, especially for hospital hotel services and night visits by GPs, might find support, with suitable safeguards. Such charges might discourage unnecessary demand on family doctors, and release hospital money for treatment. However, there is always a danger that the low charges thought reasonable by patients would be uneconomic to collect; and, in the case of home visits, that interposing a financial hurdle might penalize those least able to help themselves.

Whatever changes are made to the charges at present levied within the NHS, it is vital that they are properly thought through, and considered as a whole by a wide range of those involved in the health service, as well as by politicians.

The most serious mistake that Mrs Thatcher made when she instituted her review of the health service in 1988 was to confine it to a small group within the government. The time is ripe for a further, open, review, not necessarily a royal commission, to look at all aspects of the NHS, but above all at its funding. There is now a very great number of potential sources of valuable knowledge and opinion on tap, including many British health economists and sociologists, like Rudolph Klein, Chris Ham, David Hunter and Anthony Culyer, at least as well-informed as Alain Enthoven. There may even be another William Beveridge out there somewhere who has the knowledge, and particularly the breadth, to produce a new coherent replacement for the present botched and ideologically tainted scheme. And this time such a review should not ignore the professions who provide the health service.

The greatest fear that those who work in the health service now have is that unless something is done the fragmentation and consequent decline of the NHS will continue. These fears are shared by the public, who have seen their government failing to maintain the unique qualities that were built into the service in 1948, and leading it down the road towards privatization and decay. Continuing inroads are being made into the strongly professional values and altruism at its heart, and its cardinal principles of fairness, quality and equal availability to all are under severe threat. The National Health Service has been the greatest social advance made this century – it cannot be allowed to wither and die at the hands of an inept government which appears to have no understanding of the reasons why its founding principles are so precious to the nation.

ABBREVIATIONS

Used in the text, Bibliography and Notes

ARM	Annual Representative Meeting
BMA	British Medical Association
BMJ	British Medical Journal
CCHMS	Central Committee for Hospital Medical Services (BMA)
CCSC	Central Consultants and Specialists Committee (renamed CCHMS)
CSAG	Clinical Standards Advisory Group
DDRB	Doctors' and Dentists' Review Body
DHA	District health authority
DHSS	Department of Health and Social Security
DoH	Department of Health
DRG	Diagnosis Related Group
FHSA	Family health service authority
FPC	Family practitioner committee
GP	General practitioner
GPFH	General practice fundholder
HMO	Health maintenance organization
HMSO	Her Majesty's Stationery Office
IHSM	Institute of Health Service Management
JCC	Joint Consultants Committee
KFI	King's Fund Institute
NAHA	National Association of Health Authorities

NAHAT	National Association of Health Authorities and Trusts
NHSME	National Health Service Management Executive
NHSE	National Health Service Executive
OME	Office of Manpower Economics
PACT	Prescribing Analysis and Cost scheme
PADIV	Public affairs division (BMA)
PEP	Political and Economic Planning
PFI	Private Finance Initiative
QALY	Quality-adjusted life year
RAWP	Resource allocation working party
RHA	Regional health authority
RMI	Resource Management Initiative
SGH	Self-governing hospital
SIFT	Special Increment for Teaching
SIFTR	Special Increment for Teaching and Research
WHO	World Health Organization

BIBLIOGRAPHY

Allen, Isobel, *Doctors and their Careers*, Policy Studies Institute, 1988

Allsop, Judith, *Health Policy and the NHS*, 2nd edn, Longman, 1995

A Price on their Heads: Measuring Costs in NHS Trusts, Audit Commission, 1995

Auld, Philip, *Honour a Physician*, Hollis & Carter, 1959

Beveridge, William, Chairman, *Report on Social Insurance and Allied Services*, Cmnd 6404, HMSO, 1942

Black, Sir Douglas, *The Black Report*, DHSS, 1980 (reprinted in *Inequalities in Health*, Penguin, 1992)

BMA Health Policy and Economic Research Unit, *Hypothecated Tax Funding for the NHS*, BMA, 1994

Brittan, Leon, *A New Deal for Health Care*, Conservative Political Centre, 1988

Butler, Eammon, and Pirie, Madsen, *The Health of Nations*, Adam Smith Institute, 1988

Choices in Health Care, Government Committee on Choices in Health Care (Netherlands), 1992

Committee of Public Accounts, *General Practitioner Fundholding in England (27th Report)*, HMSO, 1995

Community Care: Funding from April 1993: Third Report of the Health Committee, HMSO, 1993

Culyer, A. J., Maynard, A. K., and Posnett, J. W., *Competition in Health Care: Reforming the NHS*, Macmillan, 1990

Department of Health, *Making London Better*, HMSO, 1993

Dowie, Robin, *Patterns of Hospital Medical Staffing: Junior Doctors' Hours: Interim Report*, British Postgraduate Medical Federation, 1990

Edwards, Brian, *The National Health Service: A Manager's Tale: 1946–1992*, Nuffield Provincial Hospitals Trust, 1993

Edwards, B., and Pennington, G. W., *Distinction and Meritorious Service Awards for Hospital Doctors and Dentists in the NHS*, Health Services Manpower Review, University of Keele, 1987

Efficiency Unit, *Improving Management in Government: The Next Step*, HMSO, 1988

Enthoven, Alain, *Reflections on the Management of the National Health Service*, Occasional Paper 5, Nuffield Provincial Hospitals Trust, 1985

Foot, Michael, *Aneurin Bevan, vol. 2 (1945–1960)*, Davis-Poynter, 1973

Garpenby, Peter, *The State and the Medical Profession: A Cross-National Comparison of the Health Policy Arena in the United Kingdom and Sweden 1945–1985*, University of Linköping, 1989

General Medical Council, *The Duties of a Doctor*, GMC, 1995

General Practice in the NHS: A New Contract, HMSO, 1989

Grey-Turner, Elston, and Sutherland, F. M., *History of the British Medical Association, vol. II 1932–1981*, BMA, 1982

Griffiths, Roy, *Community Care: Agenda for Action: A Report to the Secretary of State for Social Services*, HMSO, 1988

Griffiths, Roy, *NHS Management Inquiry*, DHSS, 1983

Guillebaud, C. W., Chairman, *Report of the Committee of Enquiry into the Cost of the National Health Service*, Cmnd 9663, HMSO, 1956

Harrison, S., and Lachmann, P., *Towards a High-Trust NHS: Proposals for Minimally-Invasive Reform*, Institute for Public Policy Research, 1996

Health Authority Costs and NHS Trust Management Costs 1994–1995, DoH, 1995

Health Finance: Assessing the Options, King's Fund Institute, 1988

Hogg, Sarah, and Hill, Jonathan, *Too Close to Call: Power and Politics – John Major in No. 10*, Little, Brown & Co., 1995

Hutton, Will, *The State We're In*, Vintage, 1996

Jenkins, Simon, *Accountable to None: The Tory Nationalisation of Britain*, Hamish Hamilton, 1995

King's Fund Commission on the Future of London's Acute Health

Services, *London Health Care 2010: Changing the Future of Services in the Capital* and Working Papers 1–12, King's Fund London Initiative, 1992

Klein, Rudolph, *The New Politics of the NHS*, 3rd edn, Longman, 1995

Lawson, Nigel, *The View from No. 11: Memoirs of a Tory Radical*, Corgi, 1993

Leading for Health: A BMA Agenda for Health, BMA, 1991

Marr, Andrew, *Ruling Britannia: The Failure and Future of British Democracy*, Michael Joseph, 1995

Muirhead Little, Ernest, *History of the British Medical Association 1832–1932*, BMA, n.d.

NHS Responsibilities for Meeting Continuing Care Needs, HSG (95) 8 and LAC (95) 50, HMSO, 1995

Owen, David, *Our NHS*, Pan, 1988

Patients First: Consultative Paper on the Structure and Management of the NHS in England and Wales, HMSO, 1979

Primary Health Care: An Agenda for Discussion, Cmnd 9771, DHSS, 1986

Redwood, John, and Letwin, Oliver, *Britain's Biggest Enterprise: Ideas for Radical Reform of the NHS*, Centre for Policy Studies, 1988

Self-Governing Hospitals: An Initial Guide, HMSO, 1989

Smith, Jane, ed., *London After Tomlinson: Reorganising Big City Medicine*, BMJ, 1993

Smith, R., ed., *The Health of the Nation: The BMJ View*, BMJ, 1991

Social Services Committee, *Public Expenditure on the Social Services*, Fourth Report, session 1985–86, HMSO, 1986

The Future of the National Health Service, Fifth Report, session 1987–88, HMSO, 1988

Resourcing the National Health Service: The Government's White Paper; Working for Patients, Fifth Report, session 1988–89, HMSO, 1989

Spiers, John, *The Invisible Hospital and the Secret Garden: An Insider's Commentary on the NHS Reforms*, Radcliffe Medical Press/IHSM, 1995

Supplementary Annual Report of BMA Council, Appendix VI: Evidence to the Governmental Internal Review of the National Health Service, BMJ, 296 6633, 1988, pp. 1411–18

Thatcher, Margaret, *The Downing Street Years*, HarperCollins, 1993

The Future of Health Care, BMJ, 1992

The Health of the Nation: A Consultative Document for Health in England, Cmnd 1523, HMSO, 1991

The Health of the Nation: A Strategy for Health in England, Cmnd 1986, HMSO, 1992

The Private Finance Initiative, Sixth Report of the Treasury Committee, HC146, HMSO, 1995

The Rubber Windmill: Contracting for Health Outcomes, Office for Public Management, 1990

The Rubber Windmill One Year On: Assuring Health Gain: A Report on Days 5 and 6, East Anglia RHA/Office for Public Management, 1991

Through the Looking Glass: Opening Up the NHS Funding Debate, IHSM, 1993

Timmins, Nicholas, *The Five Giants: A Biography of the Welfare State*, HarperCollins, 1995

Tomlinson, Bernard, *Report of the Inquiry into London's Health Service, Medical Education and Research*, HMSO, 1992

Vallance-Owen, Andrew, *The Health Debate Live: 45 interviews for 'Leading for Health'*, BMJ, 1992

Vaughan, Paul, *Doctors' Commons: A Short History of the British Medical Association*, Heinemann, 1959

Waldegrave, William, *The Binding of Leviathan: Conservatism and the Future*, Hamish Hamilton, 1978

What the Doctor Ordered: A Study of GP Fundholders in England and Wales, Audit Commission, 1996

Whitney, Ray, *National Health Crisis: A Modern Solution*, Shepheard-Walwyn, 1988

Willetts, David, *Reforming the Health Service*, Conservative Political Centre, 1989

Working for Patients: The Health Service: Caring for the 1990s, HMSO, 1989

Working Paper 1, *Self-Governing Hospitals*, HMSO, 1989

Working Paper 2, *Funding and Contracts for Hospital Services*, HMSO, 1989

Working Paper 3, *Practice Budgets for General Medical Practitioners*, HMSO, 1989

Working Paper 4, *Indicative Prescribing Budgets for General Medical Practitioners*, HMSO, 1989

Working Paper 5, *Capital Charges*, HMSO, 1989

Working Paper 6, *Medical Audit*, HMSO, 1989

Working Paper 7, *NHS Consultants: Appointments, Contracts and Distinction Awards*, HMSO, 1989

Working Paper 8, *Implications for Family Practitioner Committees*, HMSO, 1989

Working Paper 9, *Capital Charges: Funding Issues*, HMSO, 1989

Working Paper 10, *Education and Training*, HMSO, 1989

Contracts for Health Services: Operational Principles, HMSO, 1989

Contracts for Health Services: Operating Contracts, HMSO, 1990

World Health Organization, *Global Strategy For Health For All by the Year 2000*, WHO, 1981

NOTES

Introduction

1. *Working for Patients: The Health Service: Caring for the 1990s*, HMSO, 1989
2. *What the Doctor Ordered: A Study of GP Fundholders in England and Wales*, Audit Commission, 1996

Chapter One: The National Health Service: Origins and Ideas

1. *Encyclopaedia Britannica*, 9th edn, 1885
2. Chadwick, Edwin, *Report on the Sanitary Conditions of the Labouring Population of Great Britain*, 1842
3. Black, Sir Douglas, *The Black Report*, DHSS, 1980, reprinted in *Inequalities in Health*, Penguin, 1992
4. *Report on the British Health Services*, quoted in Allsop, Judith, *Health Policy and the NHS*, 2nd edn, Longman, 1995
5. Foot, Michael, *Aneurin Bevan, vol. 2 (1945–1960)*, quoted in Grey-Turner, Elston and Sutherland, F. M., *History of the British Medical Association, vol. II 1932–1981*, BMA, 1982
6. Beveridge, William, Chairman, *Report on Social Insurance and Allied Services*, Cmnd 6404, HMSO, 1942
7. *Ibid.*, para 427
8. Timmins, Nicholas, *The Five Giants: A Biography of the Welfare State*, HarperCollins, 1995
9. Churchill, Winston, quoted in Grey-Turner and Sutherland, *op. cit.*
10. *The Duties of a Doctor: HIV and AIDS – The Ethical Considerations*, GMC, 1995
11. Auld, Philip, *Honour a Physician*, reviewed in the *Lancet*, 16.1.60
12. Guillebaud, C. W., Chairman, *Report of the Committee of Enquiry into the Cost of the National Health Service*, Cmnd 9663, HMSO, 1956
13. Owen, David, *Our NHS*, Pan, 1988
14. *Patients First: Consultative Paper on the Structure and Management of the NHS in England and Wales*, HMSO, 1979
15. Griffiths, Sir Roy, *NHS Management Inquiry Report*, DHSS, 1983
16. Enthoven, Alain, *Reflections on the Management of the National Health Service*, Occasional Paper 5, Nuffield Provincial Hospitals Trust, 1985
17. *Economist*, 22.6.85
18. Redwood, John, and Letwin, Oliver, *Britain's Biggest Enterprise: Ideas for Radical Reform of the NHS*, Centre for Policy Studies, 1988

19. *Guardian*, 18.9.84
20. Moore, Stephen, *et al.*, *New England Journal of Medicine*, 309, 1983, pp. 1400–1404

Chapter Two: Lead-up to the NHS Reforms

1. Edwards, Brian, *The National Health Service: A Manager's Tale, 1946–1992*, Nuffield Provincial Hospitals Trust, 1993
2. Lawson, Nigel, *The View from No. 11: Memoirs of a Tory Radical*, Corgi, 1993
3. Edwards, *op. cit.*
4. *The Autumn Survey 1987: Financial Position of District Health Authorities*, NAHA, 1987
5. *Primary Health Care: An Agenda for Discussion*, Cmnd 9771, DHSS, 1986
6. Smith, Tony, *British Medical Journal*, 296 6614, 1988, pp. 1–2
7. *Financial Times*, 9.12.87
8. Social Services Committee, *Public Expenditure on the Social Services*, Fourth Report, session 1985–86, HMSO, 1986
9. Taylor, K. G., *British Medical Journal*, 296 6619, 1988, p. 428
10. *Health Finance: Assessing the Options*, KFI, 1988
11. Brittan, Leon, *A New Deal for Health Care*, Conservative Political Centre, 1988
12. Whitney, Ray, *National Health Crisis: A Modern Solution*, quoted in Warden, John, *BMJ*, 296 6623, 1988, p. 726
13. Warden, John, *BMJ*, 296 6624, 1988, p. 800.

Chapter Three: The Year of the NHS Review

1. Warden, John, *BMJ*, 296 6619, 1988, p. 440
2. Owen, *op. cit.*
3. BMA Council, *Supplementary Annual Report: Appendix VI: Evidence to the Governmental Internal Review of the National Health Service*, *BMJ*, 296 6633, 1988, pp. 1411–18
4. Social and Community Planning Research, *British Social Attitudes*, Gower, 1987
5. *Alternative Delivery and Funding of Health Services*, IHSM, 1988
6. Allen, Isobel, *Doctors and their Careers*, Policy Studies Institute, 1988
7. Timmins, *op. cit.*
8. Appleby, John, *BMJ*, 297 6659, 1988, pp. 1284–85
9. Social Services Committee, *The Future of the National Health Service*, Fifth Report, session 1987–88, HMSO, 1988

Chapter Four: Working for Patients

1. *The Times*, 7.2.96
2. *The Times*, 26.7.96
3. Thatcher, Margaret, *The Downing Street Years*, HarperCollins, 1993
4. *Ibid.*
5. *Ibid.*
6. Lawson, *op. cit.*
7. Dillner, Luisa, *BMJ*, 312 7027, 1996, p. 334
8. Dowell, J., Snadden, D., and

Dunbar, J., *BMJ*, 310 6978, 1995, pp. 505–7

Chapter Five: Doctors Become Angry

1. Trade Union and Labour Relations Act, 1974
2. *General Practice in the NHS: A New Contract*, HMSO, 1989
3. *Sunday Express*, 5.2.89
4. *The Times*, 20.3.89
5. CCHMS, *Self-Governing Hospitals Information Pack*, BMA, 1989
6. Marr, Andrew, *Ruling Britannia: The Failure and Future of British Democracy*, Michael Joseph, 1995
7. *Hansard*, 18.5.89, HMSO, 1989
8. *Self-Governing Hospitals: An Initial Guide*, HMSO, 1989
9. *Working Paper 9: Capital Charges: Funding Issues*, HMSO, 1989

Chapter Six: The NHS Bill Reaches Parliament

1. Griffiths, Roy, *Community Care: Agenda for Action: A Report to the Secretary of State for Social Services*, HMSO, 1988
2. Black, *op. cit.*
3. Social Services Committee, *Resourcing the National Health Service: The government's White Paper; Working for Patients*, Fifth Report, session 1988–89, HMSO, 1989
4. *Working for Patients: Contracts for Health Services: Operational Principles*, HMSO, 1989
5. *Health Service Journal*, 22.2.96, p. 13

6. Delamothe, Tony, *BMJ*, 299 6702, 1989, p. 756
7. Timmins, *op. cit.*
8. *Ibid.*

Chapter Seven: Opposition and Negotiation

1. Warden, John, *BMJ*, 300 6727, 1990, p. 369
2. Scott, Sir Richard, *Report of the Inquiry into the Export of Defence Equipment and Dual-Use Goods to Iraq and Related Prosecutions*, HMSO, 1996
3. Dowie, Robin, *Patterns of hospital medical staffing: Junior Doctors' Hours: Interim Report*, British Postgraduate Medical Federation, 1990
4. *The Rubber Windmill: Contracting for Health Outcomes*, Office for Public Management, 1990
5. Liddell, A., and Parston, G., *Health Service Journal*, 17.5.90, pp. 730–32
6. *Rubber Windmill One Year On: Assuring Health Gain: A Report on Days 5 and 6*, East Anglia RHA/ Office for Public Management, 1991

Chapter Eight: Into the Council Hot Seat

1. *BMJ*, 301 6743, 1990, p. 81
2. Cameron, J. S., *et al.*, *BMJ*, 301 6748, 1990, p. 390
3. Keen, H., *Hospital Doctor*, 23.8.90
4. *BMJ*, 301 6747, 1990, p. 307
5. *Working for Patients: Contracts for*

Health Services: Operating contracts, HMSO, 1990

6. *BMJ*, 301 6746, 1990, p. 295
7. Thatcher, *op. cit.*

Chapter Nine: Waldegrave Replaces Clarke

1. *The Newchurch Guide to NHS Trust Applications*, Newchurch & Co., 1990
2. Willetts, David, *Reforming the Health Service*, Conservative Political Centre, 1989
3. *Daily Telegraph* and *Independent*, 26.1.91
4. Smith, R., *BMJ*, 302 6777, pp. 636–40, and 302 6778, 1991, pp. 711–14

Chapter Ten: The First Six Months

1. *Guardian*, 26.3.91
2. *Birmingham Post*, 13,14,20.3.91
3. *Western Mail*, 19.3.91
4. Meek, Colin, *BMA News Review*, 3.91
5. *BMA News Review*, 5.96
6. Williamson, J. D., *BMJ*, 303 6801, 1991, pp. 499–504
7. *Daily Telegraph*, 23.5.91
8. Waldegrave, William, *The Binding of Leviathan: Conservatism and the Future*, Hamish Hamilton, 1978
9. World Health Organization, *Global Strategy for Health for All by the Year 2000*, WHO, 1981

Chapter Eleven: The Tory Victory Means the Reforms Continue

1. Vallance-Owen, Andrew, *The Health Debate Live: 45 Interviews for 'Leading for Health'*, BMJ, 1992
2. *Leading for Health: A BMA Agenda for Health*, BMA, 1991
3. *Independent* with *Doctor* and *Hospital Doctor*, 2.4.92
4. Pickard, J., *et al.*, *BMJ*, 301 6753, 1990, pp. 629–35
5. *Independent*, 12.5.95
6. Smith, R., *BMJ*, 312 7028, 1996, pp. 391–92
7. Tomlinson, Bernard, *Report of the Inquiry into London's Health Service, Medical Education and Research*, HMSO, 1992
8. King's Fund Commission on the Future of London's Acute Health Services, *London Health Care 2010: Changing the Future of Services in the Capital* & Working Papers 1–12, King's Fund London Initiative, 1992
9. Jarman, Brian, *BMJ*, 306 6883, 1993, pp. 979–82
10. Department of Health, *Making London Better*, HMSO, 1993
11. *The Times*, 14.4.96

Chapter Twelve: Five Years and Beyond

1. *NHS responsibilities for meeting continuing care needs*, HSG (95) 8 & LAC (95) 50, HMSO, 1995
2. *Health Service Journal*, 26.10.95, pp. 232–33
3. Health Committee, *Community*

Care: Funding From April *1993*, Third Report, HMSO, 1993

4. *Through the Looking Glass: Opening up the NHS Funding Debate*, IHSM, 1993

5. Efficiency Unit, *Improving Management in Government: The Next Step*, HMSO, 1988

6. Carr-Hiller, R., *et al.*, *BMJ*, 309 6961, 1994, pp. 1046–49, 1050–54, 1059–64

7. *Observer*, 26.5.95

8. *Observer*, 16.6.96

9. *The Times*, 18.6.96

10. Treasury Committee, *The Private Finance Initiative*, Sixth Report, HMSO, 1995

11. *Hansard*, 31.1.95, HMSO, 1995

12. *Developing NHS Purchasing and GP Fundholding: Towards a Primary Care Led NHS*, EL (94) 79, DoH, 1994

13. *Health Authority Costs and NHS Trust Management Costs 1994–1995*, DoH, 1995

14. *A Price on their Heads: Measuring Costs in NHS Trusts*, Audit Commission, 1995

Chapter Thirteen: Failings and Solutions

1. *BMA News Review*, 1.95

2. *What the Doctor Ordered: A Study of GP Fundholders in England and Wales*, Audit Commission, 1996

3. *Ibid.*

4. *Ibid.*

5. Committee of Public Accounts, *General Practitioner Fundholding in England*, 27th Report, HMSO, 1995

6. *British Social Attitudes, 9th Report*, Dartmouth Publishing, 1992

7. Central Statistical Office, 1994

Index